Victorian Dundee: Image and Realities

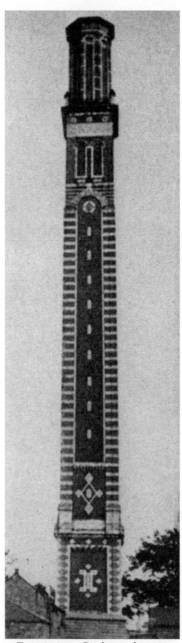

Frontispiece. Cox's stack – an emblem of manufacturing confidence in Victorian Dundee and still a notable landmark

Victorian Dundee: Image and Realities

Edited by

Louise Miskell, Christopher A. Whatley and Bob Harris

TUCKWELL PRESS

First published in Great Britain in 2000 by
Tuckwell Press
The Mill House
Phantassie
East Linton
East Lothian EH40 3DG
Scotland

Reprinted in 2002

ISBN 1 86232 171 X

British Library Cataloguing in Publication Data

A catalogue record for this book is available
on request from the British Library

Typeset by Hewer Text Ltd, Edinburgh
Printed and bound by The Cromwell Press, Trowbridge, Wiltshire

Contents

Plates

Figures

Tables

Preface and Acknowledgements

This book is the result of three years' work carried out by the 'History of Dundee' project, sponsored by the Department of History, University of Dundee. The project was begun in 1997 with support from the University's Strategic Initiatives scheme. This provided funding to employ a full-time research assistant, Dr Louise Miskell, for one year. Additional funding has been obtained from income derived from the Department of History's Distance Learning Course in Modern Scottish History (in association with the Institute for Education and Lifelong Learning and the Open University). During 1998–99 and 1999–2000 funding was also sought and obtained from the Faculty of Arts and Social Sciences, University of Dundee.

The book represents a revival of the Department of History's traditional commitment to the study of the city of Dundee. Pathbreaking work in this regard was carried out by members of the Department in the 1960s and 1970s. Important publications resulted, including Bruce Lenman, Charlotte Lythe and Enid Gauldie's *Dundee and its Textile Industry* (1969) and the late William M. Walker's seminal, *Juteopolis: Dundee and its textile workers 1885–1923* (1979). Although Christopher Whatley, Annette Smith and David Swinfen, also members of the Department, wrote a popular *The Life and Times of Dundee* (1993), this publication broke little new ground and indirectly, revealed how much new research work would be necessary in order to take Dundee's history much further forward. With the ongoing advance in urban historical studies south of the border, and the publication, during the mid- and late-1990s, of the University of Strathclyde-led History of Glasgow enterprise, as well as a number of University of Aberdeen, School of Scottish Studies-based studies of Aberdeen, it became clear that in terms both of research endeavour and methodological sophistication, Dundee was lagging. A multi-authored study of Aberdeen in which the University of Edinburgh's Scottish History Department is involved, along with historians from other Scottish universities, including Aberdeen, is currently in preparation. Of the four main Scottish cities, the least well-known in scholarly terms is Dundee, although this is not to disregard splendid recent publications on aspects of the city's history such as those by Mark Watson (*Jute and Flax Mills of Dundee*, 1990) and Gordon T. Stewart (*Jute and Empire*, 1998). The Abertay Historical Society has continued to publish significant work on aspects of Dundee's history.

From the outset, the project has been a collaborative one. A seminar series was held during sessions 1997–98 and 1998–99, in which contributors offered working papers of their chapters. Lively debate and comment at this stage were later supplemented by guidance and suggestions made by the editors on subsequent drafts of the material. In this way, efforts have been made to ensure the highest academic standards and also to identify and develop recurrent themes which emerged during discussion and reading of drafts.

Contributors were drawn from the ranks of the Department of History staff members who were interested in urban history, even though they may have had little knowledge of Dundee. We have been privileged to have had a paper from Myra Baillie, from McMaster University, Ontario, Canada. Past and present postgraduates whose work it was felt could contribute significantly were also invited to participate. It was felt that it was important to incorporate as wide a range of historical approaches as was feasible and, accordingly, visual, spacial and architectural aspects of the city's history have been key elements of the study. The Department has recently appointed both contributors in these fields to its number, Murdo MacDonald, Professor of Scottish Art History, and Charles McKean, Professor of Scottish Architectural History. Many of the ideas which have found their way onto the printed page here were first aired during undergraduate seminars on honours courses such as *The Victorian City*, and contributors are grateful to those students who have been prepared to subject them to searching and critical analysis.

It is not intended that this book should be the only material outcome from the History of Dundee project. In association with the University's Archives Department, the Department of History, though the advisory role of Professor McKean, is also involved in a Research Support Libraries Programme-funded project which will digitise architectural drawings in Scotland from the industrial revolution to the present day. Material from Dundee will feature in this innovative package of under-used research resources. Funding is being sought in order to push our research backwards in the eighteenth century. Individual members of and small teams within the project's core group have begun to publish research findings in relevant academic journals, and will continue to do so. Uniformly, the commitment has been not only to write for our peers within the academic community, but also to do so in a manner which makes the city's history accessible to its own residents and those with a general interest in it. As well as being national and international in their focus, universities must serve and interact with their region and locality. Wherever possible, we have adopted a comparative approach, and tried to place Dundee's experience within Scottish, British and, where appropriate international contexts.

The editors are grateful to the University of Dundee for its generous support for the project. The Dean of Arts and Social Sciences, Professor Huw Jones, has gone to considerable trouble to ensure the continuing funding of Dr Miskell's post, in order that this volume could be completed. Virtually every contributor has made use of the archives and other collections held by Dundee City Council. Dundee University Archives have provided invaluable assistance, not only in accessing their collections but also in providing copies of maps, plans and other illustrative material. Particular thanks are due to Michael Bolik, Jennifer Tait and Patricia Whatley. Several contributors also received generous help from Eileen Moran and her colleagues at Dundee's Local Studies Library.

The copy for the printer was prepared with superb efficiency and admirable attention to detail by Mrs Sara Reid of the Department of History. Rhona Feist, a graduate of the Department, prepared the Index. It has been a pleasure to work with the ever-enthusiastic publishing team of John and Val Tuckwell, of Tuckwell Press, who provided welcome early backing for the publication of the project team's work.

LM, CAW, BH

Notes on Contributors

MYRA BAILLIE is a postgraduate student in the department of History at McMaster University, Hamilton, Ontario, Canada. Her M.A. thesis was on the work of Mary Lily Walker in Dundee. She is currently researching and writing her Ph.D. on the experience of working-class women in the West of Scotland during the First World War.

BOB HARRIS is a Senior Lecturer in History at the University of Dundee and Fellow of the Royal Historical Society. A specialist on eighteenth-century British history, he has written widely on British politics and political culture in this period, including *A Patriot Press* (Oxford, 1993) and *Politics and the Rise of the Press in Britain and France, 1620–1800* (Routledge, 1996). A volume of essays on Scotland in the age of the French Revolution, edited by him, will be published by Tuckwell Press in 2002. He plans to write more about the early history of town planning in the future.

JOHN KEMP is a former member of Dundee City Council and a postgraduate student in the Department of History at Dundee. He is close to completing a Ph.D. thesis on 'Drink and the Labour Movement' and is a distance-learning tutor for the Modern Scottish History Open University course. His current research interests are in the history of the Temperance (Scotland) Act and pressure group politics.

WILLIAM KENEFICK is a lecturer in nineteenth- and twentieth-century Scottish and British history at the University of Dundee. His research interests lie in social, industrial and labour history and Scottish docks and dockers from *c*.1850. He has published widely, including 'Anti-Militarism and Conscientious Objection in Scotland', in *Scotland and the Great War* (Edinburgh, 1999), and 'Bread, water and hard labour? New perspectives on 1930s labour camps' (with Lorraine Walsh) in the journal of *Scottish Labour History* (2000). His monograph, *Rebellious and Contrary: the Glasgow Dockers c.1835–1932* (East Linton 2000) is part of the *Scottish Historical Review* Monograph Series.

MURDO MACDONALD is Professor of History of Scottish Art at the University of Dundee, where he teaches in both the Departments of History and Fine Art. His wide-ranging research interests include the life and significance of Patrick Geddes.

A prolific writer, he has recently completed the synoptic and highly-acclaimed *Scottish Art* for Thames and Hudson (2000).

CHARLES MCKEAN is Professor of Scottish Architectural History in the Department of History, University of Dundee. Author of twenty books including *The Scottish Thirties, Fight Blight, Edinburgh*, and *The Making of the Museum of Scotland*, he is also series editor of the RIAS/Landmark Trust series of illustrated architectural guides to Scotland. His current research work in urban and architectural history includes the architectural drawings on the sixteenth-century maps of Timothy Pont, a forthcoming book on 'The Scottish Chateau', and the selection and digitisation of 8,000 Scottish architectural drawings.

JAN MERCHANT was awarded her Ph.D. by the University of Dundee in 1998. Her research interests are based in nineteenth- and early twentieth-century British history with a particular focus on the role of women in Scotland. Having tutored undergraduates and Open University students of Scottish history, she is currently employed by the University's Archives Department where she is involved in a project charting Scotland's development through the built environment. She has co-reviewed various guides to archives and is editor of the Abertay Historical Society's journal.

LOUISE MISKELL is a researcher in the Department of History at the University of Dundee with responsibility for the Dundee Project. She researches various aspects of nineteenth-century British history with particular interest in urban elites and Irish immigrants in British towns. Recent publications include 'The Irish in Cornwall. The Camborne experience, 1861–1882', in *The Irish in Victorian Britain: The Local Dimension*, eds R. Swift and S. Gilley (Dublin, 1999) and 'Juteopolis in the Making: Linen and the Industrial Transformation of Dundee', *Textile History*, 30, 2 (1999) (co-authored with C. A. Whatley).

LORRAINE WALSH is a director of studies in the Centre for Learning and Teaching in Higher Education at the Institute of Education and Lifelong Learning at the University of Dundee. Her research interests include nine-teenth-century urban and medical history and, in the field of education, the role of assessment in higher and further education. Recent publications include '"The property of the whole community". Charity and insanity in urban Scotland: The Dundee Royal Lunatic Asylum, 1805–1850', in *Insanity, Institutions and Society, 1800–1914*, eds J. Melling & B. Forsythe (Routledge, 1999); and *Patrons, Poverty and Profit: Organised charity in nineteenth-century Dundee* (Abertay, 2000).

CHRISTOPHER A. WHATLEY is Professor of Scottish History and Head of the Department of History at the University of Dundee. He has published a number of books and articles on the history of Dundee and is head of the Dundee Project research team. He has wide-ranging research interests in the economic and social history of eighteenth- and nineteenth-century Scotland. His most recent publications are *The Industrial Revolution in Scotland* (Cambridge, 1997) and *Scottish Society 1707–1830: Beyond Jacobitism, Towards Industrialisation* (Manchester, 2000).

Introduction: Altering Images

Dundee has thrown away more opportunities for improvement than any of our other large towns. If its civic rulers and men of wealth had been humble enough to take advice we might have had a city which would have been second to none for architectural beauty in Scotland.

(Letter printed in the *Dundee Courier*, 13 March 1907.)

THESE WORDS WERE written by an Aberdonian, and perhaps one detects in them the hard edge of rivalry between the two east-coast cities. Yet their author's overall judgement of Dundee as a place, and as an urban landscape, was equally severe: 'Dundee remains unspeakably ugly'. Judgements of the city of a similar sort have dogged it throughout its modern history, and continue to do so today. Dundee, Scotland's Murmansk, the ghastliest place on earth, reminiscent of parts of Gdansk or Grozny, with its sour-faced and miserable inhabitants, has had a bad press.[1] Even Dundonians are not exempt from taking a perverse pleasure in the 'grim' story of their city and its inhabitants. An example of this appeared in *Scotland on Sunday* towards the end of 1999, when a series of Police Court photographs of persistent drunkards from the turn of the twentieth century was used to reinforce the popular image of Dundee as Scotland's centre of hard drinking amongst a nation of hard drinkers. Well-worn shibboleths were churned out, regardless of chronology and without qualification, leaving readers in no doubt that nineteenth-century Dundee was truly a wretched, drink-drenched place.[2] The pictures represented, however, the few, not the many. They were of recidivists, of individuals similar to Anne Monroe, who early in 1867 found herself in the Police Court charged with disorderly conduct; it was the ninety-first time she had been convicted.[3] Dundee, like most great industrial cities, had a drink problem at the end of the nineteenth century, but it was being tackled. It is worth noting that drunkenness amongst Dundee's female mill and factory workers was less pronounced than is suggested in some accounts.[4]

In the mid-nineteenth century, perhaps the most famous of Dundee's detractors was the High Court judge, Lord Cockburn. His description of Dundee as a 'sink of atrocity, which no moral flushing seems capable of cleansing', is the best-known of the several disparaging remarks he made. Cockburn, however, had an inherent dislike of manufacturing towns and the 'volatile god' – steam – which for middle-class Dundonians was the instrument of their enrichment and prosperity. It had also 'founded families that rival the aristocracy in deeds of charity and benevolence'.[5] Like many Tories, Cockburn's preference was for the countryside or smaller, dignified towns. In April 1842, after noting that he had 'never been so struck with the beauty of Perth', he sternly rebuked those of its best citizens who he had heard envying Dundee for its trade, 'its steam engines, its precarious wealth, its starving, turbulent population, its vulgar blackguardism'.[6] But how much were these pejorative remarks simply expressions of Cockburn's beliefs about the social and moral effects of life in burgeoning manufacturing towns, beliefs that (to him) were pleasingly self-fulfilling? This, and the likelihood that his sense of disgust may have been heightened by having had to preside over a particularly unpleasant case of incest in 1840, and the sexual nature of many of the cases which came before him, provide at least a partial explanation for his contempt for Dundee; they also suggest that his remarks cannot be taken at face value.[7]

There are, nevertheless, periods in Dundee's history when such was the grimness of economic conditions that it would be simply perverse either to deny them or indeed to inflate the significance of weak countervailing rays of light. Dundee's emergence as a major manufacturing centre, between 1820 and 1850, was, as elsewhere in Britain, marked by instability. Periodic downturns in trade were followed by over-optimistic waves of expansion and unwise invest-ment. The result was a series of acute depressions, which thinned the ranks of textile firms and threw thousands out of employment and into despair. In the early to mid-1930s the Great Depression hit hard in Scotland. Dundee, however, was more severely hurt than many of the other industrial areas. Not only were external markets flat, but between 1928 and 1935 there was an astounding 375% increase in the import of jute goods into Britain from Calcutta, partly as a result of the working of the Ottawa Agreement of 1932.[8] This was the context in which Hugh MacDiarmid portrayed Dundee in 1934 as a degraded and 'grim industrial cul-de-sac', a monument 'to man's inhumanity to man'. The later nineteenth and early twentieth centuries were also marked by growing pressure on wages and housing which left large sections of the population living in poverty and with inadequate sanitary facilities.

In many respects those who have dwelt on the negative have had an easy target. Dundee's economic foundations were narrow even in its Victorian hey-day, when it relied heavily upon the fortunes of coarse textiles, and above all jute, the world's bagging material, successful above all because of its strength and low price. In the Scottish urban context, Dundee is unfavourably contrasted in the secondary literature with Glasgow, the 'industrial powerhouse' and centre of progressive municipal government, and Edinburgh (the 'semi-capital') and Aberdeen (the 'versatile'), with their professionals and balanced economic and social structures. Dundee is the 'one industry town', torn apart by class and cultural divisions which separated the 'jute kings' from a filthy and overwhelmingly female working class.[9] The situation deteriorated with the emergence of serious competition from the

European continent and India from the 1880s. The twentieth century – the world wars apart – was a period of long-term decline for the city's staple. The last jute yarn was spun in March 1999. Only belatedly did many of the town's industrial leaders accept that the tide of economic history was running away from them.

In outlining Dundee's economic development there has been a certain sloppiness, however, even amongst professional historians. It is not unusual, for example, to read that the basis of Dundee's success in the nineteenth century was the production of low-status jute cloth. It has even been suggested that by 1850 Dundee had 'earned the nickname of "Juteopolis"'.[10] This is not only wrong – it is based on not one single scrap of evidence – it also ignores altogether the fact that until the mid-1850s the town's economy and much of the urban infrastructure depended on the wealth generated from coarse linen cloths, including canvas. The number of mills rose in a series of high steps, as in 1821–22, when twelve were built, and 1834–36 (another eleven). These figures exclude calenders (where cloth was sent to be finished), foundries, warehouses and other plant and machinery. It was during this period that Dundee took its place as Scotland's third most populous town by moving ahead of Paisley. What is also overlooked is that this was no small triumph, with Dundee leading Europe in its capture of the world's markets for machine-spun flax and the coarse linen cloth woven with it.[11] Although in volume terms Ireland, which concentrated on finer linens, had overtaken Dundee by the middle of the nineteenth century, coarse linens continued to be produced until the twentieth century, albeit increasingly overshadowed by jute. The era of jute, however, or at least the period when Dundee-made jute was triumphant, was relatively short-lived, lasting no more than three decades.

The start of the 1850s ushered in a period when three wars, the Crimean War, the American Civil War and the Franco-Prussian War, brought unprecedented prosperity to Dundee. It was during the first of these conflicts that jute overtook linen as the town's staple product. But by the 1850s Baxter Brothers had become the proprietors of the world's largest coarse linen works, while in the following decade Cox's of Lochee could boast that they were the owners of Dundee's largest powerloom factory, weaving jute. Employing more workers – around 5,000 – than any other textile company in Scotland, no works in the world turned out more jute cloth.

Like those whose focus is on industry and the economy, social and labour historians have also tended to take a gloomy view. The city's finest historian of the working class, for example, concluded that Dundee was a manufacturing centre of 'physically retarded children overworked women and demoralised men'.[12] Women workers in Dundee have rightly attracted considerable attention from historians. They loom large in folk memory and popular representations of the city which proudly recall a raucous and independent set of workers, differentiated by the superior habits of the glove-wearing weavers over the shawl-clad spinners. In the 1900s working-class women in Dundee formed the bedrock of support for women's suffrage.[13] It is not intended in this book to deny that such judgements have their place. Female mill and factory workers in Dundee, with a higher proportion of its married women in employment (23.4% in 1911) than any other comparable Scottish city, have been the subject of detailed investigations. It is impossible to ignore conclusions built upon hard and uncontestable facts, or upon timely feminist re-readings of them. Indeed Jan Merchant's chapter below, on the maidservants' agitation of 1872, builds upon Eleanor Gordon's recent re-investigation of the conditions and character of women workers in Dundee in the period 1850 to 1914 and suggests that their influence may have spread beyond the mill and factory.[14]

The sub-title of the present book has been chosen carefully to reflect a conviction that there are more faces to Dundee's modern history than the traditional and entrenched historiographical stereotypes of the city would appear to indicate. There is a need for a history of Dundee which can encompass other realities and perspectives, ones which qualify and, in several cases, directly challenge these stereotypes. How, for example, should 'pre-jute Dundee' be portrayed? This was the Dundee which had moved out of the economic doldrums of the immediate post-Union (1707) years, growing in size and prosperity from the middle of the eighteenth century as a marketing, manufacturing, and finishing centre for a coarse linen industry, an industry which spread its tentacles throughout the burgh's hinterland. In 1724, a committee of the Convention of Royal Burghs on the state of the town reported:

> That the harbour of the Burgh is in disrepair and rendered incommodious by
> sliek and sand which Deprives them of several foots of water and that the Town
> House also appears to be in disrepair. And that the streets are in bad condition
> and need to be repaired.[15]

Yet from the mid-eighteenth century, Dundee grew in confidence and ambition, as well as prosperity. This was effected both by the provision of state support for the strategically important linen industry and the astute decision by Dundee's Town Council to exempt linen brought to Dundee from the payment of petty customs. Consequently, according to Patrick Lindsay in 1736,

> Numbers of country weavers, who used to carry their cloth for sale to the
> Towns that lie nearest to them do now bring their cloth to Dundee, although it
> lies at a much greater distance from them.

By the end of the 1760s, the linen trade was providing the 'daily subsistence of the greater number of its [Dundee's] inhabitants'.[16]

Contemporary descriptions of the townscape in the later eighteenth century dwelt on the evidence of increasing wealth and, perhaps more surprisingly, the 'politeness' of Dundee merchants.[17] The 1770s saw several new, distinguished buildings – town architect Samuel Bell's Trades Hall, English Chapel (later Union Hall), and St Andrew's Church, in King Street. The erection of the first two meant that the High Street, by this time the centre of the burgh, was adorned with three pedimented civic buildings. (The other one was William Adam's Town House (the 'Pillars'), opened in 1735.) Robert Small, one of the town's ministers (and thus well acquainted with it), conceded in the early 1790s that parts of Dundee were densely packed and damp, but overall he considered it to be 'a very healthy place'. Most fevers were of the non-contagious variety and 'agues' were little known.[18] The path of growth, increasing civic ambition and urban improvement continued, and widened in the early nineteenth century as the pace of economic activity quickened. In some ways, as Charles McKean will argue in his chapter, what stands out in respect of the reshaping and improvement of the urban environment is what was not done; Dundee boasted no new town like the ones which defined a new urban order elsewhere in Scotland. On the other hand, there was also, as he points out, ample evidence of civic pride. One manifestation of this was the erection of several new public buildings – the Theatre Royal in Castle Street (1808), the Infirmary, and the Lunatic Asylum – which betokened obvious architectural ambition. By the 1830s, the sense of the pace and scope of economic change and improvement in the town was becoming a subject for memorialisation. In the 1830s, the recent changes were recorded in a series of engravings for a volume by Charles Mackie and separately illustrated by a local engraver. The *Dundee Advertiser* explained the need for a visual record of the new Dundee:

> Thirty-five years have elapsed since Bonnie Dundee invited the attention of an Artist. The ruinous harbour and tiny shipping, the lofty cones of what had been the Bottle-work, and the Auld Steeple, were then the most striking objects in the borough for the pencil of the artist. The River Tay, the Law on Dundee, and hill of Balgay, which were then the leading features of the landscape are of course the leading features still, but the changes on our borough have been many and extensive. The spacious new harbour, composed of wet-docks, graving dock and tide harbours crowded with shipping of a superior class. The splendid steam-ships of which Dundee has reason to be proud now grace the foreground of the view taken from the River; while spire above spire in all quarters of the town, emitting volumes of dingy smoke, at once resemble the spires of the city of Palaces, and the smoke exhalations of Mount Vesuvius. These vast changes having occurred, it was high time that the present state of the town should be marked by the pencil of the artist .[19]

As the quotation reveals, the river and the port figured largely in a developing civic imagery as emblems of its commercial identity. Equally telling is the use of the sublime mood – the 'smoke exhalations of Mount Vesuvius' – to capture the wonderment which surrounded the development of the port and the growth of the mills. The port improvements had been instigated by a group of ambitious merchants who overcame objections from conservative elements in the town that the plans were too grandiose and too financially risky. It was a judgement that was hopelessly wrong, and it was not long before further improvements were needed to cope with the growing volume and changing nature of shipping in the port.

Eighteenth- and early nineteenth-century Dundee was also a town where cultural provision was increasing. The presence of growing numbers of booksellers and printers; the founding of periodicals from the 1770s and a successful local newspaper in 1801; the staging of art exhibitions and art auctions; the presence of drawing and dancing masters; the provision of assemblies and theatres; and the meeting of clubs of various kinds, including an Enlightenment club, the Speculative Society, all testify to an urban culture of considerable depth, vitality, and openness, as well as increasing sophistication.[20] Liberal currents also found political expression from the later 1780s and 1790s, with the birth of Whig-radical tradition in the town. The history of Dundee Enlightenment culture has yet to be written; that it existed seems not to be in doubt.

Figure 1: Distribution of occupations of Dundee's commercial middle classes by industry, 1818, 1850 and 1870.

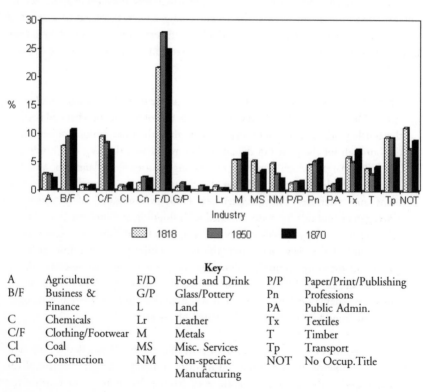

Key

A	Agriculture	F/D	Food and Drink	P/P	Paper/Print/Publishing
B/F	Business &	G/P	Glass/Pottery	Pn	Professions
	Finance	L	Land	PA	Public Admin.
C	Chemicals	Lr	Leather	Tx	Textiles
C/F	Clothing/Footwear	M	Metals	T	Timber
Cl	Coal	MS	Misc. Services	Tp	Transport
Cn	Construction	NM	Non-specific	NOT	No Occup. Title
			Manufacturing		

Source: *Dundee Directories,* 1818, 1850 and 1870.

We know surprisingly little also about the elites who presided over Dundee's emergence as an industrial powerhouse, as well as the growing middle classes who benefited from the opportunities this created. The emphasis on the working classes and a few leading manufacturers in existing scholarship is all too understandable; yet in shaping the modern town and city, members of the middle classes had an influence disproportionate to their relatively small numbers. It was a group, or series of groups, which was much more diverse than the traditional picture of manufacturing dominance suggests. Rapid population increase in the decades after 1820 generated expansion in the food and drink and in the clothing and footwear trades. Numerous opportunities for small-scale craft and retail ventures created a thriving middle-class commercial community serving the everyday needs of the burgeoning manufacturing population. It was also a middle class which remained within the town for much longer than is usually recognised. It has been too readily assumed that the wealthy moved out *en masse* as the town began to grow rapidly and as conditions, social and environmental, began to deteriorate. Various dates have been proposed for the beginning of this exodus. One commentator has suggested that movement to Broughty Ferry, a few miles to the east, was evident as early as 1801.[21] Another has claimed that 'the beginning of the middle-class exodus can be dated (with some precision) to the second half of the 1830s'.[22] Improving transport links with outlying towns and villages from this period, certainly facilitated greater residential mobility. The opening of the Dundee to Arbroath railway in 1838 and the introduction of steamers in 1821 on the Tay ferry route between Dundee and Newport improved communication links with towns and villages to the east of Dundee and with Fife.[23]

In this case, however, appearances are deceptive, or at least unrepresentative. The idea that, by the middle of the nineteenth century, Dundee's middle classes had left for more pleasant surroundings is statistically untenable, as the evidence of residential addresses in the 1850 *Dundee Directory* shows.[24] The overwhelming majority of the commercial middle classes were still resident within the burgh boundaries a decade after the Dundee-Arbroath railway line had opened. Only 1.8% of the 3,700 individuals were recorded in the *Directory* lists with separate residential addresses outside Dundee, and only thirty individuals gave residential addresses in Broughty Ferry. Still fewer resided in towns and villages like Blairgowrie, Newport, Inchture and Lochee, all within a few miles of Dundee. Where, then, did the Dundee middle classes live? The answer is partly in developing middle-class suburbs within the town. The first of these was to the west, around Magdalen Green, where town architects David Neave and Samuel Bell built detached villas. This area was particularly popular with merchants and professionals, as well as with the retired and those with independent incomes. By 1850, a second 'inner suburb' was also developing on the slopes of the Law, where new detached and semi-detached villas in Prospect Place and Laurel Bank became popular with the 'comfortable classes'. By the 1870s, this area had seen the addition of several new streets – Garland Place, Rustic Place and Panmure Terrace.

Table 1: Development of Dundee's residential suburbs, 1850–1870.[25]

	1850		1869–70	
	No.	*(%)*	*No.*	*(%)*
Magdalen Yard/Perth Rd	215	(5.8)	306	(5.5)
Dudhope/Lawside	81	(2.2)	212	(3.8)
W. Ferry/Broughty Ferry	52	(1.4)	191	(3.4)
Newport/Tayport	8	(0.2)	85	(1.5)
Total individuals in Directory	3715		5577	

Source: *Dundee Directories*, 1850 and 1869–70

Movement out of town amongst the middle classes was, in short, negligible before 1850, and while it did increase in the two subsequent decades, by 1870 it was still relatively limited. The population of Newport grew little before the mid-1850s, when the introduction of gas supplies encouraged increased settlement; before then it had primarily served as a seasonal resort.[26] Dundee experienced relatively less outward movement before 1870 than other industrial towns and cities, in Scotland and in England and Wales. On the other hand, areas such as that around Magdalen Green could not indefinitely postpone the sweeping tides of industrial activity and working-class housing. The building of the railway line from Dundee to Perth, which opened in 1847,[27] cut Magdalen Green off from its prime riverside access, thus robbing the suburb of one of its most appealing features.

The composition and residential location of this middle class had crucial implications for the character of the town, and for its civic leadership and governance. As the nineteenth century progressed, and as the town grew in prosperity and size, so middle-class Dundonians appear to have created around them a cultural, artistic and intellectual life of considerable depth and extent. Research on this is currently being undertaken by Ruth Forbes, a postgraduate in the Department of History, University of Dundee, and her findings will add significantly to our knowledge of nineteenth-century Dundee and of the role of culture in the construction of local and social identities. One aspect of it, however, was enthusiasm for art, and a wider commitment to the arts as part of the 'civilizing mission' in the contemporary urban society. Education in the visual arts was part of a programme of rational entertainment and self improvement; it also promised to improve awareness of the value of good design, of huge relevance in a textile-manufacturing centre. In 1842 and again in 1847, the Watt Institution (founded in 1824) staged exhibitions of art, which displayed paintings, engravings, prints and sculptures donated by local collectors. The first of these also included industrial exhibits. The second, which comprised contemporary art was, it is true, not a financial success. Yet it still attracted more visitors than that year's Royal Manchester Institution's Annual Art Show.[28] Twenty years later (in 1867), a major exhibition of art was staged to coincide with the visit of the British

Association for the Advancement of Science. By the end of the same decade, demands were growing for permanent public gallery space, demands which resulted in the building of an extension to the Albert Institute in 1873. There followed the formation of the Dundee Art Union in 1877 and the inauguration of annual art exhibitions which, by the 1880s, were proving a considerable success, attracting large audiences, and resulting in the sale of substantial quantities of pictures. In 1883–84, sales from the annual exhibition climbed to £8,500, a figure which, temporarily at least, 'placed the Dundee Exhibition relatively at the head of all British Art Exhibitions.'[29] From the middle of the century leading local art collectors, notably George Duncan, James Guthrie Orchar, and William Ogilvy Dalgliesh, began to donate works for the creation of a permanent exhibition in the town.[30] 1889 saw the opening of the Victoria Art Galleries, where the permanent collection was put on display. There are several noteworthy aspects of this activity, not least the commitment to public provision and wider access to art. It also relied on the enthusiasm of members of the town's middle classes, their willingness to devote time and energy to organising exhibitions, creating the permanent collection, and to raising funds to finance the building of gallery space. It is also, however, evidence for the strong sense of civic pride and ambition amongst representatives of Dundee's middle classes, a desire to show that Dundonians knew, as Thomas Couper, manager of the Dundee and Hull shipping company who proposed the formation of the Dundee Art Union put it, 'there is something higher than our mills and manufactories, our shops and our ships'.[31]

As elsewhere in industrial cities and towns in Britain, the middle classes achieved a degree of cohesion, and managed in part to project their leadership on the rest of society, through an expanding array of voluntary bodies and associations.[32] Dundee saw a proliferation of charitable bodies from the later eighteenth century, beginning with the Infirmary. This and other institutions were funded through subscription and run by committees normally formed from leading donors or from representatives of local government and civic institutions.[33] They relied, therefore, primarily on the initiative and enthusiasm of the local middle classes.[34] Through these institutions, the upper middle classes, including leading manufacturers, not only asserted their leadership in the town, they also sought to smooth the development of social relations, to defuse social and political tensions, and to promote self-help, improvement and rational recreation amongst the working classes. Before the final third of the nineteenth century, these foundations may have been especially important as instruments of civic leadership. This reflected in part the condition of local government. The burgh council, certainly before its reform in 1831, was held in low regard. In 1822, local artist Henry Harwood exhibited a picture entitled 'The Executive' in Hood's Commercial Hall, which satirised the narrow, corrupt oligarchy which was entrenched in office. In 1824, when new powers were sought for improvement and better policing of the burgh, these were conferred on a new forty-four-member police commission, the early membership of which was dominated by merchants and manufacturers.[35] It was a pattern which was familiar elsewhere, and it reflected the growing political divisions which were dividing different sections of the local elites in urban Britain in the early nineteenth century. Philanthropy attracted broad support from the middle classes; it served to knit them together in support of common goals.[36] It also attracted support from the rising manufacturers, for example, the Baxters. In this way, it brought into alignment economic and civic leadership in the town, adding to the strength of the latter. This strong local tradition of philanthropy continued into the later nineteenth century and early twentieth century, as Myra Baillie shows below. Yet whether it carried the same weight in respect of civic leadership, certainly from the 1870s, is open to doubt. This was partly because local government took on more of the burden of shaping and regulating the town's development of a providing of local services and amenities. There was a shift too in the nature of philanthropy, again one in line with developments elsewhere. The essence of this was a gradual move towards individual benefaction, which played an increasingly important role in the financing of major new initiatives in the town, such as the foundation of the University College.[37]

Dundee's civic leadership has, like the town, generally been portrayed as ineffective, and inadequate to the problems which surging growth created, especially from the 1870s. Another common criticism has been the one which was expressed in the quotation which opened this introduction – namely, that civic leaders squandered the natural advantages and possibilities for improvement which Dundee presented. This is another area which requires further, systematic research. Part of the difficulty lies in deciding what criteria should be used to assess its performance. It is relatively easy to show, for example, that in some areas of municipal activity Dundee was in advance of national trends; in others not. As Christopher A. Whatley shows in his chapter below, in the mid-nineteenth century, there is strong evidence that the elites were able to win considerable support from the rest of the population for their steering of the town's development, and for various schemes to promote the values of respectability amongst the working classes, and, as a consequence, social harmony between its different classes. Manufacturers also used paternalist measures, again with some evidence of success, to seek to win greater loyalty and quiescence from their workforces. From the 1870s and 1880s, however, social and environmental problems in the town were undoubtedly acute, and local government made only limited headway in tackling them. But was the record of local government in Dundee notably worse than other places? In dealing with the problem of water provision, for example, the Town Council's unsuccessful attempts to establish a municipal supply funded by compulsory assessment were a common experience in the early Victorian period when only ten local authorities in England, Scotland and Wales achieved municipally controlled water supplies prior to 1845.[38] In other areas of public health provision, notable successes were achieved, particularly in the wake of the

1847 fever epidemic when a hastily established Board of Health 'did much good in causing nuisances to be removed and houses throughout the town and suburbs to be properly cleansed'.[39]

A story can be told of how the reputation of the Council began to recover from the low point of the late 1810s and early 1820s, and bankruptcy in 1842, during the second half of the nineteenth century. It was a story of a town's leadership seeking to create for itself, and Dundee, a civic image which emphasised, at times somewhat relentlessly, industrial and technical enterprise and education, improvement and modernity. A turning point was 1851, when the powers of the police commission were transferred to the Town Council.[40] The move marked a growing confidence in the Council as the most suitable body to administer the watching, lighting and cleansing of the town. One contemporary commented that, 'whatever might be the defects of the Town Council . . . there was no comparison between that body and the police commissioners'.[41] In the following decades, the Council became the instrument of an increasingly well-regarded progressive, Liberal elite – men such as Frank Henderson, chairman of the town's improvement committee, William Brownlee and Alexander H. Moncur – who, together with several diligent Council officers, began to use the increasing powers of the Council to intervene more actively in the provision of services (gas, water, electricity, sanitation) and as a force for ameliorating the urban environment. In this ambition, they appear to have received active support from representatives of the organised working classes, principally through the activities of the Dundee Working Men's Association and Trades Council.[42] A key year in the process of improvement was 1871, which saw the passage of the Police and Improvement Act, under which parts of the town centre were redeveloped to aggrandise the urban fabric and to remove several notorious slums. It was a process not without tensions, and an often overt moral agenda – removing the slums meant removing the slum dwellers. Nevertheless, when in 1890 the Grand Old Man of Liberalism, William Ewart Gladstone, visited the city (Dundee was granted city status in 1889), it was an occasion for the celebration of municipal achievement since 1870. The audience packed into the Kinnaird Hall to see Gladstone presented with the freedom of the city, was delighted when the guest of honour observed that Dundee had become, 'not only an enlarged, not only an improved, but a reconstructed city'.[43] Civic leaders throughout Dundee's modern history were acutely aware of what was going on elsewhere in Scotland (and Britain) in municipal government, and they constantly measured their practices and achievements against other authorities. In the early nineteenth century, they tended to seek nationally regarded architects to design important public buildings, a tendency which continued well into the nineteenth century. In 1867, for example, Sir George Gilbert Scott, the foremost architect of the Victorian Gothic, was approached to design the Albert Institute. Undoubtedly, more could have been achieved. Yet even here we need to show due recognition of the political constraints which surrounded municipal enterprise in the later nineteenth century. The problem was political *and* financial – how to create support for large increases in rates. The extension of the burgh boundary in 1831, 1866 and 1913, increased the rateable value of property within the town and latterly city. Profits from municipal services may have been limited by a desire to keep charges relatively low. There were well-entrenched conservative forces and interests on the Council, which sought to block change or limit its impact. Indeed, as John Kemp shows, the shopocracy, the lower middle class who traditionally supported the cause of economy in local government, were very well represented on the Council. Did these factors, however, have a relatively greater impact in Dundee than elsewhere?

The following chapters do not provide full answers to all the questions raised above, although they do offer some new insights. Most focus on the Victorian era (1837–1902), when so much of Dundee's human and material expansion took place. While there has been some excellent work in the past few decades on aspects of Dundee's history, there has been no attempt to apply to it recent historiographical perspectives and research methodologies. Modern work on other Scottish and British towns and cities provides a much enhanced comparative context for such an exercise. The chapters approach the subject from a variety of perspectives. They are, nevertheless, linked by several common themes, one of the most important of which is the rich interplay between image and reality in the urban past and in the interpretation of this past.

The physical development of the town from the late eighteenth to the early twentieth centuries is assessed in chapters by William Kenefick and Charles McKean. William Kenefick's examination of the development of Dundee into a major east-coast port with direct trading links with the Baltic and North America, identifies the harbour as a key point of growth and a symbol of the town's developing civic identity. The building of a monumental dockside archway in 1849, funded by public subscription and designed by a competition-winning Glasgow architect, confirmed the harbour's status as the 'gateway' to the town. The harbour was also the location for some of the town's finest buildings and the focus of many of the street improvements undertaken in the late eighteenth and early nineteenth century. Charles McKean further explores the development of the early nineteenth-century townscape in a provocative chapter confronting the physical 'difference' between Dundee and other Scottish towns. McKean challenges the assumptions made about Dundee on the basis of its physical appearance and, in particular, its failure to adopt the grid-iron street plans that typified urban development in almost every other Scottish town in the period. In explaining the absence of a 'new town' in Dundee he explores the relationship between private initiative and public planning and highlights the diversity within the Scottish experience of urban growth.

The theme of civic leadership is taken up in chapters by Louise Miskell and Lorraine Walsh. Louise Miskell conducts the first systematic, scholarly study of the composition of local government leadership in Dundee over a crucial fifty-year period of industrial development from 1820. Her picture of a local government elite in which retailers and craftsmen outnumbered manufacturers underlines the variety within the town's middle classes throughout this period and contributes to ongoing debates about the role of manufacturers in urban life and their relationship with the wider middle classes. The status of the town's leading industrialists was based more on their wealth and their reputations as employers and businessmen than on their participation in public life, although many were prominent supporters of local philanthropy. As a result, Dundee's image of manufacturing dominance throughout this period must be qualified. Lorraine Walsh further examines patterns of participation in Dundee's urban institutions with a study of the nature of support for the Dundee Royal Infirmary, Dundee's first major philanthropic foundation financed by subscription. She assesses the impact of changing middle-class attitudes towards charitable activity from the 1870s on the financing and management of the Infirmary. Her portrayal of a working class, actively participating in the provision of their own health care, forms part of an important reassessment of the working class experience in the town which Christopher A. Whatley further develops in his examination of social relations in the mid-Victorian period. His re-appraisal of a widely-used contemporary account of factory conditions in Dundee leads to a thoroughgoing re-evaluation of worker-employer relations in the town. The mutual respect between worker and employer and a shared sense of pride in the town's manufacturing development testified less to factory exploitation and more to workplace harmony. Jan Merchant offers a different perspective on this theme of workplace relations in her chapter on domestic servants in Dundee. Here she presents a study of the events of Dundee's maidservants' agitation in 1872. This was a highly unusual example of worker protest involving an easily forgotten sector of Dundee's non-textile female workforce.

The well-documented hardships of working-class life in Dundee, in particular, the poor housing provision for the town's textile labour force, are viewed from a new perspective in Myra Baillie's chapter on the work of social welfare activist, Mary Lily Walker. Walker's solution to the challenges posed by Dundee's housing crisis in the late nineteenth century was the institution of an ambitious programme of social investigation, education and welfare provision. In Walker, Dundee possessed an impressive reforming talent. Not only was her level of influence, as a woman, over social welfare provision unparalleled in any other Scottish town, it also placed Dundee at the forefront of social reform work in this period. Through an examination of her work Baillie demonstrates the extent to which private, charitable endeavour continued to precede, and work alongside, municipal initiative in confronting social ills, even into the early twentieth century.

Two further chapters deal with issues of city management in the late nineteenth and early twentieth centuries. Bob Harris's examination of the work of city engineer and architect James Thomson, like Baillie's chapter, highlights the influence of progressive thought and practice – in this case, in respect of town planning – in the city. Thomson's singular achievement was to absorb current thinking in the early twentieth century on town planning and seek to apply it to Dundee. Perhaps the best known of Thomson's work is the Logie Housing Scheme, which was the first in Scotland to be built with Treasury subsidy after the First World War. Yet it is the totality of Thomson's vision for the development of Dundee which stands out, and the extent to which it had already been worked out before the beginning of the war. The conflicting demands and constraints of local government, however, placed strong limitations on how far ambitious plans could be implemented. Another growing constraint was political. By the second decade of the twentieth century, as John Kemp demonstrates, Dundee's working classes were abandoning Liberalism and its class alliances in favour of independent Labour representation. The representatives of Labour in municipal government opposed proposed spending on grand urban design, particularly where this promised little short-term benefit to the working classes. As elsewhere, it was the 'housing question' which was to dominate the Council's agenda from 1916.

As Murdo Macdonald's chapter illustrates, Thomson's planning vision was not the only creative energy at work in Dundee in the late nineteenth and early twentieth centuries. His exploration of the intellectual and cultural networks which fostered artistic and academic talents in the city reveals an image of Dundee often obscured by its much stronger reputation as an industrial centre. In fact the interest generated by the British Association's visits to the town in 1867 and 1912 were part of a long tradition of enthusiasm for and commitment to artistic provision in the town, evidenced in the work of the Watt Institution, the Dundee Art Union and the establishment of the Albert Institute. This chapter challenges readers to incorporate these lesser-known activities into their mental picture of Dundee. The same can be said for all of the chapters in this volume. Collectively they seek not only to challenge old stereotypes but to replace them with a new interpretation of the town as an industrial centre which had much in common, in terms of social and cultural life and civic identity, with its counterparts elsewhere in Britain. In some respects this work raises as many questions as it answers, revealing the need for further research. In its coverage, nevertheless, of the development of the townscape, the make-up of local government, the management of social problems, the relations between employers and their workforces and cultural life, it tackles themes of central importance to our understanding of not just Dundee but urban Britain in the Victorian period.

LM, CAW, BH

'Not even the trivial grace of a straight line'[1] – or why Dundee never built a New Town

Charles McKean[2]

'Quite why Dundee never acquired a New Town is something of a mystery.'
(Frank Walker, *Urban form 1750 – 1850*.)

DUNDEE IS FAR more likely to be associated with jute, jam and journalism in popular perception, than with the graciousness of early nineteenth-century neo-classical town planning. It never built a new town because, so myth has it, it had never been the kind of town that aspired to civic embellishment of that sort, and nor could it have afforded it. Indeed, by the late nineteenth century, rather than being associated with good planning, Dundee had become a by-word for bad: 'a town with the finest site in Scotland spoiled by the absence of a plan', as Sir Patrick Geddes put it. Indeed, it was the condition of *jute* Dundee that turned the mind of the young professor of botany in Dundee to town planning and the founding of that discipline.[3] By examining the condition of *pre-jute* Dundee, this paper will demonstrate how Dundee could well have afforded to build a new town but – alone of all substantial communities in Scotland – deliberately chose not to, and why that might have occurred.

There were several reasons why a Scottish town council might decide to embark upon constructing a new town in the principal 'improvement' period between 1770 and 1830 – not least that everybody else was doing it. The physical state of the centres of most Scots medieval towns had been deteriorating during the eighteenth century, leading to a fear of infectious disease accompanied, perhaps, by a growing preference for social segregation:

All over Europe, but especially in rapidly industrialising Scotland and England, with their privately driven campaigns of improvement, urbanisation and the growth of manufacturing were provoking demands from the landed classes and the urban wealthy for more exclusive living areas insulated from the disease and crime of the old centres.[4]

Moreover, the layout of the old towns was increasingly obviously at odds with the needs of the growth of commerce. Above all, and resonant in these days of competing cities, there may well have been a desire for civic embellishment.[5] The case put forward in the 1751 *Proposals*[6] for the new town of Edinburgh was based upon all of these considerations. Extensive dilapidation was discovered within the Old Town, and there was growing distaste for the social intermingling caused by sharing the same staircase – described as 'vertical streets'. The difficulty of wheeled access to the High Street had to be remedied, and the city would be embellished by the construction of as regular and fashionable a suburb as possible, in the manner of Munich and London, on a new site to the north. By this means, they sought to attract the aristocrats who had defected to London back to Edinburgh.[7]

In the eighty years following, the energy expended in the creation of some 500 new towns throughout Scotland[8] was prodigious. Albeit that so many of them remained semi-abortive,[9] new towns became a defining characteristic of 'improvement'. Before the proposals for Edinburgh had even been put to competition in 1766, plantations or new towns had begun in Callander (1735), Ullapool (1757), Whiteley (1763), New Byth (1763) and Aberchirder (1763). Some were the consequence of enclosure and relocation, such as Fochabers in 1774[10] and Cullen in 1811, and one – Ardrossan[11] – was industrial; but the vast majority were small agricultural rural villages laid out to a grid-iron rational plan.[12] A significant number, however, were planned for larger communities – although rarely for entirely new urban communities in the manner of Inveraray. They were, rather, suburbs dependant upon an existing town centre, comprising a formal plan of, usually, terraced housing laid out to a grid with axial vistas to important civic buildings. Nor were such developments the preserve solely of the larger or wealthier towns like Glasgow, Edinburgh or Perth. Arbroath, Montrose and towns as small as Langholm or as extraordinary (given its size, economy and location) as Banff, all proposed grid-iron suburban residential expansion. The ordering of society was mirrored in the ordering of the physical form. It was that for which Scotland became famous.

The most distinctive characteristic, therefore, of Dundee's urban development within its Scottish context – and a principal cause of the emergence of the Dundee myth – is that it chose *not* to build one or more new towns. The argument goes something like this: if the right sort of people had lived in Dundee, *of course* they would have built a new town. Everyone else had done so. *Ergo*, the denizens of early nineteenth-century Dundee had less foresight even than the inhabitants of Langholm. The resulting myth has come to dominate perceptions of Dundee ever since. Perhaps its best exposition, ironically, appeared as the introduction to one of the first books attempting to evaluate Dundee's built form dispassionately within a broader Scottish context:

> The eighteenth century burgh never experienced that expansion of a civilised middle class which ensured the success of Edinburgh's New Town . . . Subsequent generations [did not] possess the resources and fierce determination . . . A modest burgh with a fairly typical eighteenth century social stratification . . . became within a matter of decades an industrial city with an overwhelmingly proletarian population.[13]

Indeed the myth had taken hold to such an extent that it portrayed Dundee as little more than a proletarian mill town in 1801, whose physical condition had already so deteriorated that whatever scanty middle class it had, had already fled to Broughty Ferry for reasons of health.[14] Still believed as correct only sixteen years ago, we now know it to be almost entirely wrong. Little existed between the ferry at Broughty and the fishing village of West Ferry in 1800. A feuing plan for a 'new town at the North Ferry', drawn up in 1801, remained largely unbuilt save for Fishertown cottages lining the shore. Even once its grid-iron plan was drawn up for General Hunter of Burnside by Dundee's town architect David Neave, the feus remained mostly unoccupied even as late as 1836;[15] and Neave's rather naive 1825 plan for an extension to the north-east comprising a new Hunter Square and adjacent Hillside Crescent, all composed of detached houses, remained unbuilt[16] like so many other contemporary feuing proposals in Dundee.[17] So far as the Ferry was concerned, there was still nowhere for these mythologically fleeing *bourgeois* to roost. Even after the opening of the Dundee to Arbroath railway in 1838, George Mathewson's ambitious feuing plan for filling adjacent Barnhill with three classes of house plots – from the tiny to the grandiose – remained largely abortive.[18] The flight to this suburb, at least, was a phenomenon of the mid-century onwards.[19]

The myth then suggests that Dundee had neither the ambition nor sufficient middle classes to fuel a new town. If that had, in fact, been the case, why all the effort in preparing these grid-iron feueing plans? In any case, facts suggest otherwise.

'A spirit for literature and education manifests itself in Dundee.'[20]

In the second half of the eighteenth century Dundee had been a powerful and expanding town, processing Baltic flax imported from St Petersburg and Riga (where some of its merchants lived[21]) and then exporting it directly to America and the West Indies for use as slave clothing (Plate 7).[22] It had earlier been the second city of Renaissance Scotland,[23] and judging from the illustrations prepared for Lamb's *Dundee – its quaint and historical buildings*,[24] most of its buildings survived General Monk's sack in 1651 – even if some had been damaged and reoccupied subsequently two storeys lower. They had been fashionably refitted by around 1686 (the date on some tenements in Fish Street) with the new-fangled sash and case windows fresh in from the Netherlands. It has been typical to dismiss accounts of seventeenth-century Dundee – such as 'the buildings speak the substance and riches of the place' – as simple gratitude for civic hospitality;[25] yet is it not possible that they were telling the truth? Ships and cargoes entering Dundee harbour had increased by 450% between 1660 and 1697, a figure which was still almost double the boom pre-war years of 1637.[26] The town had built itself a fashionable hospital in 1687, and new or upgraded buildings of the late seventeenth century stalk the pages of Lamb's *Dundee*. Further evidence of quality emerges from charters such as that for David Hunter's house completed before 1697 on the north side of the Argyle Gate (Overgate) – 'a great lodging with portico, gallery, well, garden and houses'.[27]

By virtue of its refitting and rebuilding after Monk, Dundee had become arguably the most modern ancient town in Scotland, and Daniel Defoe was considerably impressed:

> it is one of the best trading towns in Scotland, and that as well in foreign business as in manufacture and home trade . . . It is exceedingly populous, full of stately houses, and large handsome streets . . . The inhabitants appear here like gentlemen, as well as men of business, and yet are real merchants too.[28]

After a shaky start to the eighteenth century, the burgh embellished the High Street with quite the finest new town house in Scotland, completed in 1735,[29] employing Scotland's leading architect, William Adam, to design it (Plate 1). Becoming the leading Scottish centre for coarse linens manufactured from low-grade Baltic flax in the 1740s,[30] the town then invested in three 'very hand-some'[31] shoreside pack houses or warehouses, designed by William Robertson of Leven in 1758. The following year, the harbour was described as 'one of the best ports for trade in all Scotland'.[32] In 1768, Dundee's port commissioners invited Britain's most celebrated engineer, John Smeaton, to give advice on how to prevent the fast-flowing Tay from silting the harbour.[33] 'Jupiter' Carlyle, chronicler of the Enlightenment, who passed through on his trip to the North of Scotland in 1765, was impressed by Dundee's opulence, although he found it 'an old town without Beauty or Elegance'.[34] It was soon to change.

The town's shift westward to the plateau of the High Street was largely complete, leaving the low-lying Seagate to periodic flooding and commerce – for it was there that clustered the whaling companies and their noisome boiling yards. Perhaps there had been a similar withdrawal from the Wellgate and Hilltown in view of the number of tanneries located there.[35] The main streets were mod-ernised by cutting back the timber frontages, sitting upon arcades, to the stone buildings some eight feet behind. It is unclear whether this cutting back of the galleries and foreworks was instructed by dean of guild or council – as had been the case in Edinburgh and Glasgow – or was a matter of individual choice.[36] There is no such instruction in the dean of guild records, as has been suggested that one might expect.[37] The Guildry Court confined itself to individual petitions for the rebuilding of properties and the inspection of dangerous ones[38] in relation to the reasonably continuous upgrading that was taking place.

In the early eighteenth century, initiative appears to have lain with Dundee's Guildry, which had been an early, if not entirely successful, pioneer of new town plantation. In 1713, it had purchased six acres of land from the lairds of St Fort and Inverdovat at Newport for the purpose of building a new port (hence its name) with houses and piers,[39] but little seems to have come of it, and the land was sold by the end of the century.[40] Nonetheless, it was clearly taking the lead in urban embellishment during the early 1770s.[41] In July 1771, the Trades agreed to fund a third part, with the Kirk Session and Town Council, of the cost of a new chapel (later church) and when the Council decided to withdraw,[42] the Trades stepped in to cover. Designed by the town's wright or architect, Samuel Bell, so that its spire faced axially down Murraygate, St Andrew's church so impressed Thomas Pennant that it was the only modern church illustrated in his volumes – which was probably the reason that the heritors of Banff decided to copy it.[43] The Trades then decided to feu out their yard facing the church between Cowgate and Seagate, held by their General Fund. Bell split it with a 22 foot-wide road, and divided it into four lots.[44] Thus it is to the Trades rather than to the Council that the credit must go for the creation of the first post-medieval street in the town. Once Riddoch came to power, however, the Trades were relegated to impotence, only to re-awaken in the acrimonious debates that emerged over the Dundee Harbour Bill in 1814. Thereafter, they extracted exemplary revenge in 1817 by being the agent of the personal attack upon Provost Alexander Riddoch's probity.[45]

Probably to coincide with the construction of the new Trades House closing the vista at the east end of the market place, a plan of the town was drawn up by William Crawford in 1776-77. The Guildry had paid Samuel Bell £42 10s for 'plans, architecting and overseeing the whole building'[46] and on its completion in 1778 let the premises as a Coffee House, which was to become the focus of the town's commercial and social activity (Plate 4). Bell's design – with its pediment and cupola – self-consciously paid homage to Adam's Town House. With the addition of Bell's pedimented English Chapel (later Union Hall) five years later (Plate 5), closing the vista at the western end of the market place, Dundee's centre was adorned by three distinguished, pedimented civic buildings which provided the necessary protection against wind to keep the town's 'dealing floor' comfortable (Plate 6).

Dundee was a flourishing, alert town of ambitious, intelligent people. It had its own Enlightenment Club – the Speculative Society – with a membership of twenty-six professionals, ministers and local lairds.[47] Similar clubs in Edinburgh, Aberdeen and Glasgow were largely dependant upon their university professoriates. To establish one in a town without a university was ambitious indeed. James Stark, one of the four booksellers in Dundee who were members of the Merchant Company[48] in 1782 (and who traded from the Guardhouse at the rear of the Town House from 1740—1800), had earlier been the servant of the poet Allan Ramsay, who had founded Edinburgh's first public library.[49] Furthermore, Dundee's numismatist, James Wright, came under government scrutiny in 1793 for having promoted a cheap edition of Tom Paine's *Rights of Man* 'that was in the hands of almost every countryman'.[50]

Some twenty-four newspapers and magazines were published in the town between 1755 and 1835 including the internationally-focused political journal, the *Dundee Repository*. Far from being parochial, it contained no news about

Dundee and virtually none about Scotland. It purported to provide, instead, up-to-date dispatches from the revolution in Paris and contributions about contemporary affairs in London.[51] It was published by the adventurous Dundee-based Colville publishing dynasty which, between 1790 and 1825, also produced newspapers, magazines, a *Gazetteer of Britain,* the *Statistical Account* of 1793 and *Dundee Delineated* in 1822. There must have been a market for such enterprises; and given that Dundee in 1821 was only a medium-sized town of 30,500 inhabitants, it must have been unusually literate. Eventually there was to be a public newspaper room on the Shore in addition to that in the Trades Hall, and eleven halls or rooms to let for assemblies, meetings or sales.[52] A further society, the Rational Institution, was founded in 1811 and equipped with a library, museum and philosophical apparatus. Its object was the diffusion of knowledge although, 'No dispute of a theological or political nature, which may have the smallest tendency to call forth party-spirit or sow the seeds of discord', was permitted.[53] In 1841, Dundee contained a higher proportion of professional people than Glasgow,[54] which was, by then, well embarked upon what may be called its fourth new town. There was a bookshop or stationer, four years later, for every 2,000 Dundonians.[55] Culturally and financially, Dundee could well compete with towns and cities embarking on a new town spree (Plate 3).

Pride in the eighteenth-century town culminated with the publication of *A Statistical Account of the Parish and Town of DUNDEE in the year MDCCXC1* by Rev. Robert Small. An important figure in late eighteenth-century Dundee, Small was a Fellow of the Royal Society of Edinburgh, and was to be one of the two originators of the Infirmary. His text had been prepared as the Dundee contribution to Sir John Sinclair's momentous enterprise, the *First Statistical Account,* where it was duly published. The enterprising Dundee Colvilles, however, commissioned a new town plan from William Crawford, junior, along with some new illustrations and additional notes from Small, and published it as a freestanding volume (sometimes referred to as a 'History of Dundee') in 1793 (Plate 7). To Small, the town was flourishing on a lovely site surrounded by 'thriving, rich and intelligent farmers'.[56] Its principal defects were the narrowness of some of the old lanes, the absence of public walks, the almost total want of adequate educational institutions and the lack of care in laying out the new suburbs. The overwhelming impression, however, was one of civic pride. A series of ten slightly boastful coins or medals were cast by James Wright, depicting Dundee's civic buildings as, the 'emblems of the "commerce" which has latterly so much elevated and enriched this very flourishing town'.

Speculative and enterprising,[57] Dundee's elite briskly set about providing the town with its principal social and public monuments. In 1794, a group planning a new hospital invited John Paterson from Edinburgh to design it. Paterson had been chief assistant to Robert and James Adam, who were probably the preferred architects – Robert having designed the Glasgow Infirmary and his father William the Edinburgh one. But Robert had died in 1792 and James in 1794, so they put up with Paterson. Nonetheless, the *ambition* had again been for the best architect in the country. In 1808, subscribers had commissioned Samuel Bell to design the Theatre Royal in Castle Street.[58] Since its taller pedimented facade differed materially from the feu requirements of two-storeyed stone and slated houses for the rest of the street,[59] a relaxation was sought on the grounds that the theatre would be 'ornamental, and beautify rather than deform that part of the street',[60] and what was effectively a retrospective building warrant was granted five years later.[61]

In 1813, the directors planning a Lunatic Asylum selected the architect William Stark. It may be that the merchant John Johnston had met him in St Petersburg whilst the latter was living and trading there[62] whilst Stark was in some way involved in its architecture.[63] However Stark, a specialist in lunatic asylums who had published on them, was nonetheless considered by Lord Cockburn to be 'the best modern architect that Scotland has produced'.[64]

Since most of the nineteenth-century additions to the town were to take place to the north, on the newly released Meadowlands and Ward Lands, Dundee's town centre still possibly retained more pre-1700 buildings and townscape than any other city in Scotland by the time of the 1871 Improvement Act. This substantial inheritance, which had survived virtually intact, was to be cut out of the town's fabric in four ambitious redevelopment programmes between 1871 and 1965. It was of no value to a community seeking a new identity. Once the old town had gone, the existence of a new town might have balanced the new perceptions of Dundee as a modern, industrial, demotic, populist, proletarian city of little charm but of couthy character. Conversely, its absence reinforced it, and played a critical role in how Dundonians rewrote their own history downwards. Yet the foundations of the myth – that Dundee had not built a new town because it lacked quality, money, ambition and class – were arrant nonsense.

Dundee merchants would have known of the grid-iron cities in the Baltic and in America with which they traded. Robert Jobson, who lived in Riga[65] probably importing 'ratikzer' or 'Russia' flax, is likely to have visited neo-classical St Petersburg, or the seventeenth-century grid-iron suburbs of Copenhagen like Christianshavn, or even the great grid-iron seventeenth-century seaport of Göteborg (Gothenburg) which, like Dundee alone, had erected a statute in honour of Poseidon.[66] So, if Dundonians were well aware of the new towns elsewhere, why did they not build one themselves? A certain feeling of smugness emerges from late eighteenth and early nineteenth-century Dundee publications, implying that the need for a new town was less urgent there than elsewhere. After all, as a consequence of its late seventeenth-century rebuilding, it was the most modern old town in Scotland, and its physical condition was probably very much better than that of Edinburgh or Glasgow – as the few dean of guild records that survived a fire imply was indeed the case. Few petitions relate to dangerous buildings, and there appear to have been no catastrophic building collapses, such as the one in 1751 in Edinburgh, which impelled the original *Proposals*. There was continuous upgrading and rebuilding during the later eighteenth century instead.

The principal advantage that the terraces of houses typical of a new town might have offered over tenement flats was an appropriate suite of reception rooms – dining room (and sometimes library) on the ground floor, drawing room and parlour on the first. It was associated with a certain status and formality of living. Inevitably, being distant from the town centre, they embodied increasing social segregation. But this desire for social segregation, so strong in Edinburgh, remained largely absent in Dundee. Of the 135 people who lived (or worked – the document is imprecise) in Murraygate in 1822, for example, fourteen merchants, three booksellers, three agents, eleven grocers and four surgeons jostled alongside four vintners, a slater, a saddler and a reedmaker.[67] Dundee street directories from the 1830s to the 1850s imply that such social intermingling continued almost until mid-century. Compare Edinburgh where, according to Robert Chambers, the last person of quality to inhabit the High Street had quit in 1817;[68] or Glasgow where, according to John Buchanan, conditions in the High Street had become so poor by 1848, that you could scarcely have given away buildings to a beggar on Glasgow Bridge.[69] Mobile Glaswegians had all decamped to one of the many new suburbs. Dundee's growth appears more to have resembled non-Scottish industrial towns such as Leeds, Wolverhampton and Cardiff.[70] Yet the difference between the town and its Scottish peers cannot be explained solely on the grounds that it was an industrial town and major port and the others were not. At this time, Glasgow was heavily dependent upon cotton, nearby Paisley (whose population overtook Dundee for a short while) was pre-eminently a weaving town, and Greenock, down the river, was a shipbuilding and trading port. All, nonetheless, had one or more new towns.

A desire for social segregation may have been less important to Dundonians. Such a social attitude appears confirmed by Small's observation that the merchants had not a male servant between them in 1792, an example of how – despite the substantial increase in their wealth – they remained 'strangers to extravagant and ruinous luxuries'.[71] Moreover, its society must have been upwardly mobile if even carters and labourers could own cottages in the industrial suburbs of Chapelshade or the Scouringburn village in the 1790s.[72] Only a few *grands bourgeois* enjoyed David Neave's pleasantly classical suburban villas on the sunny slopes to the west (Plate 18). So Dundonians, instead, elected to remain mixed within the better parts of the city centre, and in 1831, bombarded the recently appointed police commissioners with demands that something be done about the 'bands of strumpets and drunkards' parading through the streets[73] or about the more general problem of late night rowdies:

> The streets and houses of the town are at present infested by multitudes of prostitutes and pickpockets who, besides offering a constant annoyance, almost nightly commit robberies and breaches of the peace.[74]

Before the early 1830s, there was no question of conditions having driven the well-to-do to suburban exodus, and now that the police commissioners had their neatly uniformed constables on the beat, crime was actually diminishing.[75] Thus, when questioned in 1835 by a House of Commons committee on whether more public wells should be provided to the poorer parts of the town rather than areas inhabited by the richer classes, David Neave's new successor as town architect, James Black, replied: 'they are so much mixed that you cannot distinguish them'.[76]

This enthusiasm of the middle sort to stay living in the town centre indicates that it remained healthy. It was certainly so in 1793,[77] partly as the consequence of the many private as well as public wells;[78] and it was still the case in 1822: 'the whole extent abounds in wells of excellent water'.[79] Even in 1833, in the immediate aftermath of the cholera epidemic, it appears that only parts of the city centre had been identified as requiring attention.[80] Significantly, whereas the 1832 cholera had made no impact in the dense Narrows of the Murraygate at the very centre of the town, it had been particularly virulent in the Hawkhill which, until the year before, had been a suburb beyond the town boundary.[81]

There lies the clue. The continuing popularity of the city centre may have been the result of Dundee growing in a pattern inverse to other cities. Its 1800–20 expansion had taken place outside the city boundaries, mostly on land owned by David Hunter of Blackness. By 1793, 100 acres west of the West Port had been feued, and most of it for manufacturing.[82] Over 90% of Dundee's mill locations lay outside the pre-1831 boundaries of the town,[83] and no attempt had been made to bring order to such locations. Indeed, freedom from control might well have been significant in influencing where manufacturers set up; for it is patently clear from all maps of Dundee that significant parts of the town – particularly between the Overgate and the Nethergate – remained largely undeveloped and at low density up to at least 1854. As early as 1792, industry was opting for what Small described as 'the late additional suburbs' which he condemned as having been built 'without any general plan and without the least regard to health, elegance or cleanliness'.[84] By 1822, these suburbs – the Hawkhill and Scour-ingburn, laid out 'without any regard to taste, convenience or cleanliness' – had become the subject of intense civic embarrassment:

> The houses have been built generally low, and so arranged that every one obstructs or defiles the other. Some indeed are left unfinished. It is therefore, with few exceptions the receptacle of the lowest and worst part of the community; the continual abode of the typhus fever; and is converted from a fine green healthy meadow into a lazar-house, and the fixed residence of filth, disease, uncleanness and wretchedness.[85]

These warnings were to prove only too true when cholera arrived ten years later. Thus to Dundonians, the suburbs had come to imply not fashionable living but the converse. It was workmen 'from the manufactories in the suburbs' who marched to the radical protest meeting in Magdalen Green in 1819 and by 1833, the suburbs had become 'the haunt of the disorderly'.[86]

Thus three of the principal motives for building a new town – crumbling houses, fear of disease and an overwhelming desire for social stratification – appear to have been absent from early nineteenth-century Dundee. Yet there remained those two matters central to enlightenment urban thinking: civic improvement and civic embellishment. In 1777, the council entered four decades of control by Alexander Riddoch, and it is to him that one should look for the direction of the town's fortunes. Appointed treasurer in September 1776, he became provost the following year; and thereafter manipulated the sett of the burgh for his influence to remain unchallenged until the battle for the harbour was most acrimoniously joined in 1814.[87] His was the predominant hand over Dundee during the period of improvement, and when facing deposition and personal obloquy in 1817, he defended his record on the grounds of good husbandry:

> I shall be entitled to some merit for having out of a revenue more scanty than that of any town of equal size in Scotland expended very considerable sums in making new streets, widening old ones, and otherwise improving the Burgh without diminishing its public resources.[88]

He was proud of his most frugal hand.

The town he now led was enjoying growth in both population and in international trade. But it remained substantially unaltered from the Dundee of the late seventeenth century. Its harbour was small and tidal, despite the addition of new piers c.1790 and c.1804. Access was largely down the narrow curving lanes and wynds typical of the routes between harbour and market place in Baltic cities. The town centre consisted of four principal streets – the Overgate and the Nethergate extending to north-west and south-west; and the Murraygate and Seagate to north-east and south-east. They met at the Cross, a spacious 360-foot-long by 100-foot-broad wind-protected market place or High Street – effectively the 'dealing floor' of the town. Perhaps to maintain shelter against the wind, each of Dundee's streets had evolved with an unusual 'narrows' – a pinch point sometimes as tight as eight feet: the narrows of the Seagate, the Overgate, the Nethergate and of the Murraygate. Odiferous activities – the fishmarket, mealmarket and shambles – had been relegated to more wind-cleansed sites by the Shore. The Greenmarket, then in the High Street, was soon to follow.[89]

There were two principal models of new town planning that Dundee's Council could have studied. If it was unenthusiastic about following Edinburgh's – and later Aberdeen's – model of being the prime mover in the creation of a new town, it could always have followed Glasgow's example. Glasgow Town Council commissioned the surveyor James Barry to draw up 'a regular plan to the line of the streets' for the city's expansion, but left it up to private owners and developers to seize the opportunities, provided that every purchaser kept to the plan.[90] In 1792–93, Col. Campbell of Blythswood commissioned a feuing plan for Blythswood hill from a Mr. Craig which, like Glasgow's other new town plans, slotted seamlessly into the original grid-iron layout of the city's first new town plan of 1786.[91] Dundee commissioned no such plan.

Another reason suggested for Dundee's lack of a new town is 'the absence of strong-minded landowners'.[92] The initiative in Perth, had come entirely from an adjoining landowner, Thomas Anderson, who memorialised Perth Town Council in 1797 that he wished to offer to the public the lands of Blackfriars that he had purchased, for building – 'and upon such a plan as might be perfectly agreeable to the Town. For which purpose he wished to bring all the grounds within the regality.'[93] The opulent terraced houses of Rose and Marshall Streets, and the Academy, were designed by Robert Reid.

The principal proprietor of the properties surrounding Dundee, owning beautiful south-facing slopes overlooking the Tay from the sea and Magdalen Green north through Hawkhill to Scouringburn, was bluff David Hunter of Blackness (so vividly painted by Henry Raeburn). In 1777, he had the land surveyed by William Crawford but probably only for feuing purposes.[94] Rather than commissioning a strategic plan for such a prime landholding, there are all the signs of a progressive squandering of his patrimony; sporadic feuing of a cottage here, a large house there, and a manufactory in the next place. It is as though he was having to fund bank failures or bad habits by periodic sale; but whatever the reason, Dundee's greatest urban opportunity was frittered away. By 1813, a jumble of houses, villas, cottages and gardens had been built – their amenity already damaged by two ropeworks. North of Perth Road, it was much worse around the rapidly deteriorating Hawkhill. A further plan of the entire estate nine years later when David Hunter, junior, came of age, confirmed the incoherence of his father's feuing, and the extent of multiple ownerships.[95] So whilst William Burn was in Dundee anyway to design Camperdown House and the Union Bank in Murraygate,[96] young Hunter asked him to produce a plan for the western portion of his estate, comprising a crescent of terraced houses at Blackness Toll, and an estate of small detached houses spreading uphill.[97] Two terraced houses survive in the Crescent.

Between Blackness and the town centre lay the town's own lands – namely the former gardens or Kirklands of the now-demolished Hospital, leading up to the Wards and the Meadowlands which ran right across just beyond the northern boundary of the town. Herein lay the principal opportunity for a town council-inspired, neo-classical residential suburb of the type so prevalent elsewhere in Scotland. In 1793, the Council decided to roup the Kirklands to create a new street from the Hospital to West Chapelshade, and thus to the road to Coupar Angus.[98] Strikingly unambitious, they divided a single stretch of short street into twelve lots. Each house had to consist of a ground storey and two stories above, close to, and facing the new street.[99] It was to be the nearest that Dundee resembled other Scottish cities in building terraces rather than detached houses,[100] and although some were bought as speculation (the merchant John Watt bought four lots), and seven by people in the building industry, the street remained largely unbuilt for the next thirty years. Proprietors facing Tay Square were required to sow seed and contribute one seventh to the railings for the 'common benefit of all', and when they did not do so, the square became a depository of rubbish. The Council's husbanding of its new suburb can be gauged from the fact that it did not enforce the feu conditions until compelled by a lawsuit from the angry occupant of lot seven in 1806.[101]

Riddoch's biographer suggests that whereas he had not presided over the creation of a classical new town, he had nonetheless left behind a pleasantly laid out burgh with some fine buildings well suited to its commercial function.[102] So how had his Council dealt with the inherited inconveniences of Dundee's plan – the 'Narrows' of each main street opening into the High Street? The Provost's tendency was to buy small plots of land and then recoup his outlay from the town's treasurer -a habit which may well have underlain the 1817 allegations of corruption. For example, Riddoch bought two tenements and a garden at the foot of Tindall's Wynd, to remove what appears to have been a marginal inconvenience. It is not stated what he paid, and there seems to have been no requirement to present vouchers. When he assured the Council that the cost by the sale of the residual land could easily be recouped, it purchased the land back from him for £375 and offered it for the upset price of £300. Although it was offered twice, there were no takers.[103] The implication is that the land was not worth the sum which Riddoch, as provost, had persuaded the Council to reimburse him.

By 1802, the Narrows of the Nethergate had become an insupportable bottleneck in an increasingly busy street, which kept flooding.[104] Although the minutes of the Town Council depict the 'reform' of the Narrows of the Nethergate as 'an object of so much importance to the town',[105] its actions did not match the rhetoric. The Council would make a languid, periodic, opportunistic purchase of a property or two on the north side of the street from time to time over the next eight years; but showed decisiveness only when the remaining recalcitrant owners' reluctance to sell their properties drove it to secure an Act of Parliament in 1810.[106] The Narrows of the Overgate and of the Murraygate remained untouched, and those of the Seagate were addressed only by what we would nowadays call a 'road-widening line'; in other words, owners were required to set their buildings back when redeveloping.[107] No action was taken over the Murraygate Narrows and it remained to become the primary spur of the 1871 Improvement Act. This lackadaisical approach was also demonstrated in the matter of Dundee's new streets. Bell Street, along the southern boundary of Chapelshade, was merely a formalisation in 1803 of a popular track against which the Council had periodically fulminated developments over the previous decades; a slightly widened Burial Wynd was renamed Barrack Street in 1807; and in 1803, the Council accepted Riddoch's purchase for £130 of James Matthew's house in the Overgate as the first step in opening a street out to the town's Ward lands lying to the north (to emerge in the 1820s as Lindsay Street).

This unimpressive approach would have surprised few curious onlooking citizens; for that had been the way the Council had earlier set about Castle Street. In 1795, Riddoch had proposed opening a new street from the market place to the harbour blasted through the castle rock, taking advantage of a failed speculation to establish a Tontine Hotel. He informed the Council that:

> the whole subjects would be very useful and even profitable to the community as it would enable them to open a new communication with the shore and, if he was not mistaken, not only have a street of proper breadth but building stances on each side of it.[108]

In January 1795 the Council bought the land from the committee of Tontine subscribers and Samuel Bell was instructed to lay out the street, with the following minimal feuing conditions: 'buildings should be ground and two stories above, stone and slated, which should be occupied as dwelling houses and shops allenarly [sic]'.[109] But for the next eleven years, this new access to the harbour remained blocked at the foot by the owners of a riverside woodyard whilst negotiating adequate compensation.[110] Those owners were Riddoch and his partner Baillie Peddie.

During the Riddoch period, the Council was responsible for only one act of patronage – building the Steeple Church on the site of the nave of St Mary's, ruined since 1547. As though the Trades' experience of building St Andrew's Church was irrelevant, the Provost and Baillie Riddoch were dispatched to the annual Convention of Royal Burghs at Edinburgh 'to inform themselves . . . of the proper steps necessary for obtaining an erection of another church . . . the probable expenses of the same, *and if an erection of two churches could be obtained on the same expense with one*[111] [my italics]. It was not a very superior attitude to patronage. The church was designed by Samuel Bell.

Discontent with the Council's ineffectiveness amongst the town's rising entrepreneurs emerged first in 1783 when the Trades resolved to petition parliament for Burgh reform.[112] Whereas that was part of a Scottish-wide movement, it had become more serious in 1789, when a body called the Dundee Reform Committee placed before the Council a letter alleging alienation of property and mismanagement of revenue, and received barely an acknowledgement.[113] The opposition coalesced into an occasional committee of merchants, manufacturers and shipowners, who were probably behind an 1801 petition to the King complaining about harassment of the America trade by naval vessels:

> The inhabitants of this large and prosperous town and neighbourhood have long been principally employed and supported by the manufacture of linens for the West India market much interrupted by His Majesty's Ships of War.[114]

Then, two years later, a memorial from the merchants and manufacturers impelled the Council to petition Parliament to have Dundee declared a free port.[115] It was the last straw, however, when the Council decided to go to Parliament in 1811 with a proposal to widen the narrows of the Nethergate – and piggybacked onto the end of it measures for further harbour improvements: '*also* [note the 'also'] for additional piers and other improvements to the harbour of Dundee and for the augmenting of the Shore'.[116]

The Council's record on harbour development was no better that its record on town planning and civic embellishment. It casually decided to build a new east pier in 1804,[117] before checking whether it had adequate revenue. Its money was already spent – it was only a tithe of what they had spent in the purchase of a single property in the Nethergate – and they had to borrow. The new pier was a low priority. Given this record, it was hardly surprising that the potential of a parliamentary bill dealing with the harbour was keenly seized. 'A committee of respectable merchants' objected 'most materially',[118] and the harbour proposal was withdrawn for further consideration to allow the Nethergate bill to pass. As a more comprehensive harbour proposal was formulated, the principal opposition coalesced in a 'committee of merchants, manufacturers and shipowners'. In their view, the wholly uncommercial approach of the Council to the harbour was symbolised by its application of harbour income to the town's general needs,[119] as had patently been the Council practice over the preceding decades. The radicals, plotting in George Miln's bookshop in the High Street,[120] denied its right to do so, and obtained the support of the Trades, as 'representing the commercial interest of the town',[121] in opposing the Council's Harbour Bill.[122] The 1815 Harbour Act moved control of the harbour from the Council to harbour commissioners, the majority of whom represented the commercial interest of the town.

In 1819, Riddoch told the Parliamentary Select Committee that he had been utterly constrained by finance, since the total annual revenue of the town amounted to an inadequate £2,000. His biographer buys the story.[123] The town's accounts appear nowhere in an accessible and credible form – deliberately so, said his enemies – and are fiendishly difficult to check. Yet in 1808, the Council had been able to spend much more than £2,000 (with additional annuities) just on buying properties for the widening of the Nethergate.[124] Outsiders calculated the revenues in 1793 at between £2,200 and £4,000,[125] in 1799 at £3,000,[126] and not less than £4,000 in 1803, of which £2,200 was unallocated.[127] In 1815–16, that part of the harbour revenue obtainable from Shore Dues *alone* raised £4,096.[128] So Riddoch's protestations in 1819 lack credibility – never mind the evidential fact that the other cities had accepted the need to borrow capital to undertake some of their improvements.[129] The obscurity of the town's financial position tends to support the anonymous 'Monster of self-election' pamphleteer in his statement that council treasurer Alexander Keay, 'refused to serve, because, though Treasurer of the Burgh, *he was not allowed to see the accounts*[130] [my italics]. Frugality is not necessarily synonymous with good husbandry, and the town's assets had not been husbanded well.

It would be difficult to underestimate the high political drama taking place in Dundee over the Harbour Bill and the Guildry's bid for freedom from Council control between 1814 and 1819. There was meeting and counter-meeting. Rancour grew and dominated the newspapers, Riddoch attacking the Guildry supporters,[131] and the anonymous *Verax* replying by attacking 'a junta comprising the Provost and his adherents'.[132] The Guildry then issued a law suit against the magistrates. Alarmed at the damage to the town and that 'much personal abuse had been used in former discussions with the magistrates', senior Dundee businessmen sought to heal the breach.[133] They agreed to treat between Council and Guildry, Riddoch being all charm and complaisance. It came down to John Baxter of Idvies negotiating with Riddoch's right-hand man, the slippery and egregious Patrick Anderson, and several meetings were held. Whilst it appeared that a solution was possible, Baxter spotted that the Council meeting kept on being postponed. When finally challenged upon the issue, Riddoch finally exclaimed to Baxter that 'he would never yield, as first magistrate, the power to which he had succeeded'.[134] Negotiations collapsed, the lawsuit proceeded and, eventually, the Guildry succeeded. The damage done to the town's collective purpose by Riddoch's dissimulation must have been enormous. Busy and powerful businessmen, including the town clerk, had taken time to negotiate a settlement for the good of the town as a whole, and Riddoch had mocked them. It is not too fanciful to suppose that the business interests of Dundee thereafter determined to leave as little power in the hands of the Council as possible.

A burnt fragment from the Guildry Sederunt illuminates the abrupt end of Riddoch's power.[135] On 6 October 1817, Deacon Robert Mudie presented a petition to Provost Riddoch, Patrick Anderson, David Hazeel and John Gray, to the effect that the town's accounts of the last ten years and more should be made available. It was accompanied by this charge (the fragmented nature is the consequence of the burning):

> At the Head Court on Monday last, publicly and in face of the Burgesses . . . were brought against Alexander Riddoch . . . the chief magistrate of this burgh in a . . . and official manner by a constituent member of the Town Council certain heavy charges . . . of grossest malversation, – of having exposed . . . sale and turned to his own private emolument . . . offices which his political influence as . . . magistrate gave him the nomination . . . ing entered into transactions as in . . . community and afterwards appropria . . . himself the proceeds and advantages thence arising, of having squandered the public revenue in foolish and absurd speculations, and then converting to his own individual use even the little returns which those speculations offered.[136]

James Gellatly supported the motion on the grounds that 'The very Treasurer of the Town is kept in a state of such complete and utter ignorances that his office is in fact become only but a name'. Riddoch, claiming that the books were available for anyone to read, refused to produce the required paper and – worse, refused to answer the allegations. With crocodile tears, the Guildry minuted, 'the Guildry regard the conduct of Provost Riddoch in refusing all explanation on the subject of such vast and serious importance with feelings of the most painful emotion'. Realising that they, themselves, might be held complicit with the Council since 1777, and that it would 'reflect disgrace upon the town', they therefore issued a more statesmanlike exhortation to the embattled provost:

> The Guildry cannot bring themselves to believe that Mr. Provost Riddoch should have been guilty of all or any of the matters then publicly laid to his charge; but at the same time they feel themselves called upon to state . . . that it was a bounden duty not just to himself but to the public whose officer he is, not to allow them to go forward without an express and unequivocal contra-diction.[137]

Riddoch resigned as provost at the following meeting[138] almost exactly forty years after he first came to power. He had, however, a final laugh. In 1819, John Sturrock sought to persuade the harbour commissioners to raise more capital to finish the new harbour, rather than leave it half-built because the money had run out:

> If the work be completed in the manner proposed, the chance of loss from this cause will be very much lessened; and the community of Dundee will be put in possession of a harbour, which, for beauty and excellence of material and workmanship, is not equalled in Scotland, and probably not surpassed in any part of the empire.[139]

The problem was that the north quay of Telford's wet dock clipped a bit from Alexander Riddoch's building yard (a relic of his earlier, celebrated woodyard); and the commissioners had to thole a 'loss on Mr Riddoch's property' of £2,000[140] (as much as he, that year, claimed to be the entire town's revenue). The land was duly purchased, the dock completed, and Riddoch died a wealthy man.

'Such a busy manufacturing and maritime town as Dundee'[141]

Post-Riddoch Dundee was expanding and wealthy, much of its success deriving from its increasingly significant port whose new dock had opened in 1821. Vessel registration had increased several hundredfold between 1815 and 1820 – totalling 158 native registered vessels by 1822, the majority being foreign traders.[142] There was a substantial population of native sailors[143] who, with those of incoming vessels, proved very useful in filling the seats of the Castle Street and other theatres. The port and its new streets – Dock Street, South Union Street and Trades Lane – became the principal civic influence upon the south side of the town (Plate 19).

Although urban forms were already changing, Dundee's new Council had the opportunity to devise an outward-looking urban strategy for the still empty lands north of the town. The performance of the harbour trustees showed what foresight and strategy could achieve. So how did the post-Riddoch Council match up? Very like a post-communist state. Dundee displayed all the symbols of radical change whilst maintaining an extraordinary continuity of habits and personnel. William Burn was brought in to advise, and an Improvement Act followed in 1825.[144] Far from the strategic plan for the improvement of town and suburbs as claimed in the preliminaries, it addressed the city centre with the subtleties of a fragmentation bomb: a new street, 40–100 foot wide, between the Nethergate and the Harbour; a similar street from Cowgate to the Meadows (eventually Panmure Street), possibly extending west to join the Coupar Angus turnpike. Here was the chance to construct a new east-west bypass north of the historic core, and the town failed to seize it.

The main purpose of the Act, however, was the opening out and development of the marshy Meadowlands by three new, approximately parallel, streets running north and north-west from the High Street and the Murraygate to join this bypass. The first was opposite the Town House (Reform Street); the second opposite Castle Street (unbuilt); and the last half-way up Murraygate (unbuilt). School Wynd was to be widened (to become Lindsay Street), with a new street opened into the Ward opposite (North Lindsay Street). Barrack Street was to be straightened and widened, and North Tay Street extended into the Ward. *Inter alia*, the Act empowered the Council to lay out such streets in the Meadows 'for the ornament of the said town' and, as the Council should think proper, public gardens 'for the use and enjoyment of the inhabitants of the *adjacent* streets'. The description implies that there were to be enclosed gardens, solely for the enjoyment of adjacent proprietors – possibly along the lines of Edinburgh's Queen Street Gardens, or Glasgow's Blythswood Square. No plan by Burn has been found; but the Act implies some form of a grid layout with squares. From inaction, the Council appeared to have moved to over-action. But had it?

Its ancient opportunitistic habits remained strong. Well before the Act was passed, the provost purchased John Guild's house on the south side of the Nethergate 'in case it can be used' for the proposed new street – and thus fixed the line of Union Street.[145] Nor had its sense of urgency improved. Four years after Burn's visit, Neave's 1821 plan of the town was lithographed[146] probably in preparation for action. On 17 January the following year, the Council approved his plan for a 55 foot-wide new street from the Nethergate to the Harbour, and its 65 foot-wide extension southward.[147] Thus did Union Street and South Union Street emerge. That same day, it adopted Neave's plan for what became Exchange

Street through the late provost's graving dock. Given the quality of architectural advice they had sought from Burn, had their aspirations toward architectural quality improved since Tay and Castle Streets? Perhaps not:

> The corner lots restricted to the elevation proposed on Mr. Neave's plan, but no restrictions on the interior and no restriction on the other lots save that they shall not be more than three storeys in height above the cellar and shop storey. Houses must be erected before Whitsun 1831.[148]

As for the north side of Exchange Street, aesthetics got short shrift: 'the whole ground to be free of restrictions'. In the context of the strict feuing conditions of new towns elsewhere, and despite rumblings of discontent about the Council's failure to lay out new suburbs – a handsome square or even parallel street,[149] such remarkable laxity indicates a predisposition *against* central control.

Feuing of Reform Street was barely under way nine years after the Act:

> Fronting the Town Hall, a very handsome modern street has been formed, which vies in point of architectural elegance with any in the Scottish metropolis . . . There is not, perhaps in Scotland, a better classification of elegance and uniformity than that displayed on both sides of Reform Street.[150]

Not entirely so. Reform Street, laid out by James Brewster but designed by George Angus,[151] took over thirty years to complete and the Meadowlands and the Ward were never laid out with the graciousness implied by the succeeding plans of Brewster, George Matthewson in 1834 and of Charles Edward in 1846[152] (Plate 10). For the town's architects had made repeated proposals for the regularisation and rationalisation of the new lands, and their proper layout, which the town itself never appears to have supported. Reform Street itself had been intended as a neo-classical boulevard closed at each end by the porticos of the High School to the north, and the Town House to the south. The High School, being unfortunately constructed before any overall plan emerged, was built at an angle to the Town House, which meant that either one end or other of the street would open squint onto a portico. Brewster appears to have chosen to align the new street with the school – as part of a much wider scheme of gracious elliptical street blocks enfolding the school, the only relic of which is Euclid Crescent (Plate 9).[153] The school, however, was given insufficient elevation to command the vista at the north, and Reform Street burst at an angle into the High Street at the south. Likewise, in the absence of an overall plan, Lindsay Street provides but an oblique perspective to the Sheriff Court facade which, when finally complete, failed to command the vista from the Nethergate as originally intended (Plate 11).

Neither the Theatre Royal, lying flush with the facade of Castle Street, nor the Thistle Hall in Union Street had been given a setting worthy of their role as urban symbols. The Meadowlands and the Ward had provided the opportunity to redress such indifferent locations for civic buildings. Brewster's original plan had identified key *points-de-vue* for the civic monuments that the town was indeed going to build – the High School, the Sheriff Court, the neo-classical Watt Institution (later rebuilt), the Royal Exchange and the Albert Institute (now McManus Galleries). But none of the architects' plans for the Meadows were adopted, and buildings like the Royal Exchange also appeared on corners. Since they lacked the urban setting necessary for grandeur and proper civic embellishment, Dundee's pre-jute civic monuments – however dignified they might have been – lacked the added status conveyed by the stately neo-classical streets and axial vistas provided by the new suburbs adorning so many other Scots towns and cities. They thus, collectively, failed to convey the critical mass of urban ambition that they should. Moreover, the failure to use these northern lands to provide the town with a more efficient east-west route, by-passing the town centre, as provided for in the Act, condemned medieval Dundee to removal under the 1871 Improvement Act.

Few large-scale formal plans were prepared for any of the suburbs. The Hawkhill, Scouringburn, Pleasance and Blackness grew like Topsy: 'underneath the Barracks, a little town, as it were, has begun to progress and numerous mills and manufactories have risen almost by magic'.[154] It must have been black magic: for it became truly horrid. Neave proposed to open it out with a new road north from Hawkhill, and in 1846, Charles Edward produced a brave but abortive plan for a formal layout as part of his design to regularise the inconsistencies of the entire city. To no avail. Once the enthusiasm for – and pride in – the imagery of mill chimneys began to wane, the 'combination of closely packed mills and miserable unwholesome dwellings' became considered the most unsightly part of the city.[155] As for Dudhope, J. Sime surveyed the estate in 1837, and the following year George Angus designed a grandiose estate of small villas sweeping up the slopes of the Law in fine crescents. The most ambitious suburban plan of the time, it was either too extensive, or the ground too steep, or the market too low or – much more likely – it was in the wrong location, immediately above the smokestacks of Chapelshade industry. It suffered from the 'exhalations from silt and impurity of the atmosphere arising from the smoke of steam engines used in the manufactories' which had begun to make certain parts of the town unhealthy.[156] Only a few sturdy neo-classical villas with thickset Doric porches survive in Dudhope Terrace.

Between 1818 and 1830, David Neave and others had been well exercised in the preparation of serial feuing plans for small detached houses facing 40-foot-wide roads in lands on the near eastern slopes of Hillbank, Forebank, and Maxwelltown, but they remained unbuilt. The magnificent views they afforded failed to compensate for the fact that their amenity was likewise being squeezed by the industrial nutcracker of the Hilltown and Chapelshade to the west and industry clustering around the Dens Burn to the east. That might also have been the reason why only five gracious little terraced villas, possibly by Neave, emerged in King Street. Within years, a coal yard appeared a few hundred feet away. Contemporaries thought the problem to be the lack of a comprehensive plan:

> It is a matter of regret that although the situation [of Forebank] offered the utmost facility, *a disregard to general taste* [my italics] has considerably impaired the appearance which might have existed had the proprietors adopted a general plan.[157]

It was much the same on the west. The 1813 plan to develop an elite group of David Neave mansions in the old hospital's 'enclosed park'[158] – Park Place – changed from three large plots to eight smaller ones,[159] and remained only partially fulfilled because a Sugar House had been permitted at its top end. The attractiveness of Roseangle and Magdalen Green as the residence of the town's elite had been damaged by the Tay Ropeworks (in which Riddoch had an interest), and as industry had spread along Hawkhill and seeped southwards at Sinderins, little brick manufactories began to appear in the back lanes. Two smart streets north of Perth Road were laid out on lands of earlier mansions – Springfield in 1828, and Airlie Place in 1851 – and both, extraordinarily, took the form of cul-de-sacs. Normally, one would have expected them to reach north to join the cross street of Hawkhill; but the latter's condition had deteriorated to the extent that the new streets had to turn their back on it if they were to have any amenity at all. Even the town's solitary 'new town' street – Tay Street (Plate 8) – was affected by 'smoke belching from a low, cast-iron chimney in Daniel Duff's Tay Street Spinning Mill', which duly became a contested process before the Guild Court.[160] The absence of strategic plans, and the failure to prevent incompatible activities, meant that the western suburbs never retained their attractiveness; and the arrival of the railway in 1847, turning beautiful and popular beaches into railway sidings and coal yards, was to prove terminal.

So what visitors missed, when they came to Dundee, was 'regularity of plan':

> Excepting the numerous new but in general short streets . . . not even the trivial grace of straightness of street line is displayed. Most of the old streets are of irregular and varying width; and many of the alleys are inconveniently and orientally narrow.[161]

An editorial in the *Dundee Advertiser* agreed. 'We believe there is no town in the kingdom so awkwardly built . . . If a flight of gigantic crows had dropt our houses from the air, they could not have arranged themselves with more admired confusion'.[162] Conversely, visitors were most decidedly impressed by the town's appearance of economic vibrancy. The High Street wore 'much of that opulent and commercially great and dignified appearance which characterises the Trongate or Argyle-street of Glasgow'.[163] That Dundee's High Street could resemble the imperial emporium of Glasgow's Argyle Street was an enormous compliment, since the latter was possibly Scotland's premier commercial street.

Dundee had become the linen capital of Britain by the 1830s.[164] Its commercial vigour, moreover, was matched by the impressive private patronage of its elite. The plans to merge the town's three schools in a single building were funded by private subscription,[165] and the architectural competition for it was won by Edinburgh architect George Angus with a stern neo-classical Doric temple facing the Town House down Reform Street, in as grand a manner as could be found in the country (Plate14). Likewise in 1828, one merchant faction treated itself to the similarly imposing Exchange Coffee House down by the harbour, designed by Edinburgh architect George Smith (Plate15); and in that same year, the masons commissioned a new hall, the Thistle Hall, from David Neave (which doubled as assembly rooms) as the centrepiece of the west side of the Union Street, which was feued that year. The Thistle Hall was probably Neave's most sophisticated design, its splendidly glazed and pilastered *piano nobile* bearing a strong resemblance to contemporary Swedish classicism.

The following year, the police commissioners held a competition for a new Bridewell or prison, which they eventually awarded – seemingly on grounds of cost – to George Angus' design of an austere temple with flanking colonnades and wings intended to face axially (almost axially) down the new Lindsay Street with a radially-planned prison behind.[166] It was built in phases because the tenders were so high, and the classical temple at the centre was eventually to the design of a subsequent town architect, William Scott. Perhaps the most imposing neo-classical building in the town was for the harbour commissioners – the largest Customs House in Scotland (Plate 16), designed by the harbour engineer James Leslie with John Taylor in 1842. Leslie had spent six years as apprentice to the celebrated Edinburgh neo-classical architect William Playfair before diverting to engineering and harbour works; and it shows. So, by the time the Cowgate merchants commissioned David Bryce to replace the Baltic Coffee House in Bain's Square with the Royal Exchange in Panmure Street in 1851[167] (Plate 17), Dundee had adorned itself with most of the civic buildings of other Scots cities – with the particular exception of an art gallery. That was soon to follow, as the result of yet another private initiative, with the Albert Institute designed by Sir George Gilbert Scott (Plate 13). Such ambition persisted in the subsequent appointments of other notable architects from Edinburgh, Glasgow and London such as J. T. Rochead, G. F. Bodley, Peddie & Kinnear, J. A. Hansom, Coe and Goodwin and Sir Robert Rowand Anderson.

As the harbour developed after 1815, it had become the symbol by which the town was identified:

> The town and harbour of Dundee . . . present attractions of the deepest interest to all who delight to contemplate scenes of national prosperity . . . in which manufactures and commerce have attained unprecedented status and extent.[168]

The town, as one commentator put it, made up for the absence of the expected neo-classical suburb:

> by a dash of the picturesque, by its displays of opulence, and by the romance of its crowded quays the proud and opulent series of docks which are at once the boast of Dundee, the chief means of its wealth, and *the best evidence of its enterprise and taste*[169] [my italics].

Dundee's civic embellishment was therefore represented by the harbour (Plate 20) and the docks, the motor of Dundee's economy, rather than streets of douce terraced houses focused upon the odd art gallery. Here debouched both railways and the ferry: it was the primary point of entry for most visitors, and the town's principal selling point. Hence the outrage when the landed interest selected a Romanesque-arch design, redolent of ancient history, in the 1849 architectural competition for a permanent dockside royal arch to commemorate Queen Victoria's 1844 visit, rather than something that could represent the town's new identity in the eager 1850s.

Many of the pressures to build a new town were therefore absent from early nineteenth-century Dundee. It was a healthy, relatively low-density town at ease with itself, and lukewarm about the social segregation obtaining in the new towns elsewhere. On the other hand, however, the Council, under Alexander Riddoch, showed itself incapable of taking a wider strategic view, and inept in tackling improvements necessary for commercial expansion. Eventually, the exasperated commercial interest wrested control of the harbour from the Council. Moreover, since both Council and neighbouring proprietors had showed themselves uninterested in civic embellishment, any such initiative was left to private enterprise. Unfortunately, whereas private initiative proved perfectly capable of commissioning individual buildings of high quality, it could not substitute for a controlling authority preparing and giving confidence to a wider strategy.

So whereas one reason for the absence of a new town might well have been the fecklessness of adjoining landowners, the absence of a broader civic strategy that might have preserved the amenity of better-class suburbs was even more important. The consequences of that failure to regulate what planners now call zoning became evident on all sides. The absence of an over-arching plan to give guidance, confidence and – above all – control, made neo-classical suburban development impossible. Thus it was that Dundee never gained a new town.

It was only once jute became the dominant staple after 1858[170] and particularly after the enormous jute expansion in the 1860s, that the city began to develop the mill-town characteristics of the myth. That there also grew an amnesia about the town's pre-jute history, may well be an indication of just how cataclysmic the 1860–1900 transformation of Dundee into 'Juteopolis' had been. The myth holds that Dundee did not built a new town since it was in a position of weakness during the relevant decades. Civic weakness only. The reason it did not build a new town was that, in many respects, it was coming from a position of strength – a strength derived from the success of the private entrepreneurs against the Council. Ironically, this shift from civic to private initiative later came to be interpreted in terms not of an ambitious, high-quality town cursed with a short-sighted Council, but in terms of an unambitious, poverty-struck low-quality town; and thus did the legend begin.

TWO

The growth and development of the Port of Dundee in the nineteenth and early twentieth centuries

William Kenefick

THE PORT OF DUNDEE has always been an integral part of the city, sharing in and reflecting its shifting fortunes. This was as true before the advent of the jute industry as it was afterwards. While the decline in the importance of Dundee harbour in the twentieth century was inextricably linked to the demise of the jute trade, it is also clear that the growth and development of pre-jute Dundee owes much to the improvements made to the port in the first half of the nineteenth century.

Dundee's nearest trading rival was Perth and, over the years, there were numerous wrangles between the two locations 'as to the privileges of the waters of the Tay'. According to the *Third Statistical Account of Scotland*, the question of who controlled the Tay had been resolved in favour of Dundee as far back as 1404, when Dundee announced that 'Quhairfore we put to silence the yem of Perth and to yair successours upon ye siade question for evermair'. However, this was not to prove an end to the vexed question of control. In 1601 Perth was granted exclusive rights to the Tay, but only one year later the Court of Session in Edinburgh decreed that Perth's privileges only extended to that part of the Tay contained within the county of Perth. Dundee was granted similar jurisdiction in Forfarshire, but importantly this settlement covered both the north and south sides of the Tay. Dundee's rights were further underpinned in the charter of Charles I in 1642 and, thereafter, Dundee began to consolidate its influential position in relation to trade on the Tay, and strengthen its links with Europe from that period through to the seventeenth century.

For a time Dundee prospered but by the end of the seventeenth century the town and the harbour began to fall into decline. This is partly explained by the growing ascendancy of the west-coast ports such as Greenock and Port Glasgow (and to a lesser extent Glasgow docks), and a shift in trading patterns – as the west now began to exploit its geographical advantage in relation to the burgeoning transatlantic trade. Despite such drawbacks, however, Dundee was tenacious in maintaining its trading links with Europe and the Baltic in particular. This would greatly aid Dundee's economic recovery later.[1]

It was not until the nineteenth century, however, that Dundee finally gained ascendancy over Perth. This was principally due to changes in technology and the increased size of shipping entering the River Tay and local problems relating to silting. By the early nineteenth century, however, heavy silting made waterborne trade even more difficult further up-river and this helped Dundee gain ground over Perth. Moreover, improvements in harbour facilities made Dundee the preferred place for the unloading of goods and, despite Perth's importance in terms of land transport, it had to conduct much of its own trade through Dundee. Goods intended for Perth were therefore off-loaded at Dundee and transferred onto smaller vessels to be transported up-river, or moved through Dundee to Perth by land transport.

There remained a close relationship between Dundee and Perth, and this was further strengthened by improvements to the Tay shipping channels, the increased use of marker buoys and the growth and development of Dundee's textile trade – first linen and latterly jute. Both Dundee and Perth did, for a time, act as an entrepôt for the other. Between the mid-nineteenth century and the 1870s, for example, around one half of Dundee's imports of jute were being carried by rail via Perth. By the late 1870s however, the practice of shipping raw jute direct from Calcutta excluded Perth from this trade. This period marked the second main phase in the growth and development of Dundee harbour, but the growth of the jute trade was only part of the picture. In order to fully understand Dundee harbour's rise to trading pre-eminence in the late nineteenth and early twentieth centuries we must examine the period before the advent of jute.

It was the geographical and environmental endowments of Dundee that marked it out as the best site for a working harbour along the Tay and the main centre of maritime commercialism for the Tay region. Dundee was relatively sheltered and, when coupled with easy access to the sea, this paved the way for its initial growth and development. The early phase of Dundee harbour's development is perhaps best summed up by D. F. MacDonald, writing in the *Third Statistical Account of Scotland*:

> The Western ports, notably Glasgow, began to flourish on the new Atlantic commerce, and Dundee's Baltic and Continental trade dwindled to insignificant proportions. The growth of the linen industry, however, in the later eighteenth century, redeemed the situation.[2]

By the late 1790s, Dundee was 'fast becoming the linen metropolis of Scotland'.[3] The linen trade, however, only revealed the harbour's gross inadequacies, as the years of neglect following Dundee's decline in the export trade became all too obvious (see Table 2). In short, the poor condition of the harbour threatened to stifle the linen trade even before it had established a firm foothold in Dundee in the industrial era.

Table 2: Relative position of Dundee's shipping entering and clearing in foreign trade, 1760–64 and 1780–84 (using five-yearly averages).

	1760–64		1780–84	
	INWARDS	OUTWARDS	INWARDS	OUTWARDS
	tons	tons	tons	tons
Aberdeen	4,286	2,644	5,337	2,218
Montrose	2,428	789	2,438	1,011
Perth	1,094	270	2,057	94
Dundee	2,803	1,099	4,373	584
Leith	11,891	5,680	18,585	5,416
Bo'ness	3,605	4,231	14,194	12,394
Clyde Ports	24,255	28,954	27,052	22,708
Scotland	72,941	67,885	120,248	83,088
Dundee's %	3.4	1.6	3.6	0.7

Source: G. Jackson with K. Kinnear, *The Trade and Shipping of Dundee, 1780–1850* (Dundee, 1991).

MacDonald also noted that by the late eighteenth century, the harbour at Dundee had been sorely neglected – suffering from 'storm damage and apathy'. Despite a doubling in the tonnage of shipping which entered the port between 1790 and 1815–19, few improvements had been made to the harbour facilities.[4] This was due to the stewardship of port affairs, which, before 1815, was under the control of Dundee Town Council. Over a fifty-year period from 1764 to 1814 the Council collected £38,696 in harbour dues, but only re-invested £9,468 in harbour improvement. This amounted to less than a quarter of all harbour revenue raised. Thus there was a significant shortfall between what was raised in duties and what had been spent on improvement.

Before 1815 Dundee harbour consisted of little more than a tidal basin, a rough breakwater and one small wharf. The Council's efforts to improve the harbour up to that point can be best described as *ad hoc*. Essential repairs were not always guaranteed because of lack of funds,[5] but there is evidence to suggest that some minor improvements were made. Most of these are attributed to the energies of one man, Dundee's 'old hawk' and leading member of the Town Council, Alexander Riddoch. From 1787, he set in motion several initiatives to improve harbour conditions.[6] The 'Singing Pier' was improved in 1780 to help stimulate the live animal trade, and in 1781 a new landing pier was built at Craig, but thereafter the pace of improvement waned. Moreover these improvements were 'slowly and frugally carried out because the town's revenues seemed to allow no other course'.[7]

One contemporary observer was impressed by Riddoch's harbour improvements. Alexander Campbell, writing in 1802, noted that:

The pier is extensive; the docks are spacious and convenient; and the warehouses on the quay are well arranged, and commodious for the reception of the merchant's wares . . . The harbour is capable of receiving vessels of three hundred tons. The rocks which lie off the harbour have buoys or beacons annexed and the sand banks are marked to prevent hazards.

From this account Dundee harbour did seem in reasonable shape at the turn of the century. By 1792 the town had a total of 116 registered ships. Trade too had greatly increased, notably the export trade in thread, linen, leather, and the import trade in flax, hemp, timber and Swedish iron. Coastwise trade was buoyant, and included clothes, cotton bagging, all sorts of threads, barley and wheat, while imports consisted of tea, flour, porter and coals. Gross annual tonnage averaged around 8,550 tons.[8] In November 1814, the Council issued a 'Memorial on the Opinion of the Council' regarding their stewardship of the harbour. In this 'Memorial', they argued that they were of the opinion that 'they had already improved that harbour to a greater extent' – more than they had been 'bound to do'![9] Indeed, as Charles McKean noted earlier in this volume, Alexander Riddoch 'was most proud of his frugal hand' in the harbour developments.

Despite Riddoch's protestations and the Council's assertion that improvements had been made to the port, such claims did little to deflect accusations of neglect from other interested parties in Dundee. Regular reports appeared in the local press regarding the state of the port claiming that progress and development in the provision of modern facilities were being held back by the Council. This perceived neglect attracted criticism from contemporaries. One commentator, writing under the pseudonym '*The Citizen*', imagined himself a traveller, viewing Dundee harbour for the first time:

Understanding this to be a great shipping port, walked down to the quay. Astonished and confounded at the falseness of my information. Instead of the appearance of a prosperous sea-port, 'the third in rank in Scotland', find a wretched tide harbour, choked up with mud, surrounded by dangerous rocks, and the piers and quays going, first to ruin, and much liker [*sic*] the decayed walls of a county church yard 'than a harbour of the third town of Scotland'. . . returned to the Inn to ask the Landlord why things are in such a state, to which he replies, 'it is the fault of the Magistrates'.[10]

That the harbour was in great need of improvement, therefore, was obvious, despite the Council's very public claims to the contrary. Concern for the state of Dundee's harbour was most acute among local merchants and traders who feared that it was insufficient 'to accommodate the shipping and trade of the town', and also that the Council would do little to improve this situation.[11] David Blair Junior expressed the views of the merchants in a series of letters to the *Dundee Advertiser* under the pseudonym *Mercator*. He wrote that:

> The harbour which in this as in every sea-port town is the greatest consequence to the prosperity of the inhabitants, and upon consequently every expense should be laid out to make it commodious for the shipping and ornamental to the town.[12]

It was to prove a lengthy and complicated dispute, which has been examined in greater detail by McKean, but the merchants eventually succeeded in wresting control of the harbour away from the Town Council in 1815, with the foundation of the independent Dundee Harbour Commission. In May 1831, Dundee Harbour Trust was finally established by a further Act of Parliament which guaranteed that the business of the harbour would remain free from council interference.[13] The Harbour Trust was to be responsible for the transformation of the Dundee waterfront thereafter.

Many other ports around the country were busy making harbour improvements and building new modern facilities in the late eighteenth and early nineteenth centuries. The bigger ports such as Liverpool, Bristol and Leith were involved in quite large-scale programmes, but even smaller harbours such as Montrose were building quays and commissioning plans for extending port facilities.[14] From 1815 Dundee began to do the same. Brandishing the powers granted under the Harbour Act of that year, and extended under the 1831 Act, the Dundee Harbour Commissioners set about the task of creating a sea-port worthy of a town 'the third in rank in Scotland'.[15] As noted by Charles Mackie, writing in 1836:

> improvements were no sooner projected than carried into almost summary execution. Betwixt the years 1815 and 1830, £162,800 was expended on the harbour, devoted chiefly to constructing a wet dock – a graving dock attached to it – extending the tide harbour – erecting additional quays, sea walls, and other improvements . . . Most of the tide-harbour, since the operation of the perpetual act in 1830, has been converted into a second wet dock, called the 'Earl Grey Dock'.

Much of the credit for this, he noted, went to Mr James Leslie, the engineer, 'for the manner in which he conducted his scientific operations'.[16] Indeed, according to the calculations made by James Thomson (writing in the mid-1840s), between 1830 and 1833 alone a further £86,000 was invested in improvement schemes, and that in total, over the period 1815 to 1833, £248,742 was spent in harbour improvements.[17] Moreover, plans were already in place for additional port facilities, prompting Mackie to conclude, 'when further improvements are completed the harbour of Dundee [will] rank among the first in Britain'.[18]

The process began when Thomas Telford was commissioned to design a new dock. The West Graving Dock was opened in 1823, and within two years the

King William IV Dock was also completed. In the 1830s, the harbour continued to expand eastward with the completion of the Earl Grey Dock in 1834. Camperdown Dock was opened in 1865 at a cost of £100,000 and a decade later both Victoria Dock and the East Graving Dock were finished. Meanwhile, the Board of Trustees was re-cast so as to include representatives of the shipping interests at the port and members of the Dundee Chamber of Commerce.

Despite these improvements, however, problems of low water depth and a lack of quayage space continued to cause difficulties. The King William IV and Earl Grey Docks, which had been operating since 1825 and 1834 respectively, offered extensive space for vessels but lacked adequate water depth. The same was true of the Victoria and Camperdown Docks – built in the 1860s and 1870s.[19] Dundee Harbour Trust made strenuous efforts to rectify this situation. First, they lengthened the existing Western Wharf, and commissioned the building of the Eastern Wharf, which was completed in 1909. Indeed, the Eastern Wharf was initially constructed using timber but this was latterly replaced and rebuilt using reinforced concrete (the first wharf in Scotland to be built by this method). Secondly, they reclaimed land to the front of the Victoria and Camperdown Docks in order to provide deep-water accommodation for the new breed of larger steam-powered, ocean-going vessels.[20]

Changes in technology progressed quickly though, and in this sense Dundee's facilities were fast being overtaken. The second major phase of harbour expansion was in direct response to this. In 1868, one Dundee Harbour Commissioner expressed the concern that:

> The great changes which have taken place within these very few years in the size of ships and steamers have made all the old docks in a manner useless, hence the necessity of enlarged accommodation if Dundee is to maintain its position as a first class port.[21]

The ships which imported raw jute into Dundee were rapidly increasing in size, and this prompted the reclamation of land to build deep-water quays in front of Victoria and Camperdown in the 1880s. Importantly, this meant that Dundee's trading interests could finally benefit from the economies of scale.[22]

At the time of the initial phase of improvement in the 1820s and 1830s, however, future inadequacies in the West Graving, King William IV and Earl Grey Docks, could not have been foreseen – similarly, the later problems associated with Camperdown and Victoria Docks. The Trust did eventually overcome these problems and despite the drawbacks in terms of traffic, trade and finance the port was operating very effectively. Indeed, the rise in jute imports created further demand for wharf accommodation, which was largely addressed between 1903 and 1911, and work began on what was to become the George V

Wharf before the Great War (although it was not finally completed until the 1930s).[23]

By the 1830s it was widely agreed that Dundee had a harbour to be proud of. William Beattie, writing in 1838, described Dundee's town and harbour as an attraction to any who 'delighted to contemplate scenes of national prosperity'. As a result, he concluded, industry and commerce had 'attained unprecedented status and extent'.[24] There is little doubt that the people of Dundee also felt that their town was making great progress, and that there existed a real and tangible sense of pride with each new improvement made. The opening of Dundee's first wet dock in 1825 is a prime example of this and was accompanied by great public celebration.[25]

According to the *Advertiser*, 'Dundee and its neighbourhood poured out in their thousands' just to witness the first ship enter the King William IV Dock on 24 November 1825. There was a mass public procession as Dundee's 'beautiful and commodious' new dock was officially opened. Banners hailed the role of Thomas Telford the engineer and the Logan brothers who had supervised the construction work. It was generally agreed that the harbour had been transformed from a virtual ruin to an example of modern building and construction – using materials 'so durable' that the dock was likely to last for ages to come.[26] Similar sentiments were expressed as the other new projects – such as the Earl Grey Dock – were completed. All of Dundee had become enriched with the development and modernisation of the harbour, and the general impression of the town was improved as a result:

> Dundee is seen to much advantage from various situations in the neighbour-hood. The view from the Hill of Balgay on the north-west, as well as from the high grounds to the north-east, are considered beautiful; but the view from the middle of the river, or rather from the heights around Newport, on the opposite of it, is by far the most magnificent and striking.[27]

Thus the first phase of harbour improvement had transformed Dundee and prepared the town for the further improvements to come.

In terms of trade and commerce the impact of improvement on Dundee was considerable and by the mid-1870s around £740,000 had been invested in port improvement.[28] Harbour revenues, however, quickly outstripped the levels of investment. As seen in Table 3, over the period 1815 to *c*.1873, £1,151,322 was raised in port revenues and with an outlay of £740,000 there was almost £412,000 left as surplus.[29] Dundee thus became the bustling, flourishing seaport envisaged by David Blair Junior in 1815, and had for much of this time proved both 'commodious and ornamental'. The following tables clearly outline the progress of trade in terms of rising revenue and increased shipping, tonnage and employment around the port.

Table 3: Increase of harbour revenues, 1797–1873.

Time-period	Total for Period	Annual Average
1797–1800	£4,650	£1,550
1815–1825	£64,461	£6,446
1826–1830	£52,114	£13,029
1831–1840	£136,679	£15,186
1841–1850	£225,793	£25,088
1851–1860	£231,528	£25,725
1861–1870	£310,877	£34,541
1870–1873	£125,870	£62,935
Total	£1,151,972	

Source: J. Thomson, *History of Dundee, from the Earliest to Present Times* ed. J. Maclaren (Dundee, 1878), 280.

Table 4: Shipping and tonnage belonging to the Port of Dundee, 1792–1853, and employment figures for men and boys, 1843–1853.

Year	Vessels	Tonnage	Men/Boys
1792	116	8,550	–
1843	335	50,670	2,966
1848	351	54,919	3,143
1853	328	58,407	3,189

Source: J. Thomson, *History of Dundee*, 279.

As noted previously, the port of Dundee was dependent upon a very localised industry. Unlike the ports of Glasgow, Leith, Grangemouth or Greenock, Dundee did not serve an extensive industrial hinterland, but instead relied totally on local conditions and those in its immediate vicinity. Prior to the demand for sacking and the major expansion of the jute industry, the port was considered of only 'minor importance', despite increases in the manufacture of linen products. Moreover, while jute became the mainstay of the Dundee economy by the second half of the nineteenth century, it was nevertheless a low-weight, low-cost, bulk product. Tonnage of trade passing through the port reflected this.

Table 5: Net tonnage of vessels entering and clearing selected Scottish ports for foreign parts and share of Scottish totals and Scottish share of UK total, 1870–74 to 1910–3 (with cargo and ballast 000s tons).

West Coast Ports	1870–4 tons	1880–4 tons	1890–4 tons	1900–4 tons	1910–3 tons
Glasgow	1,086	2,129	2,785	4,054	7,303
Greenock	484	505	423	237	2,129
Sub total	1,570	2,634	3,208	4,298	9,432

East Coast Ports	1870–4	1880–4	1890–4	1900–4	1910–3
	tons	tons	tons	tons	tons
Leith	869	1,099	1,492	1,969	3,239
Bo'ness	211	329	384	562	–
ethil*	–	–	–	–	2,017
Kirkcaldy*	183	617	1,174	2,231	–
Burntisland*	–	–	–	–	1,346
Grangemouth	336	414	1,181	1,540	2,077
Dundee	285	322	371	293	203#
Total	1,884	2,781	4,602	6,595	8,882

*relates to all three ports Methil, Kirkcaldy and Grangemouth.
#There are no figures for vessels entering Dundee for 1910–13, figures here are for vessels clearing only.
Source: Derived from G. Jackson, *The History and Archaeology of Ports* (Surrey, 1983).

By comparing Dundee with the other ports in Scotland, in terms of vessels leaving and entering the port, it can be seen that it was a relatively minor port, even after the advent of jute. In terms of value of trade, however, a quite different picture emerges. Dundee was third only behind Glasgow and Leith in terms of value of Scottish trade, and twelfth in terms of total United Kingdom value of trade by 1914 – a position which it maintained throughout the war years (see Table 6).[30] From the 1860s, however, competition from cheap Indian goods became a major problem, and in the long term it served to 'reduce the size of the market for the Dundee industry'.[31] There was also the added and growing problem of continental jute production.[32]

Table 6: Imports and exports through individual ports in money value, for twelve selected ports, for 1913 (£ millions).

	Imports	Exports	Re-exports	Total	%U.K.
London	253.9	99.1	58.8	411.8	29.3
Liverpool	175.5	170.1	25.2	370.8	26.4
Hull	48.8	29.2	5.5	84.6	6.0
Manchester	35.3	20.6	0.5	56.3	4.0
Glasgow	18.5	35.9	0.3	54.8	3.9 [1]
Southampton	25.5	20.7	7.4	53.6	3.8
Grimsby	15.8	21.9	0.1	37.8	2.7
Newcastle	11.3	13.2	–	24.6	1.8
Cardiff	6.7	17.2	–	23.9	1.7
Leith	15.7	6.9	0.3	23.0	1.6 [2]
Bristol/Avonmouth	18.0	4.0	–	22.0	1.6
Dundee	8.0	1.0	0.3	9.4	0.7 [3]

Source: Evidence presented to Inquiry into Wages and Conditions of Employment of Docks and Waterside Labour, xxiv (PP, 1920) volume II.

None of these problems could have been foreseen in the early years of the nineteenth century. Steam technology was in its infancy during Dundee harbour's first phase of improvement. By the beginning of the second phase steam power was widely recognised as the new motive force, but not many could have envisaged just how quickly technological advances would increase the size of ships, particularly when the sailing ship was still an effective mode of transport. Prior to jute, and before the advent of significant technological change, Dundee had constructed a port that was technically sufficient for the trade of the times. Larger steam ships were most prevalent in deep-sea and foreign trade which in 1815, when the port improvements began, may not have been uppermost in the minds of the great majority of merchants for whom coastal trade was more important.

Table 7: Coastal shipping, and its percentage of total shipping, 1760–1850 (average tonnage).

Period	Tonnage entering	% coastal vessels	Tonnage clearing	% coastal vessels
1775–9	14,624	78	9,046	92
1780–4	17,586	80	9,465	94
1823–4	96,112	83	n.a	n.a
1825–9	116,686	80	n.a.	n.a
1830–4	133,446	73	n.a.	n.a
1835–9	198,749	78	n.a.	n.a
1840–4	183,356	77	91,906	67
1845–9	221,404	78	92,963	70

Source: G. Jackson with K. Kinnear, *The Trade and Shipping of Dundee, 1780–1850* (Dundee, 1991).

On average, coastal traffic accounted for over 78% of all ships entering the port up to 1850. Things began to change, however, after this date. Of the 768,000 tons entering Dundee harbour in 1913 only 339,000 was coastal trade, or a little over 44%. This was due to the larger vessels that were now visiting the port and particularly associated with the trade in jute. Indeed, after the First World War coastal trade contracted significantly to average around 29% throughout much of the interwar period.[33] As Gordon Jackson correctly points out, however, Dundee was still very important in terms of coastal trade, and as time went on Dundee, like Aberdeen, would become a main regional centre for coastal as well as foreign trade. In terms of value of trade, this made a significant contribution to the growing Scottish economy before 1914.[34]

The rise of the port of Dundee was a victory for a new generation of the town's traders and merchants, who from the early nineteenth century held to the belief that Dundee should be a seaport worthy of a town 'third in rank in Scotland'. But even with their dream realised, the port's successful development was not a foregone conclusion. The Harbour Commission and the Harbour Trust in particular played vitally important roles in ensuring the harbour's success and its continued profitable operation from the opening of the King William IV Dock in 1825 through to the early decades of the twentieth century.

The Harbour Trust was also responsible for the operation of railways and ferries at the port. The ferries carried passengers, and private and commercial vehicles, and also provided facilities for the transportation of animals. The operation of ferry services between Dundee and north Fife dated back to the seventeenth century, but it was only from the early nineteenth century that the service began to modernise and improve. It was not until 1872, however, with the passing of the Dundee Harbour and the Tay Ferries Act, that the operation of the ferry services came under the control of the Harbour Trust (paying the then owners, the Caledonian Railway Company, £20,000 for the privilege). Hitherto, the ferry service had not been a viable commercial activity and was already heavily in debt prior to the takeover.

In the long term, however, despite increased competition from the railways, the ferry service was saved by the expansion of car ownership and motor traffic. By 1914, some 6,701 motor cars, 455 motor vans, 61 lorries, and 6 charabancs had used the ferry service – bringing the total vehicle traffic to 7,225 and earnings of £7,504. By the early 1930s traffic using the ferry services increased eight-fold to reach well over 58,000 vehicles *per annum*. By 1940 total traffic handled had risen again to just under 80,000 vehicles. The ferry service was now a considerable earner and between 1914 and 1940, revenue increased by almost 400% from £7,504 to £28,792. By 1927 all outstanding debts incurred by the Trust in running the ferry service had been paid in full and thereafter it operated at a profit.[35]

The advent of the railways also had a significant effect on Dundee, and from the early 1830s the town was connected to the main Scottish railway system. The railways were largely built on land reclaimed by the Harbour Trust, and the Trust owned fourteen miles of railway in and around the port – although these lines were worked by the railway companies.[36] There was also a long history of passenger and cargo shipping services between Dundee and London, and this principally took the form of the Dundee, Perth and London Shipping Company – formed in 1836 from the fusion of two local firms. Dating from 1775, the passenger services were finally ended in 1939, although the cargo trade continued through until 1961.[37] By the mid-1930s Dundee Harbour Trust owned and maintained 381/4 acres of road, over 161/2 acres of sheds, had a total quayage length of four miles, and an operational waterfront of two miles. The Trust also operated three wharves and 56,000 square yards of shedding outwith Dundee's docks and harbours.[38]

The docks expanded in order to accommodate more ships and this meant more warehousing too, an investment thought 'compatible with the seasonal nature of jute imports'. Dundee only secured the direct importation of jute in the 1870s because those same ships could be utilised on the return journey. Once a ship had unloaded at Dundee it then proceeded to the Tyneside coal ports and loaded with coal destined for the coaling stations along the Suez Canal. Dundee also handled general goods but, like the links with Indian jute and Tyneside coal, its trading connections often proved complicated, if ultimately beneficial. Dundee boasted links with other general cargo ports, particularly London, Glasgow, Liverpool, Antwerp, Hamburg and the Baltic ports, and these maintained its continued commercial viability from the turn of the century through to the 1920s.[39]

According to S. G. E. Lythe, had it not been for Dundee's direct access to the sea, the city would not have sustained the growth experienced from the early nineteenth century onward. The harbour and the improvements made to it were therefore central to the town's industrial growth and development and helped generate new spheres of economic activity. During the first half of the nineteenth century, for example, shipbuilding grew in importance and from the 1830s onward it was a major employer of labour in the town. Often subject to 'violent fluctuations' in trade, however, shipbuilding at Dundee had a troubled history and struggled to compete with the west coast in particular. Much of this was due to location, and to the demand for larger ships, which the Dundee yards were in no position to produce. Whaling and fishing also became significant employers of labour and this too increased the importance of the port. During the 1860s and 1870s Dundee was one of Britain's leading whaling ports. By the 1890s, however, the industry was on its last legs, while the fishing industry only regularly employed around 200 men in total – many of these operating from Broughty Ferry.[40]

Despite the changing nature of Dundee's commercial enterprises, the port had attracted considerable investment. Under the stewardship of the Dundee Harbour Commission the waterfront around Dundee was to be transformed. Locally owned shipping, for example, increased in tonnage from around 8,500 in the late eighteenth century to reached 50,000 tons by the middle of the nineteenth century.[41] Local shipowners also provided passenger-vessel services which from the early nineteenth century not only competed with stage-coach traffic, but later with the railways, and also provided direct sea-going passenger/cargo services between Dundee and London. The waterfront around Dundee, therefore, was the focus of some considerable commercial activity and was of significant importance to Dundee's trade. The Harbour Trust also undertook the reclamation of land along the town's waterfront. During the nineteenth century it was responsible for reclaiming some 188 acres – substantially more than the 124 acres reclaimed by Dundee Town Council. Reclamation created 'flat lands' which were much sought after for the siting of industrial premises.

'King Jute was a mighty Monarch', reported the *Dundee Advertiser* in 1872, but at the same time it questioned how long 'this reign [could] be expected to last'. By the interwar years the Dundee jute industry was seriously threatened by foreign competition. The harbour continued to operate profitably, but after 1918 the pattern was essentially one of slow but sure decline. There is little doubt, however, that the growth and development of the harbour contributed significantly to Dundee's status as a textile town during the nineteenth and early twentieth centuries and played a vital role 'in shaping the emerging industrial town' – long before the jute industry became the economic staple.[42]

THREE

Civic leadership and the manufacturing elite: Dundee, 1820–1870

Louise Miskell

IN 1868, DUNDEE's annual local council election generated intense public interest. In the weeks leading up to the poll, the Dundee Working Men's Association and Trades Council organised a campaign to persuade the town's leading manufacturers to stand for election. The *Dundee Advertiser* reported that, 'Showing how good a feeling exists between employers and employed, the latter are now looking to the former to set aside business considerations and assist in giving new dignity, weight and influence to the Council'.[1] Dundee's emergence as a major centre for textile manufacture, however, had begun some fifty years earlier. Studies of the development of the town in the nineteenth century have invariably emphasised the dominance of manufacturing over the economy, the labour market and the townscape.[2] The mill and factory owners at the forefront of this industrial growth attained unrivalled positions of wealth and status as the leading employers of labour in the town, but they did not take over the reigns of power in local political institutions. The aim of this chapter is to account for this apparent reluctance, on the part of Dundee's manufacturing elite, to play a leading role in local government.

Although Dundee has not previously benefited from any detailed study of civic leadership of the kind that has been carried out for other industrial towns and cities,[3] a few historians have offered interpretations of the contribution of manufacturers to town life in Dundee. In doing so, however, they have created a picture of a remote manufacturing elite, which abdicated responsibility for the needs of the working population. According to one interpretation, Dundee's manufacturers, to a far greater extent than their counterparts elsewhere, were guilty of diverting the profits of their businesses into lucrative overseas investments rather than channelling them back into the town for the benefit of their employees and the community at large.[4] Similarly, while building themselves residential 'palaces' in desirable suburbs, they have been accused of failing to address the housing needs of their workers by neglecting to build low-cost worker accommodation for rent.[5] As a result, the gulf between manufacturer and worker was a widening one based on opposing class interests.[6] The resulting picture is one of a remote and disinterested manufacturing elite with little input, outside of their businesses, into the rapidly changing urban society.

As an explanation for the low profile of manufacturers in mainstream municipal government, however, this is unconvincing. The idea that manufacturers distanced themselves from town life and aspired to gentrified lifestyles[7] has recently been undermined by city-based studies reasserting the influence of industrialists on urban society.[8] This chapter will contribute to these major historical debates on the place of manufacturers in nineteenth-century urban society with an examination of the role of Dundee's manufacturing fraternity in the life of the town during the fifty years of industrial growth from 1820 onwards. Throughout this period it will be shown that manufacturers did not dominate the ranks of the town's commercial middle classes from which the local government elites were drawn. Instead, civic leadership in mid- nineteenth-century Dundee reflected the diverse range of retail, trade, commercial and service occupations in which this section of the population was engaged. In addition, an examination will be made of the social and commercial networks operating in Dundee, which provided avenues into public life. It will be argued that the work and family connections of Dundee's leading manufacturers were largely separate from these local government circles. It was partly because of this that the manufacturers did not dominate local government institutions but instead developed status and notoriety in the town through their business achievements and their reputations as employers.

Dundee was already an important centre for the east of Scotland linen trade some fifty years before the introduction of steam-powered spinning mills in the 1820s. By the 1770s the town had an estimated 2,800 flax-weaving looms.[9] Its other principal branches of trade included leather tanning, shoemaking, rope-making and the corn trade.[10] Primarily though, it was the market centre and port serving the spinning and weaving population of its rural hinterland.[11] From 1820 onwards, however, the introduction of steam-powered flax-spinning machinery saw the production of yarn and linen cloth concentrated much more heavily in the town itself. The number of new steam-powered mills in Dundee increased from seven in 1820 to forty in 1832.[12] New docks, catering for larger and more numerous trading vessels, were opened in 1825 and 1834 to handle the increased volumes of imported flax and exported linen cloth generated by this industrial growth.[13] In addition, the population of Dundee, which had grown little in the first two decades of the nineteenth century, more than doubled in the next twenty years to reach over 63,000. In the decade after 1831 Dundee experienced a 40% increase in its population – a growth rate which exceeded that in any other major Scottish town in the same decade.[14] By 1851 Dundee had clearly emerged as Scotland's third largest town, with a population of 79,000.[15] It had forty-three spinning mills, eight powerloom factories and sixty-two handloom factories employing 11,382 people, over 8,000 of whom were women.[16] A further phase of growth in the decades after 1850, however, brought even greater change. This second industrial transformation saw jute replace flax as the town's economic staple and turned the thriving mid-nineteenth-century linen town into an industrial city mythologised as 'juteopolis'. By 1867, the town had seventy-two factories manufacturing flax, hemp or jute products[17] serving vast North-American markets for sacking and supplying canvas goods to army and navy customers during the Crimean and American Civil Wars. This expansion attracted heavy immigration from the surrounding countryside,[18] especially in the two decades after 1861 when the population of Dundee rose from 90,568 to 140,239.[19]

Despite the extent of economic and demographic change, and the fact that by 1850 Dundee was a major centre for linen manufacture, the personnel of municipal government in the town did not undergo a parallel transformation. The shape of local government in nineteenth-century Dundee had, along with that of other Scottish towns, been established by the Convention of Royal Burghs in 1705.[20] The main arm of local government was a twenty-member Town Council, which consisted of representatives of the burgesses or chief proprietors whose property was pledged against the town's debts.[21] Every year, eight members were re-elected from among the retiring council. This meant that there was a good deal of continuity in the personnel of local government. The career of Alexander Riddoch (examined earlier in this volume by Charles McKean) symbolised the dominance of the Town Council by the property-owning merchant elite. His time in office spanned the period 1776-1819 during which time he alternated the provostship with various supporters.[22]

Gradual reform of this system had been underway since 1815. Pressure from liberal reformers within the local merchant community loosened the Council's hold on power, notably by forcing them to concede to the establishment of an independent Harbour Commission in 1815 and the restoration of independent Guildry rights three years later. Pressure for further reform was sustained throughout the 1820s until in 1830 a disputed election result led to the disenfranchisement of the burgh, presenting reformers with the opportunity to apply to parliament for a poll warrant, allowing the election of a new council by the burgesses.[23] This effectively marked the end of self-election in Dundee. The new franchise arrangements were confirmed in 1831 and extended by the passing of the Scottish Municipal Reform Act in 1833.[24] Despite the fact that these developments coincided with the early growth of mechanised linen manufacture in Dundee, they did not herald a new era of dominance for the town's manufacturing elites in local government.

Table 8 illustrates the decline in the dominance of the traditional merchant elite and a gradual increase in manufacturing representation, but by 1850 the manufacturers were still not the largest occupational group on the Town Council, despite three decades of industrial expansion in the town. There were examples of textile manufacturers who pursued successful careers in local government. James Brown who, along with his brother William, developed their flax-spinning operations at East Mill in Dundee, became provost of the town in 1844. Likewise William Hackney, who went into business as a mill spinner in 1821 with Charles Chalmers, held the provostship from 1839–40.[25] More notable however, were the absences of prominent manufacturing families from the ranks of the Town Council in these years. William Baxter, founder of the highly successful firm of linen manufacturers in the Dens, and James Cox, head of Cox Brothers Camperdown Works, were two notable absentees. In fact, the only member of either family to hold a council post in the first half of the nineteenth century, was William Baxter's eldest son Edward, who had left Dens Works to establish his own export business in the mid-1820s.[26]

Table 8: Occupational status of Dundee Town Council members in the first half of the nineteenth century.[27]

	1820	1834	1850
Merchant	10	6	3
Manufacturer	1	3	6
Professional	2	2	5
Trade/Retail	8	5	7
Shipowner/Shipbuilder	3	0	2
Banking	2	1	1
Other	0	3	1

Source: *Dundee Directories* 1820, 1834 and 1850.

The place of manufacturers in other local government institutions in the period was similar. The Harbour Commission (which became known as the Harbour Trust from 1830) had the same number of manufacturer members in 1850 as it had thirty years previously (see Table 9). Membership of this body was made up of a fixed number of representatives from the Town Council, Guildry, Trades Incorporations and the shipping industry, together with county representatives,[28] and so its make-up was unlikely to alter dramatically over time.

Table 9: Occupational status of Dundee Harbour Commissioners/Trustees, 1820–1850.[29]

	1820	1834	1850
Merchant	8	4	4
Manufacturer	3	1	3
Professional	2	1	3
Independent	4	4	4
Retail/Craft	4	5	1
Shipowner/builder	2	2	4
Banking	0	3	3

Source: *Dundee Directories* 1820, 1834 and 1850.

The town's Police Commission on the other hand, founded in 1824 and responsible for the watching, lighting, paving and cleansing of the burgh,[30] was rather differently composed. Compared to earlier improvement commissions such as those in Birmingham, Manchester and Bradford, which tended to be dominated by traditional ruling oligarchies,[31] Dundee's Police Commission was, from its inception, elected annually by ratepayers. Initially its members included a number of high-profile mill owners such as William Brown and James Tawse. Over time, however, the composition of the Commission changed perceptibly, with a shift towards greater representation for retailers and tradesmen at the expense of merchant and manufacturing members.

Table 10: Occupational status of Dundee Police Commissioners, 1824–1850.

	1824–5 No. (%)	1840–41 No. (%)	1850 No. (%)
Merchant	19 (43)	3 (6.8)	4 (9)
Manufacturer	11 (25)	8 (18.2)	5 (11.3)
Professional	0	3 (6.8)	1 (2.3)
Independent	1 (2.3)	0	0
Retail	9 (20.4)	13 (29.5)	17 (38.6)
Craft/Trade	4 (9)	17 (38.6)	16 (36.3)
Other	0	0	1 (2.3)

Source: *Dundee Directories,* 1824–5, 1840–1 and 1850.

Taken together, the occupational data on members of these three municipal bodies reveal that the rapid growth in textile manufacturing in Dundee since 1820 had made comparatively little impact on the make-up of local government institutions by the middle of the nineteenth century. Shopkeepers, lawyers, merchants and tradesmen rather than manufacturers occupied the bulk of municipal posts throughout the first half of the nineteenth century. In exhibiting this pattern of municipal representation in the first half of the nineteenth century, Dundee differed from larger regional capitals such as Glasgow, Leeds and Manchester where major manufacturers played a more prominent part in local government and other civic institutions.[32] Even in smaller textile towns like Bolton, Rochdale and Salford, manufacturers tended to form the largest occupational group among councillors and members of other municipal bodies.[33]

The prominence of representatives of the retail and trade sectors among local government personnel in Dundee reflected the diverse make-up of the town's middle-classes. Despite the fact that, by 1850, Dundee's status as a leading linen-manufacturing town was firmly established, the commercial activities of the local middle classes were not dominated by textile manufacture. Figure 2 illustrates this with information from the 1818, 1850 and 1869–70 *Dundee Directories.* The *Dundee Directories* listed the economic activities of some 4.5% of the population involved in the retail, industrial, business and commercial sectors, as well as those of independent income. The comparison of *Directory* data from 1818, 1850 and 1870 allows the impact of fifty years of industrial transformation on the business activities of these commercial middle classes to be assessed. The manufacturers listed were involved in large-scale production, often in a mill or other works. They were most commonly engaged in the manufacture of textile goods including rope, sail, twine, cloth or flax yarn, but there were others who simply described themselves as 'manufacturer' without reference to any particular product. Figure 2 shows that manufacturers formed a comparatively small proportion of the business community in Dundee. Moreover, their significance declined despite the rapid expansion of the local textile trade in this period. In 1818 manufacturing accounted for 9.4% of the occupations listed in the *Directory*. By 1850 this had declined to 5.7% before increasing again to reach 6.5% in 1870.

To a degree these figures must be treated with caution. Methods of collecting and recording data in nineteenth-century trade directories were neither transparent nor consistent.[34] Nevertheless it is likely that the dip in the proportion of manufacturers between 1818 and 1850 reflected changes in the organisation of the industry. In the early days of mechanisation, textile manufacture in Dundee was characterised by keen competition between a host of small mills, but trade depressions such as the slump in the American market for cotton bagging in 1836, affected small firms particularly badly. The result was that there were 'very numerous failures, both amongst importers and exporters'[35] and, by 1850, larger operations capable of producing yarn or cloth in bulk and shielding themselves from trade fluctuations became the norm.[36] Comparisons between towns based on directory figures are even more problematic because of the variety of ways in which data was compiled for different directories.[37] Nevertheless, it appears that similar trends were evident in Bradford which, like Dundee, experienced rapid growth in textile manufacture after 1820.[38] Bradford's 1850 directory listed proportionally fewer worsted firms (11.5%) than were recorded in 1826 (15.2%).[39] In contrast, manufacturers formed 'the backbone of the middle-class' in Manchester in the first half of the nineteenth century.[40] In fact, figures for Manchester, Leeds and Glasgow in the 1830s suggest that manufacturers were a more important section of the middle classes in all three towns, constituting 30%, 17% and 9.6% respectively.[41]

In Dundee, far more middle-class business activity was generated in sectors that provided for the feeding, clothing and housing of the population. The growth of this 'urban-service economy'[42] was a by-product of rapid industrial and demographic growth, and opportunities for commercial ventures in these areas were plentiful. The 'craft' and 'distribution and processing' sectors, in particular, had far more scope for small-scale entrepreneurial activity than the textile industry with its growing emphasis on bulk output. Occupations designated as 'crafts' were typically those involving small amounts of capital to produce goods in a workshop or similar premises. Shoemakers, tailors, and cabinetmakers all fell into this category, as did those engaged in the production of more substantial products, such as shipbuilders, machine-makers and millwrights. The 'distribution and processing' category incorporated all those involved in retailing, including grocers, booksellers, ironmongers and those simply listed as shopkeepers. In addition, it included those who were also involved in some degree of product processing as well as sale, such as bakers, confectioners and brewers. This category necessarily included businesses of varying size, but in the main small-scale retailing was the norm.

Figure 2: Principal occupational status groups found in Dundee Directories, 1818, 1850 and 1870.

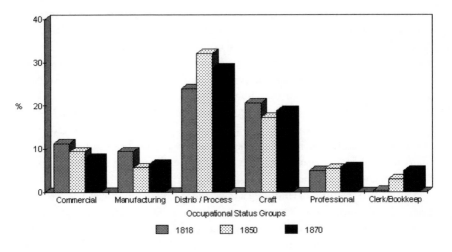

Source: *Dundee Directories*, 1818, 1850 and 1869–70.

In Dundee, the proportion involved in 'distribution and processing' grew from 24% in 1818 to 32% in 1850. By 1850, for example, Dundee had 438 grocers, 348 engaged in the beer, wine and spirits trade (including brewers, innkeepers and spiritdealers), seventy-six shoemakers, ninety-one tailors and sixty-one bakers.[43] By 1870, the proportion of directory occupations in this category fell back a little to 28.7% but it still remained the largest sector and formed a more significant portion of middle-class economic activity in Dundee than in Glasgow, Leeds or Manchester.[44] Again, however, Bradford, where the pattern of growth in the textile economy bore a much closer resemblance to that of Dundee, had similarly thriving retail and trade sectors. There the proportion of firms engaged in the distributive trades increased from 41% to 52.9% between 1826 and 1850.[45] Although it is difficult to make direct comparisons it appears that the expansion of the textile industry in the two towns created similar opportunities for the rapid development of businesses serving the needs of the growing urban population.

Further evidence of diversity within Dundee's middle-class economy can also be seen in Figure 2. 'Commercial' occupations remained an important outlet for the business activities of the town's middle classes throughout this period. Many who described themselves as merchants were engaged in branches of the staple trade, dealing in raw materials, yarn or finished cloth. In addition, there were also plentiful commercial opportunities in the growing shipping industry. Ownership or part ownership of vessels became an increasingly important source of middle-class wealth and the number of shipowners listed in the directories rose from just eleven in 1818, to thirty-two in 1850.[46] In addition, insurance brokers and others involved in handling large units of finance were also numbered among the 'commercial' occupations. The 'professions', meanwhile, included those engaged in legal, medical or religious work.[47] The rise in the proportion of professional occupations in Dundee over the period was small but significant. The share of this occupational status group increased from 4.9% in 1818 to 5.4% in 1850 and 5.8% in 1870. In contrast, only 2.3% of occupations in the 1834 Leeds Directory were classed as professional, and Manchester in 1832 was not far ahead with 6%.[48] Similarly, white-collar occupations were becoming more significant in Dundee. The proportion of individuals recorded in the directories as clerks or bookkeepers rose steadily from 0.3% in 1818 to 3% in 1850 and 4.9% two decades later. The expansion of the harbour, in particular, fuelled a growth in white-collar occupations such as clerkships and managerial positions in the local branches of shipping companies like the Dundee, Perth and London Shipping Company and the Hull Shipping Company.

This varied picture of middle-class economic activity is easily overlooked given the dominance of the textile trade as a source of employment for Dundee's workers. Although the dependence of these sectors on the growth generated by the textile trade should not be underestimated, their strength illustrates the degree of diversity in the local middle-class economy. Textile production has tended to mask the importance of other sectors, which were in fact vital to sustaining the urban population at a time of unprecedented demographic and industrial growth. Moreover, when the diversity of middle-class commercial activities in the town is considered, the validity of Dundee's image as a town dominated by manufacturing is undermined. Similar revisions of the place of manufacturers within the urban middle classes have already changed perceptions of industrial towns and cities in the north of England and Scotland.[49] The numerical inferiority of manufacturers to representatives from the craft and retail sectors within the ranks of Dundee's middle classes, and their failure to dominate posts on local government institutions in the town, suggests that a similar re-evaluation is needed of Dundee's traditional mill-town image. An examination of the place occupied by the town's leading textile manufacturers in town life during its phase of industrial expansion is central to this reassessment.

Although the growth of manufacturing had a relatively small impact on the make-up of Dundee's middle-classes in the first half of the nineteenth century, the decades after 1820 did witness the emergence of a small group of elite mill and factory owners who became key employers of labour in the town. Comparatively little work has been done on the characteristics of these men.[50] Studies of manufacturers and other early nineteenth-century entrepreneurs elsewhere in Britain, however, have helped to shed light on their role in urban life and their relationship with other middle-class elites.[51] In Bradford for example, a new leading group of urban entrepreneurs had emerged by the middle of the nineteenth century. Typically young immigrants to the town, from nonconformist religious backgrounds, these men took over the mantle of urban leadership in the wake of the decline of traditional Tory Anglican elites after 1825.[52] Dundee's emerging manufacturers, however, cannot be categorised in such distinct religious and political terms.

Information on a sample of thirty leading manufacturers who established businesses in Dundee between 1820 and 1870 is presented in Table 11. Their birth dates show that they represented a new generation of textile industrialists. Only four were born more than forty years before the first take-off of mechanised spinning in 1820. More than one-third were born between 1800 and 1820 and were thus at the beginning of their careers during a period of rapid organisational and technological change. This was not to say, however, that they lacked first hand knowledge and experience of non-mechanised, domestic textile production. As the section on parental occupations in Table 11 reveals, many of Dundee's new manufacturing elite came from established backgrounds of family involvement in the textile trade. William Baxter, who founded the Baxter's first Dundee mill in the Lower Dens, was the fourth generation of a family of merchant-weavers engaged in textile production.[53] James Cox was also the fourth generation of a family of bleachers and manufacturers based in Lochee, just outside Dundee. When he took control of the business in 1827 he inherited an extensive network of local weaving families built up by his father and grandfather.[54] Other key players in the growing linen industry in Dundee also came from established backgrounds in the trade. The Browns of East Mill were sons of James Brown who had built up a rural flax-spinning business. Peter Carmichael's father James, meanwhile, had a spinning mill in the Upper Dens in Dundee.[55] Given Dundee's history as a port and market centre serving a large textile-producing region, it is not surprising that such backgrounds in the industry were so common.

Table 11: Dundee's manufacturing elite. Characteristics of thirty leading manufacturers (businesses established between 1820 and 1870).

Year of Birth		Birthplace		Politics	
Pre-1780	4	Dundee	13	Lib	16
1780–1800	7	Fifeshire	5	Cons	2
1800–1820	11	Forfarshire	5	(Unknown	12)
1820–1840	4	Perthshire	2		
(Unknown	4)	Other	1		
		(Unknown	4)		

Religion		Father's Occupation	
Free Church	2	Spinning	7
Established Church	7	Manufacturing	8
United Presbyterian	1	Professions	2
Congregational	6	Other	2
Baptist	2	(Unknown	10)
Episcopalian	3		
Other	1		
(Unknown	8)		

Sources: Norrie, *Dundee Celebrities*; Millar, *Eminent Burgesses*; DPL, Obituary Books 1 and 2; DPL, LC 398, obituaries of well-known Dundonians, *Dundee Year Books* and *Dundee Directories*, various years.

These strong links with the regional economy are also evident in the birthplaces of the manufacturers examined in Table 11. Unlike Bradford's new generation of entrepreneurial elites, Dundee's manufacturers were not predominantly newcomers to the town. Thirteen of those examined in Table 11 were born in Dundee and, of the remainder, the neighbouring counties of Fifeshire and Forfarshire were the most common places of origin. Rather than long-distance migrants, they were the sons of local families or natives of nearby rural districts. Dundee's leading manufacturers cannot be viewed as outsiders bringing with them new political and religious values to displace those of the traditional elite. Instead, they shared many of the values and beliefs espoused by the town's urban middle classes as a whole. In political terms, their allegiances were overwhelmingly with the Liberal Party and the cause of Reform, but in this they were no different from the majority of the town's urban elites. By the mid-1830s, liberal political views 'embraced the great body of the burgesses and middle-classes in the town.'[56] Neither did their religious affiliations mark them out as a distinct group like Bradford's predominantly nonconformist entrepreneurs. Dundee's leading manufacturers belonged to a range of religious congregations throughout the town. Established Church (Church of Scotland) membership remained strong, even though, in the town as a whole, the Free Church was the largest denominational group by 1851 with a 32.2% share of the church-going population.[57] This defection rate, however, was not quite as high as in other Scottish towns where the Free Church gained a formidable power base among the upwardly-mobile middle classes.[58] Among Dundee's manufacturers, membership of much smaller dissenting bodies, in particular, the Congregationalists, was more common.

Although in terms of their origins and affiliations, the small textile manufacturing elite in Dundee had much in common with their counterparts among the town's middle classes, the networks of contact and association that they established in the town were largely separate from those of the local government elites. Figure 3 illustrates the distinctive networks developed by these groups.

Section A of the diagram includes families predominantly engaged in textile manufacture or in its sister industry, engineering. These families developed intricate social and business links through their shared experience as pioneering textile manufacturers. In the early days of mechanised mill spinning, local industrialists frequently visited each other's premises and developed a detailed knowledge of one another's businesses.[59] This close contact also manifested itself in the form of business partnerships such as the early collaboration between William Halley and James Gilroy in the establishment of Wallace Craigie Works,[60] and the longer-running partnership between Alexander J. Buist and the Don Brothers, which commenced in 1865.[61] Marriage links between manufacturing and engineering families were also common. Both James Cox, of Cox Brothers Camperdown Works, and Peter Carmichael, manager at Baxter Brothers, married daughters of the engineer James Carmichael, whose Ward Foundry supplied much of the machinery used by local linen manufacturers from the 1820s.[62]

Figure 3: Elite Networks in Dundee
    Business, marriage and apprenticeship ties between families prominent in
    business or public life, 1820–1870.

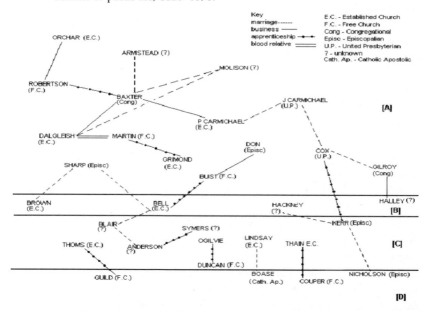

Source: Norrie, *Dundee Celebrities*; Millar, *Eminent Burgesses*; DPL, Obituary Books 1 and 2; DPL, LC 398, obituaries of well-known Dundonians; *Dundee Year Books* and *Dundee Directories* for various years.

Links were far less common, however, with families prominent in local government (Section [C]). Here, a different set of networks operated which fostered close connections between successive generations of municipal leaders. This trend was particularly evident in the frequency with which the same families supplied members for the Town Council. The glover George Rough was a member of the 1820 Town Council. His son, also called George, inherited his father's business in the High Street and also his interest in public life. His career on the Town Council began in 1849 and within four years he was elected to the post of provost. The Thoms family, meanwhile, maintained a presence on the Town Council for an even longer period. George Thoms was an early nineteenth-century councillor during the Riddoch era.[63] His eldest son, Patrick Hunter Thoms, was appointed town chamberlain in 1817, a post which he held for fourteen years. He was then elected to a council seat in 1843 and held the post of provost between 1847 and 1853.[64] His younger brother William, meanwhile, was elected dean of guild and entered the Town Council in 1844.[65]

As these examples suggest, links between successive generations of local-government post holders were often strong. These links were not only evident within families, but also within the commercial sphere. It was not uncommon, for instance, for mid-nineteenth-century council members to have spent a period as a clerk or apprentice with a previous councillor. Nineteenth-century clerkships were often filled on the basis of personal recommendation via 'informal but widespread networks of patronage'.[66] The idea that clerks could derive status from a prominent employer and use their association with him as a route to their own social or financial advancement, was particularly prevalent in the first half of the nineteenth century.[67] Figure 3 illustrates the frequency of these links in Dundee. George Duncan, for example, began his business career as an apprentice to Archibald Ogilvie, draper and town magistrate. Duncan's own political career began in 1836 when he was elected to the Council and later saw him returned as Member of Parliament for Dundee.[68] Similarly, John Symers, a native of Alyth, gained a foothold in the banking business with Patrick Anderson, a council member from 1804 to 1823, including a period as provost. Symers' own council membership began in 1820.[69]

Marriage ties between families involved in public life were also common in Dundee, as in other industrial towns.[70] Such connections linked a number of elite Dundonian families. The daughter of David Blair, who held the prominent post of Board of Trustees' stampmaster in Dundee, as well as the positions of magistrate, JP and patron of a number of local charitable institutions,[71] married the banker and merchant Patrick Anderson. Long-serving town clerk, Christopher Kerr, meanwhile, married the sister of an early political rival, William Hackney, who entered the Council in 1837 and became provost in 1839.[72] As this case suggests, marriage links often cut across potential sources of division posed by different religious or political backgrounds and Figure 3 provides further examples of families united across the denominational divide. In fact, marriage links between families had the potential to evolve into lifelong friendships spanning generations. The three textile-manufacturing families of Bell, Brown and Sharp, all featured on Figure 3, provide a case in point. Thomas Bell, senior, married Grace Brown, the sister of fellow flaxspinner and Town Council member, James Brown. The lasting link between the two families was evident in Bell's will, in which he named James Brown as one of his executors,[73] and also in the will of his son, Thomas Bell, junior, who died in 1887 and who named Andrew Brown, James's son, as an executor. The connection with the Sharp family was forged with the marriage of John Sharp's daughter to Bell junior's son. This link was also evident in the younger Bell's will, with the nomination of Sharp as another of his executors.[74]

Of the manufacturing families featured, only four also participated in the Town Council in the first half of the nineteenth century (Section [B]). The others developed few lasting links with the town's political elites. Prominent local government families were themselves more likely to forge contacts outside public life with those in the financial and commercial sector rather than with the manufacturing community. Some examples of these contacts can be seen in the connections between Sections [C] and [D]. Charles Boase, manager of the Dundee New Bank, which amalgamated with the Dundee Banking Company in 1838, married Margaret Lindsay, daughter of William Lindsay, corn merchant, town councillor and early advocate of liberal reforms in burgh politics.[75] The accountant Thomas Nicholson, meanwhile, who became manager of the Dundee and Newtyle Railway Company and served as treasurer for a number of local institutions, married a sister of town clerk, Christopher Kerr.[76]

The extent to which such links of kinship, marriage and business shaped urban life in Dundee was by no means unusual. In Manchester, for example, similar networks were also evident in the provision of business capital, electoral support and social contact among urban elites.[77] The strength of these networks in Dundee helps explain the relative absence of the new manufacturing elite from local government, despite the growth of the mechanised textile trade in the town since 1820. Established routes of entry into public life were durable enough to survive industrial transformation and municipal reform and to foster close links between one generation of local-government post holders and the next. This did not mean, however, that the manufacturers were excluded from public life against their will. For many, the long hours and close attention they devoted to their businesses deterred them from seeking public office.[78] Participation in local government demanded time and energy and many with large business commitments regarded it as an encroachment on their own work.[79] Neither did it mean that they were remote from town life. Men like George Gilroy, Joseph Grimond, David Baxter and Alexander J. Buist, were highly visible public figures in Dundee. Their participation in town life came not so much through mainstream local government, but rather through organisations more closely allied to their businesses. Grimond, Buist, Gilroy and Baxter, for example, all served as directors of the Chamber of Commerce during the height of their business careers. Gilroy, during his time as a shipowner, also held a seat on the Harbour Trust. Charitable work was also common. The major benefactions of David Baxter who gifted Baxter Park to the town in 1863 and, along with his sister, endowed the University College of Dundee are some of the most celebrated examples.[80] Support for the work of charitable institutions, however, was commonplace amongst the manufacturing elite. In particular, the Industrial Schools Society, which helped promote education among the children of the poorer working classes, was well supported by the manufacturing fraternity. One-third of the thirty leading manufacturers examined in Table 11 held positions on its board at some time during their careers.

Moreover these men enjoyed positions of unrivalled status and respect in the town. Although wages were low and facilities such as employer-built housing were scarce,[81] employer-worker relations in Dundee were good. The Grimonds employed some 3,000 hands at their Bowbridge Works in Dundee's Dens Road. They gained a reputation as good employers and were said to have designed every aspect of their works 'with a view to the health, comfort and self respect of the workers.'[82] Such was the esteem with which Alexander J. Buist was regarded by his employees, that his retirement in 1893 prompted a demonstration by workers in protest at his departure.[83] The close association of the Cox family with the weaving village of Lochee, where they had presided over the textile trade as old-style merchant-manufacturers for generations, earned them an elevated position of respect and influence among the local population.[84] James Cox, who oversaw the massive expansion of the business at Camperdown where over 5,000 workers were employed by the 1870s,[85] continued traditions begun by his father and grandfather such as a New Year supper for the head weavers.[86]

The prominence of leading manufacturers in the town and their links with urban life were also furthered by their tendency to reside close to their mill or factory. Men like Peter Carmichael, manager at Baxter Brother's Dens works, chose to live near to the mills where they spent so much of their time. During his working life, Carmichael was tempted to move out of Dundee to the neighbouring seaside village of Broughty Ferry only temporarily in 1847 when his wife was in poor health, but by 1850 he was back in his house at Dens Brae.[87] James Cox also moved with his family to Broughty Ferry temporarily in the 1840s, but in 1848 returned to Dudhope Terrace in Dundee 'to be near the works'.[88] This preference among manufacturers for residing close to the workplace did not diminish until after 1850 (see Table 12). By 1870 increasing numbers of them, along with their counterparts in commercial occupations and the professions, were opting to live further afield. Alexander J. Buist, for example, moved from Hawkhill Place in Dundee to Reres Mount in Broughty Ferry in 1856. Harry Walker, whose firm ran the Caldrum Works in Dundee, moved from Dudhope Terrace, on the slopes of the Law Hill, to Newport in Fife in the same period.

Likewise, William Halley moved from the Hilltown area of Dundee, a stone's throw from his Wallace Craigie Works, to take up residence in Carnoustie in 1864. Despite the distance, his contact with the town and the workplace did not diminish. He drove daily to Dundee by carriage and pair, returning home by train in the evening.[89]

Table 12: Residential addresses of thirty leading Dundee manufacturers in 1850 and 1870.

	1850	1870
Dundee (centre)	11	3
Inner Suburbs	(8)	(3)
Magdalen Green/Perth Rd	3	2
Dudhope/Lawside	3	1
Mayfield/Craigie	2	0
Outer Suburbs	(2)	(10)
Broughty Ferry/West Ferry	1	7
Monifieth/Carnoustie	1	1
Fife	0	2
Not Applicable*	3	11
Unknown	2	0
Other	2	3

*No longer in business or deceased.
Source: *Dundee Directories*, 1850 and 1870.

Dundee's manufacturing elite also derived status and notoriety from their wealth. Although on a nation-wide scale, manufacturing wealth has been shown to have been less significant than commercial wealth in nineteenth-century Britain,[90] in the context of individual towns and cities the picture could look quite different. Those who built up the most successful businesses during Dundee's phase of unprecedented industrial expansion amassed huge fortunes. Eleven of Dundee's thirty elite manufacturers left over £100,000 in wealth at the time of their deaths. These men included Joseph Grimond and Robert Gilroy, who both left over £200,000; James Cox, who left over £300,000; John Sharp and William Ogilvy Dalgleish, who each left over £700,000; and David Baxter, of Baxter Brothers linen works, whose wealth was valued at £1,200,000.[91] This level of wealth was unrivalled in the town. In 1881, less than 1% of the personal estates of deceased Dundonians were valued at more than £10,000.[92] The leading manufacturers thus clearly dominated the upper echelons of Dundee's economic elite. The wealth of Town Council members, by contrast, was typically much lower (see Figure 4). Only two members of the 1850 Town Council left over £100,000 at the time of their deaths. The majority, who came from occupational backgrounds in retail and trades, had accumulated wealth of less than £10,000 by the end of their lives.

Figure 4: Comparative wealth of leading manufacturers (1820–1870) and 1850 Town
Council members in Dundee.

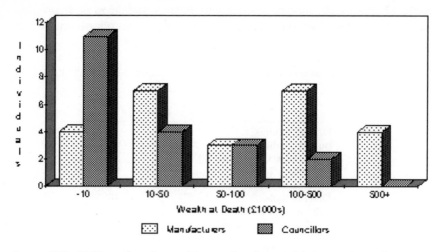

Source: SRO, SC45, confirmations and inventories of personal estates, various volumes.

In Dundee then, the absence of many leading manufacturers from the Town
Council also meant the absence of some of the town's wealthiest citizens. This had
significant consequences for the shaping of perceptions of local government in the
town. Unlike Glasgow where the 'wealthiest and worthiest citizens' were 'to the
fore in civic activity'[93] Dundee's council members were neither the richest nor the
most respected members of the urban middle classes. In contrast to Aberdeen,
where the economic elite and the political elite of the town were comprised of the
same families,[94] wealth and political influence were largely separate in Dundee.
There, council representatives were often people who, but for their spell in public
office, would not have been widely known among the population at large.
Members were often accused of seeking office in order to serve their own vested
interests rather than to use their status and influence for the good of the wider
community. This charge was most commonly levelled against representatives of
the spirit trade who had gained council posts thanks to nominations by the Spirit
Trade Association and were seen as using their subsequent authority to serve the
interests of that body.[95]

Up to the middle of the nineteenth century, however, criticisms such as these
had little impact on the organisation of local government in the town. Traditional
patterns of municipal representation prevailed and the divisions between the
manufacturers and the local political elite remained largely intact. The implications of this were that municipal leadership became increasingly divorced from the
industrial face of the town. This became even more apparent when Dundee
underwent a second phase of rapid industrial expansion and demographic growth
from the 1860s. The disruption to Baltic flax supplies during the Crimean War

was the final push many Dundee manufacturers needed to switch production to cheaper jute goods.[96] Meanwhile the outbreak of the American Civil War generated huge demand for coarse textile products, a market which Dundee firms were able to monopolise.[97] Accordingly, jute imports increased from 15,400 tons in 1853 to 58,474 by 1868[98] and a rapid period of new mill building and heavy inward migration transformed the town into a burgeoning city of over 100,000 inhabitants by 1871.[99] The balance of council representation in Dundee in favour of retailers and craftsmen rather than manufacturers seemed increasingly out of step with these developments.

At the same time, changes in the organisation of municipal government were placing increasing responsibilities on town councils. The trend towards rationalisation in local government saw councils taking over the work of previously separate municipal bodies such as improvement commissions. This process was well underway by the middle of the nineteenth century. In Leeds, for example, the municipal council took over the powers of the improvement commission in 1842.[100] In Dundee, the transfer of police commission powers to the Town Council was achieved in 1851.[101] The local gas and water companies were also municipalised in 1869[102] and a host of other services such as the tramways, slaughterhouses and public baths were transferred to the corporation in the same period so that the Town Council became 'about the largest employer of male labour in the city'.[103] These developments meant that council members of high calibre were needed to cope with the new demands and responsibilities of this growing local government portfolio.

The combination of Dundee's growing stature as an industrial city and the increase in council powers also coincided with the sweeping franchise reforms of 1868, which saw Dundee's electorate soar from 3,000 to 15,000 voters.[104] Large sections of the skilled working classes were enfranchised for the first time and it was from this sector that an impetus came for an overhaul of Town Council membership. The desire for reform quickly crystallised into an organised campaign spearheaded by the Dundee Working Men's Association and Trades Council with enthusiastic support from the *Dundee Advertiser*.[105] The aim was to bring forward candidates for council election who better reflected the economic growth of the town and who enjoyed the confidence and respect of large sections of the population. By general consensus, these were the manufacturers:

> It is amongst the intelligent working men of Dundee that the anxiety to see our local parliament made worthy of the town is leading to active exertions, and it is they who are now looking to the most able and public spirited of our citizens amongst our great industrial chiefs to come forward and help them in raising the character of what should be our most respected civic institution.[106]

Those targeted for nomination included the textile manufacturers James Cox, Alexander H. Moncur, George T. Graham and H. C. Briggs, and the merchant and manufacturer Frank Henderson, of Ladybank Leather Works. These men were favoured not only because of their importance in the town as employers and the considerable business skills they had to offer, but also because they were regarded as men of learning and culture who would bring status and dignity to council proceedings. Cox, Briggs and Henderson were all involved in the establishment of the Albert Institute and the movement to set up a Free Library in the town. Henderson, in particular, was renowned for his abilities as a reader, thinker and public speaker. A close associate of George Gilfillan, he had delivered many public lectures in the town, including a talk on 'Leather, its history, manufacture and uses', on the occasion of the British Association's visit to Dundee 1867.[107]

The Working Men's Association and Trades Council campaign proved an overwhelming success when all bar one of its seven nominees were successfully returned to Council posts in the poll held in December 1868. The significance of this achievement was noted not only locally but also in other industrial regions where the Dundee example was hailed as a model for other towns to follow. The *Sheffield Daily Telegraph* carried a report of the election result and commented that, 'To get the nominations out of the hands of nobodies, to make the local parliaments esteemed where now they are treated with levity and rudeness, to cause seats in councils to be accepted by men of weight and culture are not small things to have been accomplished'.[108] The success of the 1868 campaign to reform council membership, however, did not see an end to debates over the character of Town Council representation in Dundee. As another chapter in this book reveals, the issue of the status of participants in local government continued to cause controversy into the late nineteenth and early twentieth centuries.[109]

What the campaign does reveal is how the newly enfranchised Dundonians perceived their town in this period and, moreover, how they wanted it to be perceived by the outside world. The determination with which council membership was overhauled reflected a mood of confidence and self-esteem among large sections of the working population. Dundee was riding high on an unprecedented wave of industrial growth and the move to propel the people in the vanguard of this growth into public office was driven by a sense of shared pride in their achievements. The *Advertiser* commented that the nomination of leading manufacturers to council posts 'shows the real community of feeling between all classes amongst us, the absence of jealousy and the confidence of the employed in those known to them as honourable employers'.[110] Although the expression here is somewhat dewy-eyed, the wider point about the town's worker employer relations is a valid one, as Christopher Whatley demonstrates in more depth elsewhere in this volume.[111] The scale of industrial development since 1850 seemed to have shifted perceptions of Dundee, from a bustling, mid-nineteenth-century textile town to a thriving industrial city on a par with the metropolises of Leeds, Glasgow and Manchester. The campaigners for Town Council reform argued that, like these other great cities, Dundee had leaders of outstanding ability who were fitted not only to serve on the local political stage but also in the national parliament. Frank Henderson was already being described as 'destined to attain more than local distinction' even before he had secured his Town Council seat.[112]

That it took a determined campaign in 1868, to attempt to place the civic leadership of Dundee in the hands of the manufacturing elite, illustrates the problems inherent in attempting to view the town prior to this date as manufacturer-dominated. Throughout the fifty-year period of industrial growth, Dundee developed a diverse middle-class economy in which textile manufacturers made up only a small proportion of the commercial urban elites engaged in providing food, clothing, transport and financial services to the burgeoning population. Their place in the evolving urban setting of Dundee was thus not a significant one in a statistical sense. The manufacturer's contribution to urban life, however, cannot be measured purely in numerical terms.[113] In Dundee, just as in other industrial towns, their prominence and status far outweighed their statistical importance within the urban middle classes. The reformed Town Council with its new, high-profile manufacturing contingent presided over an era of far-reaching urban improvement. Henderson, Cox, Moncur, Graham and the other new recruits played a key role in overseeing the implementation of the 1871 Improvement Act which aimed to 'make Dundee one of the finest and healthiest towns in Scotland'.[114] The opening up of new streets and crescents and the widening of existing thoroughfares transformed the town centre, ridding it of some of its worst areas of cramped medieval housing.[115] Through this work they played a key role in fashioning an urban environment befitting the status of a significant industrial city. They also unleashed a powerful new image of manufacturing dominance, which defined Dundee for decades to come.

FOUR

Altering images of the industrial city: the case of James Myles, the 'Factory Boy', and mid-Victorian Dundee

Christopher A. Whatley

FEW HISTORIANS OF Victorian Dundee have omitted from their portrayals of what they perceive to be a grim industrial town either quotations from or references to the 'anonymous' *Chapters in the Life of a Dundee Factory Boy*. So compelling is the testimony in *Chapters*, that historians whose interests have been in wider aspects of British industrialisation have also drawn material from it. Their reliance on this source, which purports to have been 'written by [the 'Factory Boy'] himself', is understandable, as it provides investigators with what appears to be one of a very small number of first-hand accounts of the early decades of the mill and factory system in Scotland, written by an operative.[1]

The description in *Chapters* of masters and managers adjusting factory clocks forwards in the morning and backwards at night – 'cloaks for cheatery and oppression' – was used by the late Edward Thompson for example to support his condemnation of the use to which time-discipline was put by unscrupulous early capitalists.[2] This is not the only piece of damning evidence in a book which, in autobiographical mode, tells the tale of a young country lad, Frank Forrest, who is brought by his widowed mother to work in Dundee. Such were the poverty-stricken circumstances of mother and son around 1815 that he was forced at a very young age to enter a mill. There he endured a catalogue of horrors which included unrelenting work, exhaustion, beatings, and exposure to lewd songs and crude suggestions on the part of the female mill workers, facets of Forrest's experience – the authentic voice of Scottish labour's suffering in the early industrial revolution – which have now become ingrained in a secondary literature which has been criticised for its negative assessment of the nineteenth-century Scottish cities.[3] Bleak and terrible places, they were spurned by the country's stunned middle-class writers in the nineteenth century, whose novels were 'suffused with nostalgia for a lost green world'.[4]

The first section of this chapter examines the authenticity of *Chapters*. The revised account of the provenance and purpose of the book will reveal that the real author of *Chapters*, James Myles, had a rather different view of early industrial Britain than that with which he has usually been identified by mis-readings of his text. Myles was in no doubt about the superiority of urban life. However, the chapter is more than an essay in textual analysis and bibliographical criticism. The investigative process of tracing Myles's career and examining his ideas about industrial society will modify received wisdom about the nature of conditions and social relations, and more importantly, working-class attitudes – popular menta-lité – in Dundee in the mid-nineteenth century.

Leading on from this, in the second section of this chapter, it will be shown that depictions of Dundee as a 'frontier town', lacking 'traditional and stable relation-ships' and severed by class division, are deficient.[5] In British history the years from *c.*1851 to 1873 are often described as 'the age of equipoise'. In Scotland too the absence of significant class conflict has been observed, while it has even been claimed that, in general, Scottish towns were more orderly than their English counterparts.[6] Myles's values and attitudes, it will be argued, were to a greater or lesser extent shared by a significant body of the working classes in Dundee. This is not to deny the existence of a sub-strata of alienated and dissolute urban dwellers, but as will be seen, this group was in the minority. The third and final section of the chapter will offer an explanation for the emergence of relatively peaceful social relations in the two decades which followed the final Chartist uprising.

Hitherto, attention in Scotland has largely been directed towards this issue in the context of Glasgow and its surrounding heavy-industrial region, with emphasis being placed upon the importance of a skilled, masculine, Protestant culture in determining the mid-nineteenth century mood of consensus and conciliation.[7] While, as will be seen, in most respects this explanatory model can be applied to Dundee, because of its higher proportion of female workers in textile mills and factories where their work was formally classified as unskilled, it requires modification. Indeed in some depictions of Dundee it is the 'raucous shawl-clad mill-girl culture' – bawdy, boisterous and bad – which predominates. Clearly the issue of where Dundee's female textile workers are to be placed within the context of mid-Victorian consensus also requires to be explored.

'What ordinary people thought, and the way in which they expressed it, matters', it has recently been argued, 'and ought to be taken seriously by historians'.[8] The approach, not a new one, has had many adherents, and, in a modest way will be adopted here. It is recognised that there are potential dangers in drawing upon testimony which may fail to convey the fluidity and complexity of social identity, for some critics an elusive and undefinable fiction. Myles, it will be seen, was an articulate, respectable, young working man, and it can be argued that he was necessarily unrepresentative of the 'historically silent and perhaps disreputable masses'.[9] But the case which will be made here is that there is sufficient corroborating evidence to suggest that Myles – and individuals who were part of his circle – represented an important (but by no means the sole) component of working-class identity in Dundee. Notwithstanding the limitations to the explanatory possibilities of what, broadly speaking, has been called the 'linguistic turn', such an approach has the merit of enabling historians to comprehend more clearly than behaviourist studies alone, working-class perceptions and identities. Thus other first-hand testimony, including poetry, diaries and reminiscences will be incorporated, as well as new material gleaned from more traditional sources such as newspapers, and local authority minute books. Although materialist analyses which link greater prosperity and the emergence of an 'aristocracy of labour' with greater political and social quiescence now tend to be discounted, the evidence from Dundee suggests that economic conditions cannot be excluded from the equation, nor how these were experienced and perceived by those who lived through them.[10]

It was only in the twentieth century that *Chapters* began to be utilised as an authentic autobiographical account of working-class experience during the industrial revolution. Although the author's true identity was not revealed to readers when *Chapters* first appeared in weekly instalments in Dundee's *Northern Warder* in January 1850, strong denials were issued when any parts of the series were judged to bear too close a relation to contemporary people and events.[11] Published in a single 'handsome little volume' in May 1850, it was no secret that the author was James Myles, who conducted a correspondence with readers of the *Northern Warder*. Myles was a fairly prominent local artisan with literary pretensions, who perhaps as early as 1843 but certainly by 1845 had become the proprietor of a bookshop and a news agency in Dundee's Overgate.[12] Owing to some possible confusion about the book's provenance in 1903, the Dundee-based *People's Journal* published some information about its author and declared that not only was the sole autobiographical section of the book that which dealt with Myles's early life in the rural hamlet of Fowlis, outside Dundee, but that the author had never in his life worked in a spinning mill or factory.[13] None of the other facts the paper revealed about Myles were new: it had long been known that he had been born in Liff parish (which bordered Dundee) in 1819 and died in Dundee in February 1851, at the comparatively young age of thirty-two.

What were Myles's motives for writing *Chapters in the Life of a Dundee Factory Boy?* It has been argued that Myles took up his pen owing to his 'fierce resentment' at 'the misrepresentations' which were being made about the conditions of child workers.[14] This is partially corroborated by the knowledge that Myles was indeed concerned about contemporary working conditions, and in August 1849 spoke out angrily at a public meeting called to oppose the 'relay system', which had been introduced by some employers as a means of circumventing the restrictions imposed on working hours by the Ten Hours Act. Myles's opposition was based on his concern that the system would interfere with the education of young factory employees, the absence of supervision and the 'disarrangement that will be caused in the domestic economy of families' by its use. Accordingly, *Chapters* was dedicated to Richard Oastler, and in its final paragraph the author records his hope that the 'old system' had been 'for ever blasted with the detestation of the wise and good', never again to be imposed 'on the young females and helpless children of our country'.[15]

The greater part of the explanation however almost certainly lies in the development of Myles's social and political ideas. During or after serving his apprenticeship as a stonemason in Lochee, a quarrying and weaving village adjoining Dundee, Myles had evidently become interested in Chartism. An impressive, even charismatic, speaker, he had been encouraged to abandon his trade and become 'a public lecturer on the people's rights'.[16] Although the details and timing are hazy, by September 1841 he had adopted the increasingly well-supported cause of Owenite socialism, on behalf of which Myles spoke at sizeable and sometimes heated meetings and debates in Glasgow, Falkirk, Fife and Forfarshire.[17] Although retaining links with Dundee's small band of hand-loom-weaver, artisan and petty-bourgeois literary Chartists, a religiously inclined and strongly principled collection of men otherwise known as the Dundee 'Republic of Letters', Myles became increasingly hostile to physical-force Chartism. He poured scorn on Chartist meetings in Dundee, at which, he asserted, 'all the insanities of political fanaticism [were] entertained and respected'. The town's Chartist council he described as 'the skep where the honey of O'Connor democracy was collected, and around which fluttered drones, demagogues and fools'.[18] Doubtful about the prospects of Chartist success, Myles committed himself instead to moral reform. In 1840 Dundee was the location of one of the four main Scottish branches of the Owenite Universal Community of Rational Religionists. Unlike hardline Owenites, however, Myles was also a strong supporter of protestant Christianity.[19] By the end of the 1840s he had apparently turned his back on Owenite solutions too and, convinced that the clergy had 'lost all hold' on the affections of the lower orders (whom Myles viewed with considerable distaste), had committed himself to the cause of Christian evangelicalism.[20]

It was in this context that *Chapters in the Life of a Dundee Factory Boy*, set mainly in the 1820s and 1830s, was written. The mid-century years were particularly creative ones for working-class writers in Britain, especially amongst Chartist circles, with much stress being placed on self-education as the route to working-class achievement as the likelihood of radical political change diminished. The apprentice-tale format adopted by Myles was not uncommon and indeed appears to have provided one of the antecedents of the industrial fiction which enjoyed a surge of popularity in the 1840s and 1850s.[21] *Chapters* is a didactic novel, one of the earliest in a 'wave' of serialised, purposeful fiction which in Scotland was to become a feature in the newspaper and journal press in the 1850s.[22] Working-class readers – for whom it was mainly written – were offered ingeniously plotted fiction, often set in familiar settings, much of it laced with liberal evangelical values and millenarian in tone. The factory was clearly a popular subject around which to construct a fiction: the title of the best-known novel written by the leading serial novelist in nineteenth-century Scotland, David Pae, was *The Factory Girl; or, The Dark Places of Glasgow*. This novel, whose author's moral concerns were similar to those of Myles, was written during the late 1850s, and published in serial form in 1863–4.[23]

Radical but reformist, the roots of the genre have been traced back to the movement to distribute cheap religious and improving tracts which was formally begun in Scotland in 1793. The fictional narrative was a screen behind which the author worked his real purpose. Thus in *Chapters* a prominent theme is reconciliation between the classes. Employers are exhorted by the narrator 'to cultivate a good understanding with the employed, and show forth kindness and brotherly love'. Kindness was 'cheap, sweet and pleasing' and shed 'a halo of felicity over all who move within its holy circumference'.[24] Too few modern readers have read beyond the early pages of the book which describe conditions in the early mills, or paid sufficient attention to the narrative of which these early experiences were but part. Forrest and his mother were forced to flee to the industrial town because his father, a country shoemaker, had been transported for seven years following a drunken brawl at a fair during which Forrest senior, his mind 'unhinged by the whisky demon', had killed a fellow reveller. Drink and the ruination brought in its wake, is a recurring and insistent theme of the book. On one occasion the narrator himself yields to the temptation of a glass of whisky, and as a result is nearly drowned. Indeed, it is as a temperance tract that *Chapters* can at least in part be understood, although paradoxically, some of its earliest readers had taken umbrage at what they had mistakenly judged to be its anti-temperance stance. By mid-century temperance was widely supported by the working classes in Scotland.[25]

Frank Forrest, encouraged by his mother, finds knowledge and wisdom in reading and, in common with countless other Scots, is inspired by the 'fiery patriotism' of Blind Harry's *Wallace*, and the numerous other, easier-to-read versions of it which were published in the nineteenth century.[26] Further reading on the part of the largely self-taught Forrest leads him to *Robinson Crusoe* and other texts, but none was more influential than that 'glorious dream', *Pilgrim's Progress*, the staple fare and source of inspiration for numerous working-class evangelists in the nineteenth century, and one which made its mark in Dundee too.[27] After serving an apprenticeship as a shoemaker, finding some success as a writer, and then marriage to a woman whose 'modesty and good sense' he had long admired (rather than the 'snare' of physical beauty), the tale culminates in Forrest's discovery that his father is still alive in Australia. His punishment borne, along with his son's struggle to adulthood and respectability, he was now the proprietor of a modest-sized farm, on which he was to be joined by Forrest and his wife. Forrest, like Myles, planned to launch a newspaper, *The Banner of Scotland.*

Readers were presented in *Chapters* with a series of homilies, based upon Myles's own view of how society should be ordered. Examples abound. The appearance in print of Forrest's first essay leads him to conclude that though a 'poor orphan boy' with a limited education, he had 'by an indomitable spirit of perseverance, overcome educational barriers and social adversities' and been 'enabled to convey my thoughts in respectable English'. The reader is then addressed directly:

Achievements such as these . . . I am not ashamed to be proud of and I relate them with a lively faith that they will kindle in some poor boy's mind the flame of hope, and spirit of emulation.[28]

On his return to Dundee as a shoemaker, Forrest reflects on his presence at 'the scene of my former trials and sufferings' and could not help but feel 'a deep sense of gratitude on what I was compared to what I had been':

True, I was only an operative, but who is more independent and happy than the unmarried, temperate, and good workman. He has less anxiety of mind, and fewer troubles than any class I know of. If he attends to his work, is prudent, and cultivates his mind, he undoubtedly occupies a felicitous position, the sweets of which are only known to those who have tasted them.

Earlier, the 'young of the working classes' had been advised that the 'pride, independence, and even happiness' of working people 'depends upon their ability to . . . work expeditiously and well; hence the importance of industry, anxiety, and care on the part of apprentices'.[29]

Chapters is certainly not worthless as a primary source. The descriptions of factory conditions owe much to the findings of Sadler's 1832 parliamentary report on children in factories, which included evidence taken from workers in mills in and around Dundee. Testimonies of straps being employed, beatings, tampering with clocks, of bothy sleeping arrangements, the impossibility of escape from the country mills and of links between mill work and female prostitution were plundered by Myles and redeployed in autobiographical form, as too was the language and imagery of slavery. Yet other references in *Chapters* do relate to Dundee from the 1820s to the 1840s, as either witnessed or understood by Myles, and there is a suggestion that a model for Myles's narrator and central character, Frank Forrest, was provided by a John Deans from Lochee, 'in whose life there was a strange admixture of tragic romance' and who 'resided with a deserted, poverty-stricken mother', just like the fictional Forrest.[30] Actual places and events are skilfully woven into the narrative, as for example the collapse in 1832 (when Myles would have been about thirteen years old) of the banking firm of John Maberley & Co, which caused considerable havoc and some bankruptcies in Dundee and the linen towns of east Scotland.[31] There are parts of the book too which appear to be autobiographical, not only reflecting Myles's views but also reporting his practices, as for example when through the voice of his narrator he extols the virtues of discussion groups formed by 'young men of the operative class', and almost certainly reveals his delight in his membership of the 'Republic of Letters' when reporting on weekly meetings at 'Denham's Hotel', to talk about 'our hopes and aspirations . . . indulge in gentle tilts on our favourite dogmas', 'the hot and burning scintillations of liberty-loving and imaginative souls'.[32]

Chapters in the Life of a Dundee Factory Boy should not be read therefore as a critique of industrial capitalism. Its author acknowledged ills in the system, but was confident that legislation and the Christian spirit had expelled the worst of these. In this respect Myles's conclusions were not unlike those reached by most Scottish Chartists, who had rejected violence and believed that cooperation with the middle classes would produce greater benefits than class struggle.[33] Rather, *Chapters* is a mid-Victorian guide book for the attainment of a successful life by the diligent male worker, no matter his background. That this is the aim is made clear in Chapter 1, where the narrator condemns most existing accounts of factory work as being 'compiled by literary scavengers – a mere collection of sickly, nauseous, unhealthy rubbish'; Myles's readers by contrast were offered a

> truthful history of a poor boy, who has drunk pretty deeply from the cup of misery, but who has, by perseverance, industry, and a strong will, surmounted many obstacles, and triumphed over many difficulties.

Readers were invited to consider that those who 'outstripped us at school, and possessed hereditary social advantages' may now be 'far behind us in the race for respectability and comfort'. The 'careless clever' were often left in the rear too, while 'now and then' the poor supplanted even the rich, and 'the plodding and the dull' frequently achieved more than 'the dawning of their manhood promised'.

Indeed, by the end of the 1840s (if not earlier) the author of *Chapters* had become an adherent of and advocate not only for British capitalism and its civilising influences but also of industrialism and the industrial city. The first (and probably only) issue of *Myles' Forfarshire Telegraph* in January 1851 contains a lengthy hymn of praise to British military prowess and economic progress in the first half of the nineteenth century. Notwithstanding the anti-urban stance of *Chapters*, and indeed Myles's awareness of the harshness of urban existence and the moral depravity of what he called the 'lowest type of the poor', elsewhere in his writings he reveals his enthusiasm for the city and all that it could offer.[34] While his narrator in *Chapters* reflects that the countryside cottage in which he was born 'was the sweetest spot on earth', and describes the confusion he felt when arriving in the town, a 'mysterious social enigma, a complete chaos of houses and crowds', Myles elsewhere was in no doubt about the superiority of the town over the countryside. The town, he declared, was 'brimful of interest', 'the focus of refinement and art, the centre of all religious and political stamina, the great laboratory of intellect', and the 'grand problem of civilisation'.

As has been seen, Myles was familiar with several of the Scottish industrial towns, and although he admitted that he enjoyed the 'simplicity of agricultural life', he much preferred to contemplate the 'wonderful arcana of life as un-bosomed in the every-day movements of a large town'. Every street, he wrote, contained some 'material objects of interest . . . milestones on the highway of local and general progress'. This was no less true of Dundee, with its spinning mills and workshops. Think 'on the vast and complicated schemes', he urged his readers, and the

> cares that are ever active in the mercantile management of such leviathan 'hives of industry'; and when you know that the regular motion of their engines and wheels gives employment and bread to thousands of our townsmen, are they not objects of interest more intense than the silent woods, sunny dells, and moss-covered ruins of the country? Look at the coffee houses, reading rooms, hotels, lodging houses, mechanics' institutions, libraries, literary clubs, debating clubs, young men's societies, missionary societies, churches, chapels, in one word, all the intellectual, religious, and social apparatus of a huge town wherein nearly a hundred thousand mortals "live, move and have a being", and then ask yourself the question – Can there be any scene or object in the country so interesting as all this? The reply must be in the negative.[35]

In expressing his admiration for the industrial city Myles was in a minority amongst working-class writers, but he was not alone. Many broadsides for instance celebrated the entertainments available in towns.[36] Popular novelists writing for the press in Scotland – such as David Pae – often set their stories in an urban setting; industrial capitalism was not in itself to be condemned, what was were those who abused it and placed mercenary values and the cash nexus above divinely-inspired morality.[37]

Nor indeed at the local level does it seem that Myles was out of step with other sizeable sections of the working class in his positive response to recent developments in Dundee. Contrasting with the views of historians reported earlier, there is a solid body of evidence from Dundee to suggest that as in much of the rest of industrialising Britain, the third quarter of the nineteenth century was one of considerable social harmony based on a 'shared commitment to the values and ethos of liberal capitalism'.[38]

One indication was the virtual absence of working-class political activity after the final defeat of the Chartists in 1848; the first body of any significance, the Dundee Working Men's Association, was not founded until 1864 and struggled to attract many delegates from the town's 'public works' until the end of the decade.[39] So peaceful was a gathering of some 1,300 Roman Catholics (mainly from Ireland, and usually described in the most disparaging of terms) to mark St Patrick's Day in 1863 that one contemporary declared himself astonished, 'as they presented the appearance of an ordinary assembly of the respectable working classes'.[40]

In retrospect, what was most notable about the mid-Victorian decades in Dundee is the apparent warmth of social relations within the workplace. Works' outings were commonplace. In June 1859 for instance 1,100 well-dressed employees of Cox Brothers marched off in an orderly fashion from Camperdown Linen Works accompanied by four bands of music for a day out to St Andrews.

Once there they visited the historic sites and danced, raced and played other games. By 1865 the number involved had risen to 2,000, with two trains being booked to take Cox's workers to Stirling for the day. Four instrumental bands accompanied them to the station.[41] At numerous works, large and small, festivals, soirees, balls and dances were held at New Year.

Female mill and factory workers were participants too, with reports of women workers singing songs or reciting poems at soirees held to mark the departure of a favourite overseer for example.[42] Textile workers of both sexes, notably the Irish, were much-criticised for crowding onto the streets in the evening, singing 'immodest songs', using obscene language and oaths and curses, particularly as those concerned were often attractive-looking females who were failing to show the moral lead expected of Victorian wives and mothers. Myles was convinced that the morals of mill girls were 'very low', and that many of the wives of the 'lowest types of the poor' were former mill workers who had 'no idea of domestic comfort and industry'. But public opinion was divided about the character of Dundee's female textile workers. 'One who was Once a Mill Girl' opined that the picture of the prematurely-old, pale-faced and shiftless mill girl no longer applied (following the reductions in working hours), and that close comparison of the character and habits of shopgirls or domestic servants with mill workers would show that the last-named were 'not so bad after all'. If this was deemed to be an over-optimistic claim by some observers, there were those who were prepared to concede that the appearance of mill girls had improved since they had first begun to arrive from Ireland, and that they 'were still in the way of progress'. There were those who defended the factory weavers – the 'tidy steam-loom lassie[s]' who were widely regarded as being superior in their habits to the spinners – on the grounds that they 'cultivate the social virtues to a marvellous degree, their ways and means considered', but even the mill spinners had their advocates. That they talked 'loud and free' was in part due to the difficulty of being heard in the mills, and they were worthy of respect, it was argued, as they 'gloried' in their work.[43] Nor did they exclude themselves from the officially-sanctioned political life of Dundee: during the General Election campaign of 1868 'bands' of mill girls were seen parading the streets arm-in-arm, singing abusive songs about the Conservative-inclined, reluctant secret ballot supporter J. A. Guthrie, and displaying 'Vote for Armistead' (one of the two successful Liberal candidates) tickets.[44]

Perhaps the most telling sign that Dundee was a town outwardly at peace with itself however was the opening by Earl Russell of Baxter Park in 1863. Looking back from the vantage point of 1902 Sir John Leng saw it as a key turning point in the town's history. The 36 acres of ground for the Park was donated to the town by Sir David Baxter, of the Baxter textile dynasty: it was designed by Sir Joseph Paxton (designer of the Crystal Palace) and created by Frank Richard, who had undertaken a similar project in Bradford, when he laid out Peel Park. An estimated 70–80,000 people were in attendance at the opening, a figure equivalent to around three-quarters of Dundee's population. Visitors had thronged to Dundee, but they were very much in the minority. A procession some 7,500 strong had marched on what had been declared a half-day holiday, through a town decorated with 'great walls of verdure', a series of floral arches, and past flag-bedecked mills, factories and foundries. Many bore placards which celebrated Queen Victoria, leading employers, Dundee's prosperity, industry, free trade and the poets Burns and Byron, the former portrayed as a self-taught peasant farmer who had attained universal respect through perseverance and hard work, and whose popularity in the nineteenth century owed much to the nostalgia and part-patriotism his poems and songs invoked for a vanished and largely imagined Scottish rural past.[45] Underlining Myles's enthusiasm for steam power, the statue of James Watt which topped Baxter's Dens Mill was crowned with laurel leaves. (Dundee lacked running water sufficient to drive mill wheels and so the steam engine and the name of James Watt had a special resonance for the nineteenth-century Dundonian.) Most of the town's main works and trades were included in the procession, in which banners declaring trade solidarity and worker independence were carried along with numerous models of steam engines, looms, ships and other representative works' productions.

While few females joined the march, their role in the town's economic and social life was vividly displayed on flags which showed them working at spinning frames and powerlooms. They feature too in illustrations of the opening and in song celebrating it ('the mill lassies, all looking so fine/With their mantles, and bonnets, and trig crinoline'). One of their number, Ellen Johnston, a whisky-drinking powerloom weaver, wrote and had published in the local press a commemorative poem which in the awfulness of its metrical rhythms and rhyme foreshadows MacGonagall. 'The Opening of the Baxter Park' begins with the lines:

> The ninth day of September
> The sun arose in splendour,
> His glory to surrender
> To Sir David of Dundee.
> The Trades came forth in grandeur,
> Each led by its commander,
> Bold as an Alexander
> Of eighteen sixty-three.[46]

Also unveiled on the same occasion was a statue of Sir David Baxter, the costs of which had largely been borne by the working classes who comprised most of the 16,731 subscribers, including females, in what was apparently a spontaneous show of appreciation for Baxter's generosity.[47]

The peace was not altogether complete however. There were outbreaks of disorder, more often when trade conditions were poor, but in most cases they were predictable, and tended to be short-lived and confined to particular parts of the town. New Year produced a flurry of drunkenness and drownings of the inebriated at the harbour, and the July Stobbs Fair was renowned for its drink-induced turbulence and the scuffles 'of the lower and rougher classes' with police. 'Flit Friday', when farm servants arrived in town to engage with new masters, produced 'pernicious habits' when the young of both sexes gathered together in public houses.

The Monarch's birthday, traditionally a part-holiday and occasion of civic celebration in Scotland, was always troublesome for the authorities and sometimes the cause of considerable anxiety. The disturbances on the evening of 23 May 1853 were notable for their severity, with the sacking of the Town House, numerous windows on the High Street broken and police officers injured. But there was almost universal agreement that the main reason that the crowds had been 'more than usually boisterous' was that the holiday had been held on the Monday, when many weavers were off work anyway, and had money to spend on drink and fireworks. Demands that hat wearers remove their headgear when walking on the High Street, temporarily under the control of the crowd, were to be expected, as was the seizure of some hats to be used as footballs; what was galling was the degree of violence and that middle-class control of the town's public spaces continued to be challenged. Nor was there any surprise that the districts where unruly crowds had gathered were those in which there were concentrations of working-class housing. Outrageous the proceedings may have been, but some comfort was derived from the fact that the main offenders had been 'ragamuffins' and 'the lowest and most ignorant grade of working lads'. The editor of the *Advertiser* was relieved to discover that the 'mob in Dundee' was not 'far more debased and a cause of much greater alarm to the community' than it was. After all, it had been estimated in 1850 that some 20–25,000 people in Dundee did not attend any church, and that there were some 7–8,000 destitute children.[48]

There were workplace tensions too, and industrial disputes and strikes continued to punctuate the relative social calm of the 1850s and 1860s. Skilled workers such as the engineers, builders and shipyard employees can be found forming trade societies and, periodically, exercising their industrial muscle.[49] Generally, however, their growth was slow and faltering. Amongst textile workers, probably the most militant in Dundee during the 1830s and 1840s, there were few signs of organisation between 1850 and the mid-1870s, and even the spontaneous walk-outs which typified the female mill and factory workers' approach to industrial action were rare prior to 1874.[50]

But what the events of May 1853 had revealed was a town in which respectability was in the ascendant, many adherents of which were to be found leaving the town, for an excursion on foot, by horse, cart, rail or boat, or simply watching or participating in the street gatherings passively. As was noted earlier, there was also a smaller 'rough' element but, significantly, this appears to have comprised comparatively few textile workers. A pioneering study of criminality in

Dundee in the 1840s has shown that in 1845, for example, most of the female millworkers who appeared in High Court precognitions did so as witnesses and not as suspected thieves or prostitutes. None were tried for crimes which can be categorised as forms of social protest. There are suggestions that it was females who were unable to find work in the mills or factories who were more likely to turn to crime in order to survive.[51]

That the civic mood in the 1850s and 1860s should have been so harmonious is at first sight surprising. As was seen in the Introduction to this book, both before and during the period in question Dundee continued its rapid expansion as a manufacturing centre, with all the potential for class conflict this created.[52] As in many British towns, social relations in Dundee in the 1830s and early 1840s had appeared to have been highly confrontational, and for the urban elites, the situation was distinctly uncomfortable if not downright threatening. Just over twenty years prior to the opening of Baxter Park, during the depressed conditions of 1841–2, with unemployment rife and relief measures scanty, Dundee's Chartists had embarked on their renowned but ill-fated 'march to Forfar', an event which had been preceded by siege-like preparations on the part of the civil authorities who, in addition to the police force and soldiers from the 92nd Regiment, had recruited the shore porters and 755 special constables in readiness to repel an anticipated attack on the town's mills.[53] In 1837, so concerned had the hard-pressed military authorities in Scotland been about the potential there was for disorder amongst the 'large Manufacturing Population' in Dundee that troops were moved there from Perth.[54] Even by 1850 the Chartist fires had not been entirely extinguished.[55]

Workplace struggles over the control of processes and new technology had scarred worker-employee relations in the heckling trade over more than two decades until most hand hecklers were finally replaced by machine operators during 1845 and 1846, while in weaving Peter Carmichael of Baxter Brothers had taken advantage of widespread unemployment in the slump of 1842 to introduce the practice of double-loom working for females in his powerloom sheds.[56] Handloom weavers, struggling against the introduction of the powerloom from 1836, were prominent supporters of the Charter. Some groups of workers, notably the shipwrights, had turned their back on capitalist employers and attempted to set up what were short-lived co-operative ventures between 1825–31 and 1848 until around 1851.[57]

The rest of this chapter however is concerned to account for what *seems* to have been a remarkable transformation. The emphasis on appearance is deliberate. The extent to which large sections of the working class in Dundee collaborated with and shared many of the moral and political values of the town's Liberal leaders was not unprecedented. Cross-class radicalism had been a powerful force in Dundee politics in the period which preceded the Reform Act, and while weakened subsequently, the tradition survived the disruption caused by the Chartist agitation.[58] Conditions in Dundee according to one manufacturer were not so 'difficult' as in Glasgow and some of the English manufacturing towns.[59] If productive relations are the key determinant of the emergence of a consciousness of class, with the first real boom in mill building not occurring until the 1820s, and the later adoption of factory weaving and the powerloom, it is arguable that this was in its infancy in Dundee compared to Glasgow and some other textile towns in the West of Scotland. Even as mill construction was getting under way, newcomers noticed how much housebuilding was taking place too, and were impressed by Dundee's affluence and the tastefulness of its citizens.[60] Well into the second decade of the nineteenth century it had been possible for Provost Alexander Riddoch to walk amongst and persuade meal rioters to disperse. In Glasgow by contrast public order was on the verge of collapse, notably in 1820 prior to the threatened radical rising, necessitating the use of force.[61]

Chartism in Dundee had had its ugly moments, but after the defeat of 1842 and the imprisonment of the movement's local leaders, it was something of a damp squib. Feargus O'Connor, associated with a more robust route to Chartist success than the bulk of the movement's Scottish sympathisers, excited little support. Working-class politicians, although divided over a number of issues, favoured discussion and conciliation as the best means of dealing with working-class grievances.[62] Pragmatism, and sectionalism, a tendency to prioritise occupational or trade interest over class (through a return to trade-union activity), were in the ascendant. Chartist-run meetings called during 1848 could attract only small audiences (except in October, when O'Connor had returned to Dundee to drum up support for his Land Scheme), which were reported to have comprised mainly the Irish. Stronger pulls were exerted in Dundee by the more moderate adherents of Chartism, several of whom, along with James Myles, belonged to the 'Republic of Letters' referred to earlier, and through their prolific and widely-read writing and other activities, worked to end class war and with the middle classes to extend the franchise. Even the weaver-poet William Thom – also a 'Republic' member – who had endured years of brain-numbing misery and 'moral horrors' in an Aberdeen weaving factory which he entered at the age of ten, and suffered severe poverty at times thereafter, condemned the 'mutual ignorance' of rich and poor. He could rage against starvation wages and inequality, but even in his angriest poem, 'Whisperings for the Unwashed', he dismisses 'bludgeon' and 'blow', and awaits instead the coming of Heaven-borne 'Truth' and rights.[63] The significance of this group of men and their connections with their patrons and supporters such as Gilfillan or, in the case of James Gow, another weaver-poet and sometime Chartist, Lord Kinnaird and Richard Gardner of Dudhope, should not be underestimated in explanations for class collaboration in mid-nineteenth century Dundee.

Considerable emphasis in the Scottish context has been placed on the resurgence of paternalism within the workplace as employers attempted to eliminate the hostility which had marked industrial and social relations in the 1830s and 1840s, and in the wider arena as the middle classes mounted an intensified assault on the undesirable behavioural patterns and values of the working classes.[64] This strategy, a civic gospel which stressed the virtues of philanthropy and recognised that labour had legitimate needs within the industrial system, was also adopted in the woollen-manufacturing town of Bradford where, as in Dundee, rapid and socially de-stabilising expansion had occurred during the first half of the century. As elsewhere, its purpose in Dundee was less to eradicate class divisions than to secure them through what Theodore Koditschek has described as a 'strategy of negotiated class alliance', and by subtle reminders to the working classes of their different and subordinate social status. Thus Baxter Park had been purchased by Sir David Baxter, 'with a view to affording the working population with the means of recreation and enjoyment after their hard labour and honest industry', and as a 'common ground' where all the inhabitants of Dundee could 'meet in mutual acknowledgement of their dependence the one upon the other'.[65]

Balgay Hill, Dundee's 'local Lebanon', a wooded hill purchased by the burgh in 1869, was to serve a similar purpose. Previously in private hands and inaccessible, what was advertised as the 'People's Park' was 'pre-eminently for the working classes'. The wealthy had their country houses, the middle classes their villas and gardens, but now, working people and their children could, 'after the toils of the day and week . . . breathe a purer atmosphere than is to be found in the densely populated town'. Its acquisition not only generated considerable civic pride within Dundee, the town now boasting five such 'breathing spaces', but also the admiration of outsiders from towns less well provided for, including Sheffield. Paternalism in Dundee, as in Paisley, incorporated a strong and consciously-nurtured sense of locality, identification with which further served to blunt the sharp edges of class hostility.[66] This was not the Town Council's first attempt to provide Dundee's citizens with land for leisure purposes, and in 1851 the Council agreed with the Royal Engineers that the townspeople should have access to Barrack Park, improvements to which were made over the course of the following decade. In July 1856 permission was granted to the Dundee Instrumental Band to play on Saturday evenings in the town's bleaching green as the municipal authorities sought in limited ways to enhance civic provision.[67]

That change was taking place was noted by Myles: the 'influential classes', he wrote in 1850, had in the past decade 'exerted themselves in . . . schemes of benevolence for the exclusive benefit of working men, with a view to increasing their comforts and elevating their character'. Compared to the other Scottish towns, Dundee's record in this regard had hitherto been unimpressive.[68] The town's leading employers too publicly declared their commitment to the new approach in words and less frequently in deeds, such as the 'considerable' sum of money which was distributed amongst the handloom weavers of Messrs Graham and Mitchell in the cold January of 1865. Along with neighbouring landowners who retained an interest in Dundee, such as Lord Kinnaird, and individual members of the Town Council, they engaged in a campaign of class bridge-building no less impressive than that launched in the English cotton-spinning town of Ashton-under-Lyme, and as radical as the sea-change led by entrepreneurial liberals in the woollen-manufacturing town of Bradford, with a barrage of improving provision in the form of coffee and reading rooms, model lodging houses, ragged schools, allotments, walking grounds and temperance societies.[69] Continuing concerns about the morals and habits of the working classes and the possibility that such rottenness as there was in Dundee could taint those easily led astray, ensured that the 'cultural offensive' was sustained.

The reforming and collaborationist message was clear and articulated through the spoken and written word, as well as by the employment of unambiguous symbolic devices. Although Dundee's Watt Institution closed its doors in 1849, owing to unacceptable financial losses, its membership in the mid-1840s was as high as at any time in its history, and its programme of public lectures was well-attended, including one by Ralph Waldo Emerson which condemned the individualism of the age and the 'decay of . . . mutual feelings'.[70] The need for an equivalent facility was recognised, particularly for the purpose of guiding apprentices, but in its absence resort was had to speeches at work (and on outings), and the use of influential men to whom the working classes could more easily relate, like Myles. Providing links between intelligent artisans and the leading benefactors were sympathetic figures such as the Rev. George Gilfillan, of the United Presbyterian Church, one of whose self-adopted roles was to act as patron, critic and a guide to the content of the poetry of aspiring working-class writers, who were encouraged to enter remarkably well-subscribed poetry competitions run by the *People's Journal* and, from 1869, the *People's Friend*, both of which were published by the radical Liberal, John Leng, of the *Dundee Advertiser*. Included amongst the most popular were several poems on urban themes, as 'In the Street', 'In a City Square' and 'A City Song'.[71] Personal contacts of the sort described here were easier to maintain in a spacially restricted urban environment like Dundee, which tended to thicken in population density in the centre and within a one or two mile radius. Even for the middle classes, the town continued to have its attractions. One merchant, observing but by no means disapproving or fearful of the spread of Lochee and the housebuilding that was taking place on the lower slopes of the Law in 1830, within a mile of the town's centre, reflected that the houses were 'distant from all Markets' and during the winter would be 'an uncomfortable residence'.[72] As the Introduction to this book showed, the exodus of the middle classes from Dundee did not commence until mid-century, compared to a city like Glasgow (which was 4.6 times more populous in 1861), which spread westwards and south into the suburbs some decades earlier. Although not identical to it, Dundee had more in common with the smaller textile town of Paisley, even though Paisley's population was not far short of half of Dundee's 90,000 in 1861.[73]

'Company cultures' too were much in evidence. At a supper held by the proprietors of Baldovan Bleachfield, workers were treated to an address 'on the mutual relations between master and workman, and the benefits flowing from a proper understanding of them'. Elsewhere, at Tay Works, after a supper of cake and fruit, those present were advised by the overseer 'to go quietly home, and . . . avoid the use of strong drink'. Ironically, prosperity tended to lead to an increase in liquor consumption. Female workers were singled out for special attention. On 24 May 1862 a public lecture was held in the Corn Exchange for 1,000 of the town's female mill workers, where from a platform packed with employers and their managers and overseers those present listened to advice which emphasised the importance of self-respect and women's household duties.[74]

But if the most regular attenders at social events of the sort described here tended to be male artisans it should not be assumed that the lower ranks of the working classes were excluded from this orchestrated nurturing of pride in workplace, locality and nation. Few employees could have avoided the powerful symbolism of the sort displayed at the Baltic Linen Works' New Year festivities in 1867, where above the platform was a 'large crown' composed of over 500 gas jets. Throughout Dundee recurring themes on banners and in toasts and speeches were the future success of the firm and the good health of Queen Victoria. Significant events in the town's progress were marked by a holiday, as on 22 July 1852, when the foundation stone of the new Royal Infirmary building was laid.[75] The opening of new mills and other works or the completion of a new – and higher – chimney stack were also occasions which were used to reinforce commitment to particular employers, as at the vast newly-built Manhattan Works in July 1874. Following the official speeches, the workers were 'entertained', and then 'by them the firm was enthusiastically toasted'.[76] Their local power and authority was emphasised visually through devices such as the 'monster pediment' erected by Gilroy Brothers on their massive Tay Works in 1865 (which had the longest mill frontage in Britain), upon which were carved the names of the three principal partners, along with the rose, thistle and shamrock of England, Scotland and Ireland respectively.[77] Employing more workers (around 5,000) than any other textile company in Scotland, no works in the world produced more jute cloth than the Cox's of Camperdown Works, and their 282 foot-high Italianate chimney vied with a handful of others in Bradford and Leeds to be the best and most fashionable in Britain.[78] Nor was the potential of cosseting the aural senses of working people ignored: in 1867, responding to a long-standing demand, the Cox's unveiled a public clock in Lochee – 'said to be the largest in Scotland' – the chimes of which, unlike the 'harsh clatter' of the typical mill bells were 'sweet and pleasant'.[79]

Paternalism of this character however, with its emphasis on exhortation, ritual and symbols, did have its limitations, of which some critics were acutely aware. Historians too have been conscious that paternalism had less purchase in the urban environment than it did in the countryside.[80] Arguably it worked best during peak years of economic activity, as between 1863 and 1865. Indeed the attention of the working classes of Dundee was brought to their good fortune during the American Civil War, when the price of linen had soared, along with the availability of work, while in places such as Blackburn and Preston, the operatives – for whom collections were held in Dundee – were 'literally starving'. That fewer works' excursions were organised in 1861 was ascribed to the difficulty workers were having in meeting the costs.[81]

Paternalism could do little to soften the harsh realities of working-class life: periodic unemployment, injury, sickness, old age – and in Dundee, poor and overcrowded housing and a polluted and inadequate water supply.[82] Public baths were only a part-solution, although the number of users did rise from just under 14,000 to over 20,000 between 1861 and 1866. The failure of Dundee's textile firms to provide housing for their workers is noted elsewhere in this volume. The working classes however were not simply passive recipients of middle- and upper-class benevolence, and brought pressure to bear from below, thereby negotiating the form which charitable provision took. Contributions from the working classes to Dundee's Royal Infirmary had been an important aspect of its funding from the 1820s.[83] Nor was the creation of Dundee's urban identity solely the work of the middle classes.[84] It was in part the working classes themselves who had made public space for walking and other forms of recreation an issue. And notwithstanding the initial intention of the benefactors that Baxter Park would be closed on Sundays, the decision was quickly reversed. This was in spite of the protestations of some ministers, outraged by the 'levity, carnal mirth, and profanity', exhibited by the young who assembled there on the sabbath, 'as in a theatre, to see and be seen'. Defending their decision, the Park's trustees argued that Sunday opening had been 'the will of the people', a reference to the appearance on consecutive Sundays of 'several thousands of people [who had] issued from the narrow lanes and closes of the town', and forced their way into the Park through a gap in the fencing.[85] Artisan pressure too resulted in cricket, bowls and other pursuits (but not football) being allowed on the town's parks, while in 1862 a working men's committee was set up to press for a free library.

Nor was it always easy to keep the working-class genie in the bottle. The residents of Lochee who had forced their way illegally into Balgay Park and cut timber, had justified their actions on the grounds that 'the Park is their own, i.e. the public's'.[86] And beyond the reach of paternalist ideology were the 'lowest rabble of the town' who even in 1863 resisted paternalism in practice by engaging in what was a fairly serious riot – instigated by sailors – against the efforts of the police to close their shebeens.[87]

The acts of generosity reported above, as well as the town's successes, were written about in glowing terms and avid detail by Dundee's 'advanced' Liberal newspapers. Their very success indicates that, like other British mass-circulation weeklies of the time, and the better-selling regional newspapers, their 'pronounced political identity' and the editorial lines taken on other issues were in keeping with the inclinations of their readers.[88]

The most popular was the *People's Journal* (it sold more copies than any other weekly paper outside London), which from 1861 was edited by William Latto, a former Chartist who remained a committed reformer throughout the rest of his life.[89] Like Myles, Latto had artisan roots (he had been a handloom weaver), was largely self-taught and had become a writer. The *Journal* not only spoke to the working classes, but it also listened, debated with and opened its columns to them. A consequence was that the *Journal*, the *Northern Warder* and the *Advertiser* not only reflected working-class concerns but also on occasion acted as their advocate, shaming the ratepayers on the grounds that they would do little to tackle the outbreaks of cholera which swept the town as long as only the poor were afflicted, and prodding the town's Liberal leadership to go further than they may otherwise have been inclined to do. Sometimes such appeals fell on deaf ears, as in February 1850 when the *Northern Warder* urged Lord Kinnaird to provide houses as well as allotments for the working classes. On the other hand the energetic campaign for access to land for recreation in Dundee was successful, first with Barrack Park, public access to which had been fought for by the *People's Journal*, the *Northern Warder* and, as has been seen, the *Advertiser*. The *Journal* was active too on the part of the 'lads and lasses of Dundee', who lacked parlours, drawing rooms and pleasant gardens in which to make love, and who therefore resorted to the town's bleaching green which, much to the paper's chagrin, the Town Council had threatened to close.[90] The same paper had published a letter which attacked the practice of naming parks after individuals, proposing instead that they were 'the people's parks', paid for by 'the sweat of their brows and their empty stomachs'.[91] But limits were imposed on such radicalism, and attempts by workers to act collectively either to resist the introduction of machinery and therefore the 'progress of improvement', or to raise wages, were condemned. Should the significance and purpose of an event such as the Camperdown Works' workers' excursion in June 1859 been lost on their readers, the *Journal*'s editor made good any failure in this regard by praising both employers and employed and anticipating that the outing would 'serve to strengthen the bond that binds both parties to each other'.

And there were many issues in Dundee which served to unite large numbers of employers, some civic leaders and sizeable sections of the working classes. The degree of conformity however differed from question to question, and over time. Crucial was a deep sense of religiosity which characterised much of the indigenous handloom weaver population: James Gow for example became a regular attender at Gilfillan's church. Like many others in his circle Gow had been raised in a religiously devout family environment. Latto, the *People's Journal* editor, had been a founder member of the Free Church in his native parish of Ceres.[92] Such individuals often developed a heightened political awareness and, like Myles, adopted an asceticism which provided them with the energy and courage to act publicly and become involved in reforming activities, incorporating what to their listeners and readers were the familiar language and images of New Testament radicalism.[93] Myles for example was a bitter critic of Church of Scotland ministers, who he regarded as being out of touch with and blind to the sufferings and moral degeneracy of the poor in certain quarters of Dundee. In their attachment to religious faith and their association with dissent and opposition to the established Church of Scotland, men like Myles shared a common cause with considerable numbers of Dundee's employing and governing elite.

Little is currently known about working-class religious affiliation in Victorian Dundee, but there is little reason to suspect that the proportion of the working classes belonging to dissenting congregations would have been very different from the two-thirds found in Edinburgh and Glasgow.[94] Active church affiliation however did not preclude support for and involvement in militant Protestant activities and the 'No-Popery' movement which swept much of industrial Lowland Scotland from the 1830s until the late 1870s.[95] Although Orangeism was weak (but not absent) in Dundee, there is evidence of a strong 'common presbyterian culture', including a fondness for John Knox and other Scottish martyrs who 'shed their blood for their religion and their liberty', and Dundee may have been the only town in Scotland where branches of both the Protestant Association and the Protestant Operative Association were formed, some time between 1836 and 1844, while in common with many centres the Scottish Reformation Society, founded in 1850, also had a presence.[96] The anti-Catholicism upon which these organisations was partly based was endemic in Dundee as in much of the rest of urban Britain, and prone to express itself in more extreme fashion at the lower levels of the social scale. Thus it was the 'Lower Class of People & Boys' (led by the clergy) who were reported to have been most strongly opposed to Roman Catholic emancipation in 1829. On the other hand, the devout millwright John Sturrock did at least attend a Roman Catholic mass at Christmas in 1864 before concluding in disgust that he had witnessed the 'merest trumpery', and questioned whether 'such ceremonies were acceptable to God.'[97]

Anti-Papacy however was but one of the impulses – albeit an important one, and millennialist in nature until the end of the 1860s – which persuaded men of this rank to embrace the cause of Italian independence from Rome.[98] The charisma and plain-speaking oratorical powers of the Rev. Alassando Gavacci were attractions for Dundonians who flocked to his meetings and subscribed to the cause of Italian nationalism, motivated too by a deep-seated sympathy with the idea of liberty struggling against tyranny which was released by Giuseppe Garibaldi on his periodic visits to Britain in the twenty years after 1854.[99]

Scottish patriotic sentiment too, reflected and bolstered in the mid-century years by events such as the building of monuments to Sir Walter Scott (completed in 1844) and William Wallace (completed in 1869), and the national celebrations to mark the centenary of Robert Burns' birth in 1859, also served to bring together people from all ranks by affirming Scotland's place within Britain and the wider world.[100] They were figures with which men of Myles's ilk could readily identify and from whom they drew inspiration. Thus there were frequent references to Scottish icons and influences in their writings with which their readers could identify. Significantly, as has been seen, Frank Forrest's newspaper in *Chapters* was to be called *The Banner of Scotland*. Although never a mass movement, either in Dundee or elsewhere in Scotland, the broad thrust of the National Association for the Vindication of Scottish Rights (established in 1853) was adopted by the Town Council which during the 1850s voiced many Scottish grievances. The Council adopted an anti-centralising position on education for example, and were forceful defenders of the rights of local authorities in Scotland to manage their own affairs, and ardent advocates of a 'large and liberal' extension of the franchise in Scotland on the grounds that the 'Scottish nation is entitled to the same proportionate representation as the people of England'. The demand and campaign for a second MP for Dundee was one which allowed the town's representatives locally as well as nationally to boast the town's achievements and thereby further fuel civic pride.[101] Myles's sense of wonder at the expansion of manufacturing in Dundee is understandable, and he was by no means alone.

There were many sights about which both residents, including at least some from the artisan class, and visitors, enthused. The 'grandeur' of the Royal Arch attracted much notice, as did the quay, while the townspeople were urged to take pride in 'the most spacious Cross that any city might envy'. A visitor from Edinburgh in the autumn of 1860 described Dundee as 'a large, prosperous city, full of life and activity, like a hive of busy, busy bees; full of people intent . . . on making not honey, but money'. It was 'full of shops' and large factories, but unlike Princes Street in Edinburgh there was little evidence of idle opulence; instead, everybody, 'either rich or poor . . . seemed to have something to do, and be doing it'.[102] The town's civic leaders, businessmen and newspapers derived enormous pleasure when flattering comparisons were made between Dundee and other leading British cities; Dundee's growth rate was a matter of particular pride (and a powerful weapon in the struggle to secure a second MP), leading the *People's Journal* to report on 15 August 1868, that it was 'doubtful if, excepting some of the cities in western America, you will find anywhere an example of commercial development to come up to Bonnie Dundee'.

An issue alluded to more than once earlier, access to land, provided another common cause. Chartist animosity in Scotland had shifted towards the landed class, with the land question, as has been seen, attracting considerable if probably fleeting enthusiasm.[103] But in Dundee this took the form not only of interest in schemes for peasant resettlement and opposition to 'feudalism' in the countryside and support for rural workers, but more significantly, of support of rights of access to land within the newly-industrialising town.[104] Only twenty or thirty years earlier, town dwellers in Dundee had had easy access to the countryside and common ground within and on the borders of the burgh. The 'principal playground of the young' had been the Meadows and the Wards, to which there were established walkways.[105] There was clear recognition of the need for such a facility when so much green land was being built over – so that working-class families could 'enjoy a pic-nic . . . without incurring any travelling expenses'.[106] It was a sentiment which was marshalled and incited by the *People's Journal*, which in 1860 declared its support for 'the workmen of Dundee' in the efforts they had made to keep open, sometimes with the use of force, rights of way within Dundee, up the Law, through Dudhope and Craigie estates, and on Balgay Hill. If the duke of Atholl could be 'humbled and made harmless' by the Right of Way Defence Association in its campaign on behalf of walkers in Glen Tilt, it was argued, surely similar action in Dundee would successfully counter 'the aggressions carried out by the comparatively little lairds . . . of Dundee'.[107] This was an alliance however about which some middle-class Liberals clearly felt uneasy – the *People's Journal* had exhorted the workmen of Dundee to organise collectively in defence of their land rights – and in July 1874 for example some of the public speeches made at the opening of the large Manhattan Works were directed to, and in support of, the landed interests in Forfarshire, with the hope being expressed that good relations between them and the town of Dundee 'would long continue'.

Thus far the explanation for the relative tranquillity of mid-Victorian Dundee has mainly focused upon political and cultural factors. Also part of the equation however, were material factors and the economic and social processes by which the industrialising city was created.

As in the other Scottish cities, in-migration to Dundee undoubtedly occurred on a substantial scale, notably during the three decades after 1821, with the population rising by 15.6%, 38.6% and 25.6% per decade respectively. By 1851 over half of Dundee's population of around 79,000 had been born outside its boundaries. For most of the period the greatest proportion of the incomers was drawn from the surrounding county of Angus, along with Perthshire and Fife.[108] Although the movement of Irish migrants had begun to be noticeable in the 1820s, it was only after the effects of the potato-crop failures from 1845 that the trickle became a flood. Between 1851 and 1871 the population rose by some 40,000 people, thereby justifying the Town Council's claim that Dundee's 'peculiarity' was its great 'influx of strangers'.[109] As has often been noted, by 1851 some 19% of Dundee's population was Irish-born.[110] There was also a much smaller inward stream from the Highlands, mainly Highland Perthshire but there were also fairly strong flows from Cromarty, Dingwall and Tain.[111]

The transition from rural to urban life however may have been less traumatic and alienating than has usually been supposed.[112] Not only was most movement into Dundee short-distance, or stepped where Scots migrants had come from further afield, but there is evidence that the shock of cultural discontinuity may have been much less real than apparent. Thousands of females in rural Angus for example had been engaged since the eighteenth century in hand spinning flax and at least until the 1820s had been used to bringing their yarn into the yarn market for sale to urban merchants.[113] There was some initial resistance to mill work and the loss of independence and status this entailed, but the indications are that female workers managed, partly through the conduit of song and informal collective action, to protect within the urban context those values of the pre-industrialised system they held in high regard.[114]

Textile mill and factory work within the burgh itself was relatively new and had required the introduction of steam power, but in 1804 it was claimed that there were some sixty-three mills of varying sizes on the Dighty water, all within five miles of Dundee. Several spinning mills inside the burgh boundaries had been converted from other uses.[115] Both cushioned the shock of regimented, closely-supervised employment. It is certainly the case that the early country mills outside Dundee drew on the labour of pauper children. Within the burgh, 'hard driving' employers, anxious to maximise yarn output at the lowest prices, resorted to employing whatever labour was available. Contrasting with this however is the testimony of a millowner like William Brown who instructed his managers to employ 'as good hands as possible', including spinners, to whom he declared he 'would always be willing to give liberal wages'. Persons of good character and regular habits only were recruited, the 'bad ones . . . quickly got rid of'. Other employers too, even at some of the biggest works, including Baxters, made determined efforts to cultivate good relations with their workers on an individual basis well into the nineteenth century, with regular visits to the works school being made by both partners and managers.[116] Allowance has to be made for variations in labour management practices and the fact that periodically, when labour was in short supply as the town's industrial army was being recruited, workers were in a stronger bargaining position, as for example in 1873, when linen weavers left their employers to enter the rising jute trade. Conditions could change quickly. In 1847 workers were being laid off, with miserable conditions being aggravated by 'the influx of hands still poorer from famine-stricken Ireland', but between 1848 and 1851 workers were scarce and wages rose. Between 1864 and 1867 some eleven new firms came into existence, while the workforce in textiles increased by over 5,000 people.[117] Downturns in trade were not always uniform in their impact. Spinners might still be in work when weaving was in the doldrums, or vice versa, while the markets for the numerous varieties there were of linen and jute cloths were far from homogenous.[118]

Although there were setbacks and slumps in the textile trade which brought production – and full employment – to a grinding halt, by and large, for both employers and employed this was a period of considerable prosperity. Firms could well afford to indulge their workers through acts of benevolence referred to earlier. The Dens Works had been 'better than a gold mine', reflected Peter Carmichael in 1880, and while few if any workers would have used this metaphor to describe their circumstances, the wages and living standards of skilled workers – male artisans, of whom there were some 3,000 in the 1860s – did rise over the period 1853 to 1872, while working conditions also improved. The best estimates available suggest that for the typical mill worker the situation was less buoyant, although significantly (and this would have mattered to those who had moved into the town from the uncertainty and lower wages of the countryside), mill and factory earnings were much more regular, even if the rates paid showed relatively little improvement.[119]

The difficulties of shifting from one way of life to another could be eased too where family ties were strong. These could be exploited in creative ways to assist in the process of adaptation to the new environment. In 1846 the Drysdale family, which comprised a mother, her three daughters and a lodger, moved *en masse* from a recently-closed mill in Monifieth to one in Dundee.[120] John Sturrock, a millwright in Dundee during the 1860s, was one of several urban dwellers who at weekends or at the annual fair holiday returned to visit their parents and other family members and friends in nearby parishes. They continued to reside there either as farm tenants or agricultural workers.[121] Often, considerable distances – fifteen miles and more – were covered by foot. Earlier, the parents of Alexander Moncur, a weaver, warper and subsequently a manufacturer, had moved into Dundee in a step-wise fashion from outlying parishes, with his father eventually finding work as a ploughman on a farm on the border of the burgh, while his mother, formerly a domestic servant, worked as a hand spinner for Dundee merchants. The family's first 'urban' home was in Step Row, then on the very edge of the thinly built-up area to the west of Dundee's burgh boundary.[122] Up to mid-century it was not uncommon for urban workers to abandon work for the harvest, and in some trades, including factory weaving, the Scottish equivalent of Saint Monday was honoured.

There were of course 'push' factors at work, driving both country-dwelling Scots and the Irish into the towns. Yet for both, towns like Dundee offered employment, higher living standards and somewhere to live.[123] For the Irish, faced in west and south Ulster with the demise of handspun flax yarn owing to the growth of machine spinning in Belfast, the industrial centres of Britain looked like an attractive alternative, more easily reached than America.[124]

Such was the resentment of handloom weavers resident in Dundee at wage cuts and the degree of employer hostility to trade unionism that they organised a major strike in 1834, but there was no shortage of new recruits.[125] Towns too were also places of consumption, with circuses, theatres, steamship and later rail excursions, shows and shops – those selling shoes and clothes were particularly popular – providing welcome commercialised diversions and spending opportunities for the working classes. Easily overlooked, but as has been seen, emphasised by Myles, towns were places too for social interaction and both informal and formal association.[126]

For young Irish adults, particularly females, and family groups where a male was present, with experience in hand spinning and handloom weaving respectively, Dundee provided matching work opportunities (albeit within an urban context) and improved family incomes within a familiar household structure. Some handloom weaving in Dundee was carried out in or near the home, and although real wages were falling, and periods of unemployment were increasingly common, the trade survived longer than in the west and there was some room even for the factory weaver to dictate his own working hours. A practice said to have been 'common' amongst the Irish handloom weavers was to take in such large numbers of lodgers that some of them were able to amass modest savings, while others found escapist pleasure in the pain-numbing relief of whisky-drinking binges.[127] For the large proportion of the migrants who were single, an attraction was the greater opportunities there were for indulgence and enjoyment which accompanied regular working hours. Thus it was their 'half-day's freedom' spent at the town's Greenmarket on Saturdays, which 'lighted up' the faces of 'comely matrons' and 'industrious millworkers' (not all of whom were Irish), observed one correspondent in 1868.[128] During the 1830s and 1840s, prior to the Famine, a work and residential pattern was established by the Irish in Dundee, which its victims could subsequently follow. During the 1840s at least, the housing into which they moved may have been hastily built and of a poor quality but in one of the two main concentrations, the Scouringburn, it was mostly new, and both there and in the Hilltown the inhabitants were less densely-packed in their semi-rural locations than their counterparts in Paisley.[129]

It is true that migrants had to endure taunts directed against Roman Catholics and the barbs of anti-Irish abuse. Myles was one of a number of Dundee residents who blamed the Irish for lowering wages and creating much of the town's squalor. There were occasional incidents of physical violence against the Irish, but these were partly compensated for by better material conditions and access to the town's welfare institutions, such as the Royal Infirmary.[130] They were welcomed and indeed valued by most employers who had little hesitation in promoting the most reliable males to the rank of foreman (although men 'with the fear of God before their eyes' evidently found favour whatever their ethnic origin).[131] Opposition too was absorbed through high levels of residential segregation and the mutual support which their ethnic identity provided within the textile mills in which they were both concentrated and predominant. Kinship, friendship networks and the bonds of debt and credit (with local shops for example) which had developed before mid-century were supplemented in the 1850s and 1860s by the comprehensive efforts of the Roman Catholic church to place a spiritual, cultural and political ring fence around the Catholic Irish community in Dundee.[132]

It would be flying in the face of the evidence to deny that industrialising Dundee did not suffer from some of the worst of the social consequences of that process. The excess of stomach-churning squalor, wretchedness, disease and overcrowding apparent in the industrial cities struck contemporaries forcibly and can be supported by the findings of modern historians.[133] The inadequacy of housing conditions for the poor was recognised early on, and remained a constant thorn in the side of the much-abused Town Council. The events on the queen's birthday in 1853 for example had driven the editor of the *Advertiser* to declare that, 'you cannot coop up hordes of human beings in narrow pestilential closes, hemmed in on all sides with whisky shops, and pawn shops'; if 'amusements' were not provided for them, he warned, 'they may be expected to amuse themselves . . .

without much consideration for public order and quiet'. Unless Dundee's housing problems were tackled, to the churches the people 'will not go, and to ministers they will not listen', a clear criticism of ratepayer parsimony and of the inflated hopes of evangelicals – including Myles – that alone they could effect large-scale moral reform.[134]

Yet caution is required. The Rev. G. Lewis's dire descriptions of Dundee at the turn of the 1840s – he had 'looked in vain' for evidence of deeper degradation in Manchester and elsewhere than he had seen in Dundee – refer largely to a single district, St David's parish, where within the space of two decades a conglomeration of mills (twenty-one for spinning flax alone) and workers had swamped what was formerly a greenfield site. Lewis too was a passionate moral reformer, in whose interest it was to portray a city scarred by the consequences of unregulated industry, housing and drinking, and in which he feared that conditions would worsen as more and more female workers neglected their domestic duties.[135] Investigations into living conditions and higher than average mortality rates in Dundee tended to focus on three locations, two of which, the Overgate and the Meadowside-Murraygate-Seagate intersection in the central district, were unimproved and increasingly squalid quarters of the medieval burgh, now over-run by incomers. It is notable that the millwright John Sturrock could walk untroubled by unseemly sights through virtually all parts of Dundee in the mid-1860s. Only in the Overgate did he find himself so disgusted by the smells and sights that he felt compelled to stay away, although he may have been equally appalled had he visited the Scouringburn and the adjacent Hawkhill, the heart of the textile industry in Dundee's west end and, like the Overgate, liable to experience chronic destitution during downturns in trade.[136]

The three decades between the later 1840s and the early 1870s do not comprise a forgotten golden age in Dundee's history. It is one however which is very different from that which has been portrayed by historians hitherto, and it compares well with what was to follow. James Myles, aspirant novelist, is an inadequate guide to early industrial Dundee. But Myles the social observer and activist had rightly sensed the mood of the times. He also contributed in a minor way to the changed relationships between masters and employed. He was an artisan in Dundee and an autodidact and in both respects therefore, unusual, although less so than might be assumed. In 1841 for example, only 32.8% of Dundee's registered occupied population was female, compared to 33.9 and 36.3% in Glasgow and Edinburgh respectively. Even in 1871 males were still in the majority (although much less so than in the other main towns).[137] Even although females had long been disproportionately prominent in the town's textile industry, most of the figures which show the extent to which Dundee was unusually skewed in the direction of women, women workers and married women in the workforce, come from after 1871.[138] The 'women's town' became a reality rather later than is often thought.

For an emergent manufacturing centre which was sucking in large numbers of strangers, social relations were remarkably good. The paternalist policies of Dundee's employers and urban elite were similar to those adopted in Paisley, but they were successfully introduced earlier and in much less stable demographic conditions.[139] Paternalism, philanthropic gestures and municipal endeavour continued to be favoured as means of civilising and containing the inhabitants of the industrial city.[140] Some firms – Baxters for instance, and other 'better class mills' – managed to secure considerable loyalty from their workers into the twentieth century. Such was the concern for respectability on some of the spinning and weaving flats that workers who were deemed socially unsuitable were cold-shouldered.[141] The popularity in Dundee from the later 1870s of the broadsheet verse of William MacGonagall, with its celebration of the town, its leading citizens, great events in Scottish history (the battle of Bannockburn for example) and empire, is testimony to the continuation of at least something of the earlier class-bridging harmony to which the working classes themselves contributed a great deal. Later Victorian, published working-class poets such as George Watson, the 'roper bard', were prepared to deplore the unevenness of capitalist society and oppressive 'princes made o' jute', but like his artisan-predecessors, it was to heaven he looked for salvation, not class war. God would judge their masters' fate, while the working classes should accept theirs, have brotherly regard for each other, eschew hard drink, and hope and pray that Parliament would provide temporal relief.[142]

Growing numbers however were overwhelming the city's provision of low-rented housing, even though the rate of population increase slowed after 1871. Paternalist strategies within the workplace in particular were to be less effective from the mid-1870s. Dundee had recruited its industrial army – to excess – and with reserves readily available to replace dissidents and the dissolute (more so in the less highly-skilled occupations such as the preparers in the low mills), employers could more readily apply the constant downward pressure on wage costs which was necessitated by the growth of international competition in the coarse linen and jute industries, first from India and then Europe.[143] By the 1880s conditions in Dundee's jute mills could with some justification be compared to those in India, notwithstanding criticism of them by Dundee employers. Labour grew more restive, and was less prepared to adopt the deferential stance which had predominated during the mid-Victorian years. Increasingly, as the differential between male and female wages widened, gender differences, in attitudes to work, wages and organisation, drove male and female workers apart.[144] However, while in some respects social relations sank into a chaotic kind of civil war, there were powerful continuities from the mid-Victorian period amongst which, as will be seen in a later chapter, were pride in place and a determination that Dundee should be able to hold its head high in relation to other cities in Britain, Europe and the United States.

FIVE

'From the Grampians to the Firth of Forth':[1] the development of the Dundee Royal Infirmary

Lorraine Walsh

THE INFIRMARIES WERE the largest and most successful of the many charitable organisations and bodies in nineteenth-century Scotland. Their immediate object was simple: to provide medical services to a working class increasingly menaced by the prospect of industrial injury in the industries on which contemporary middle-class fortunes were built. For the middle classes who provided the money and organisational skills which underpinned their foundation and survival, they offered different rewards – confirmation of their benevolent stewardship of the 'common good' and, more subtly but no less importantly, a powerful means of reinforcing 'respectable' values and behaviour amongst the working classes.

By the end of the nineteenth century, however, the role of the infirmary in Scottish towns had changed, or at least the distribution of influence which governed its operations had. Put simply, the working classes were no longer the passive recipients of middle-class help, but had come to assume much greater control over the place of the institution in their lives. Founded on middle-class wealth, concerns and hopes, by 1900 the infirmary was only continuing to flourish because of the capacity and desire of the working classes to use the institution's services to help themselves. It was a shift which was symptomatic of wider changes in the nature of society and of relations between the classes.

The origins of Dundee's Infirmary, which was founded in 1798, lie in existing sources of charitable care for the sick in the town in the later eighteenth century. A Dispensary had been established in 1782 and a Society for the Relief of the Indigent Sick was founded in 1797. The Dispensary would appear to be the earliest organised source of medical care in the town, and it was from its supporters that the idea of founding an infirmary grew. The initial step was the formation of an infirmary committee in 1793, and of a subscription. The membership committee comprised a cross-section of the older and rising elites in the town, including merchants, manufacturers and town officials. It also included the local Angus landowner, George Dempster of Dunnichen. The search for support extended far beyond the town and its environs. In 1794, 2,000 handbills were printed for distribution to 'proper persons' in London and the East and West Indies with a view to raising funds.[2]

Why did these individuals perceive there to be a need for an infirmary at this point? One explanation might be the limitations of existing medical charities. The

Dispensary was devoted to out-patient care. It was economical to run, and met a wide range of health needs. Its value was demonstrated by the fact that, as in other Scottish towns, it continued to operate when the Infirmary was founded. It also treated more patients than the Infirmary. In its first year, for example, the Infirmary admitted forty-five patients while the Dispensary treated 734.[3] Yet what the Dispensary and the Society for the Relief of the Indigent Sick did not offer was institutional care. One of the earliest comments in support of the establishment of Dundee's Infirmary drew attention to the 'straitened' nature of many dwellings in the town and the effects of poor housing on the condition and likely recovery of the sick.[4]

Despite the medical need, however, this was not the most compelling motivation for the establishment of the Infirmary. Its early years were marked by the provision of a relatively small number of beds and by their generally low use. More important in prompting the establishment of the Dundee Infirmary was the prestige such an institution would confer on the town and its supporters. In this, as in so much nineteenth-century philanthropic activity, there was a strong element of inter-civic rivalry. By the 1790s, most other major Scottish towns boasted infirmaries. Glasgow's was established in 1792 and smaller towns such as Dumfries, Montrose and Paisley opened similar institutions even earlier. As this examination of the Dundee Infirmary will show, these hospitals were major symbols of civic pride. They also served to reinforce the dominance of towns over their hinterlands. By the early 1820s, patients from Kirriemuir, Forfar, Blairgowrie, Alyth and Forgan were all receiving treatment in the Dundee Infirmary.

The early history of the Dundee Royal Infirmary was not without difficulties, particularly with regard to securing adequate levels of financial support. Before its first year of operations was complete, expenditure was already outrunning subscription levels and a loan had to be arranged to cover expenses. Even before the Infirmary's foundation, the need to bolster funds through admitting paying patients had been acknowledged even if it meant threatening the reputation of the institution for only treating what the middle classes viewed as 'deserving' cases – in other words, ones which did not offend their notions of propriety and moral conduct. Cases of venereal disease were treated, at a price, although prostitutes found the door barred to them. In 1796, that is two years before its opening, it was agreed that the Second Battalion of Breadalbane Fencibles could have the use of one ward and a nurse's room for the sick. Soldiers were also to be admitted to the ward on payment of a proper sum. It was to prove an unhappy arrangement, not least for the Infirmary's apothecary, Thomas Nicoll, who found himself abused by members of the militia and, on one occasion, threatened by the sergeant armed with a bayonet.[5] Not surprisingly, the governors of the Infirmary later reviewed the arrangements for the admission of private, paying patients. It was agreed that they would only be admitted 'during the pleasure of the Committee' and at the rate of 10*s* 6*d.* a week for a full diet or 7*s* for what was described as a 'low' diet.[6]

As well as the income derived from the admission of private patients, the governors of the Infirmary also sought to increase revenue from an ever widening range of fundraising activities. In an attempt to induce wealthy individuals with Dundee connections to make financial donations, the governors announced that the names of all donors of £20 or more would be inscribed in gilded letters on a board displayed in the hall of the Infirmary.[7] They were also successful in attracting donations from municipal bodies in the town. A petition to the Town Council realised a donation of £50.[8] Contributions of this kind were insufficient, however, and in order to maintain the Infirmary's viability the governors adopted increasingly novel forms of fundraising. Public events were a useful means of raising the Infirmary's profile and generating funds. A dinner and procession through the streets of Dundee to celebrate the establishment of the institution was held annually until 1818. The Infirmary's own resources were also utilised for fundraising purposes. Their bathing machine was offered for hire at the rate of 6d. per day. Income was also generated by the use of Infirmary funds to provide financial services. A loan of £350, for instance, was made to James Cabel, senior, a shipowner in Dundee, on the security of his property in the Seagate.[9] This commercial use of funds was not unique to the Infirmary. Other large charitable institutions in the town including the Lunatic Asylum and the Orphan Institution also saw interest on loan repayments as a source of much needed income.

The imaginative efforts of the governors were occasionally supplemented by large financial gifts from high-profile local figures. In 1839 the governors received the Panmure Endowment. This was a donation of £1,000 by Lord Panmure to be invested for the benefit of the Infirmary. It generated an annual payment of £50 and testified to Panmure's 'continued interest' in the institution and his 'regard for its stability and permanence'.[10] Another significant bequest was received in 1849 from James Soutar and his sister. This was a one-off donation of £7,570.[11]

Gifts of this size enabled the governors to contemplate the expansion of accommodation and facilities to meet not only the increased needs of the growing population, which numbered 79,000 by 1851,[12] but also to ensure that the Infirmary secured a high profile in mid-nineteenth-century Dundee's changing townscape. By this period, the town had some fifty spinning or weaving mills and a further sixty handloom factories.[13] It could also boast an increasing number of impressive public buildings including the new Custom House and the Royal Exchange, designed by the renowned architect David Bryce for the Chamber of Commerce in 1854. The site secured for the new infirmary, however, commanded a prominent position near Dudhope Castle, overlooking the town. A civic ceremony was held to celebrate the laying of the foundation stone by the duke of Atholl and the new Dundee Royal opened for the reception of patients in 1855.[14] Its English baronial-style design, with towers, gables and an imposing gatehouse earned some criticism from contemporary commentators,[15] but it was a triumph of image-promotion and the championing of middle-class philanthropic values.

If the Infirmary had, by the mid-century, come to occupy a much more prominent position in the local townscape in the minds of Dundonians, its improving financial position and episodic large donations from local notables could not disguise an underlying financial instability. It was this which promoted a marked change in fundraising tactics which was to have far-reaching and long-term consequences for the role of the institution and its relationship to the local working classes. The essence of this change was an increasingly open appeal to the working classes themselves to provide more money to support the Infirmary.

As early as the 1820s indications of this desire to secure increased worker contributions were clearly evident. In the Infirmary's 1828 annual report it was noted that:

> The Institution is intended for them [the labouring classes], for their families, and for their friends; and it is surely most reasonable, that, in the season of health and strength, they should contribute something to its aid . . . let them only reflect how different their situation would be if, in the midst of the accidents and diseases to which they are liable, this Institution by any means should fail, or be limited in its means of usefulness.[16]

Appeals of this kind carried considerable weight in a town where industrial injuries were a feature of life for workers of all ages. Early nineteenth-century mills fitted with new and unfamiliar equipment were dangerous places to work. Machinery was liable to break down and 'fly about like Grape Shot', imperiling life and limb.[17] Throughout the nineteenth century the Infirmary dealt with the victims of many 'severe accidents connected with railways, shipping and machinery'[18] and consequently, its appeal to the self interests of workers and their families was a powerful one.

The role of employers, however, was also important in increasing worker contributions to Infirmary funds. The workplace was the obvious venue for the organisation of worker collections such as the one taken at East Mill in Dundee in 1819. There, around seventy workers contributed about a day's wages from their weekly earnings and raised a total sum of £5 5s. In this case the mill manager, William Brown, claimed that the collection was taken on his initiative, but the reasons for the workers' enthusiasm were:

> First, that most of them at the time were making good wages by their extra work and could without much difficulty spare a little; second, that they were perfectly aware of the usefulness and neediness of the institution, how beneficial it had been to the public and to some of themselves, and how soon and much it might be so again; third, how honourable a subscription would be, as it would appear in the newspapers and be taken notice of by the public, and perhaps be the means of bringing forward the hands of other works to do a similar deed.[19]

Whether the impetus came from employers or employees, increasing levels of support for Dundee Infirmary came from the local working classes. As the town and its employment base expanded so did the potential contributors to the institution. Textile workers, harbour porters and dock workers, contractors and employees of the Dundee Water Works and Gas Company, railway and tram workers, and workmen generally employed at various occupations including brass founding, plastering, furniture- making, brush-making, photography and newspaper publishing were all contributors to the Dundee Royal at some point over the nineteenth century. Not surprisingly, the largest single collections originated with the major textile employers. In 1875 more than £80 was collected by the employees of the Gilroy Brothers' Tay Works, over £110 from the Baxter Brothers' employees and over £200 from the workers at Cox Brothers' Camperdown Linen Works in Lochee.[20] These were the largest collections raised that year, and the total contribution of the textile workers, of almost £400, comprised between a fifth and a quarter of the monies raised in 1875 from collections made in public works.

The consequence of this flurry of workplace-based fundraising activity was that, by the 1870s, working-class contributions were increasingly becoming the main source of funding for the Dundee Royal Infirmary. In 1875 the value of workplace collections exceeded middle-class subscriptions to the institution for the first time. Thereafter, the gulf between the two forms of funding widened. In 1890, funds raised from middle-class subscriptions amounted to approximately £1,160 while monies collected from public works, mills and factories totalled over £2,360.[21] This level of reliance on worker contributions does not appear to have been typical of Scottish infirmary funding in the period. In Glasgow, for example, working-class contributions never overtook the subscriptions of the middle classes in terms of monetary value.[22]

The increasing reliance of Dundee Royal Infirmary on working-class financial support was a consequence not only of increasing workplace collections but also of a marked decline in the levels of middle-class subscriptions to the institution. The reasons for this decline in support from the traditional subscriber are difficult to pinpoint. It is likely, however, that the trend was part of a general shift in attitudes towards charitable activity. The Charity Organisation Society [COS], in particular, encouraged the channelling of charitable efforts into social work rather than financial donation. A branch of the COS was founded in Dundee in 1885, and other organisations such as the Dundee Social Union, established in 1888, promoted similar ideas and ensured that notions of charitable activity rather than charitable donation took a firm root in the town.[23] One outcome of this was the greater involvement of women in charitable activity, as Myra Baillie demonstrates elsewhere in this volume.[24]

These changing notions of charitable endeavour did not put an end to fundraising initiatives altogether. In 1874 a new Infirmary money-raising event organised around local church congregations was held in Dundee for the first time. The 'Hospital Sunday' idea, originally pioneered in England in the 1850s, was repeated annually in Dundee until the early 1880s. The donation of goods in kind also remained a popular form of support for well-established charitable institutions such as the Infirmary. Gifts of fruit, flowers, children's toys and other donations to the Dundee Royal increased significantly in this period. The effects of the demise of the traditional middle-class financial subscriber were felt more keenly by newer charitable institutions. Attempts to launch new ventures in this period, however worthy the cause, were met with a lukewarm response. In 1900, for example, the Dundee Convalescent Home in Barnhill could muster only six subscribers, even though the need for funds was evident with 1,055 patient admissions taking place over the year 1899–1900.[25]

The extent to which working-class collections were becoming the financial mainstay of the Infirmary in this changing charitable climate, however, was never formally acknowledged by the institutions' governors or by other contemporary commentators. David Lennox, in his *Working Class Life in Dundee*, noted that 'To some extent . . . the contributions of operatives in public works to Dundee Royal Infirmary may be regarded as insurance against accidents and sickness, although the sum contributed is far from covering the cost of the benefits received'.[26] The Infirmary governors, meanwhile, appeared to pay progressively less attention to working-class contributions as their monetary value increased. In 1846 they were acknowledging the 'numerous and handsome contributions' of the working classes, but by 1892 the sum of £2,390 raised from workplace collections was placed only fourth among the items listed in the annual account, behind much smaller sums donated from other sources.[27]

Other working-class fundraising activities also failed to merit any attention in the Infirmary's annual reports. While the Hospital Sunday was essentially a middle-class venture the working classes launched their own fund, the Hospital Saturday. This method of raising funds involved street collections as well as workplace contributions and was a nationwide fundraising event under the control of working men, the main aim being 'to collect small weekly subscriptions from the classes who cannot give considerable sums at one time'.[28] In two years, almost £280 was raised from Hospital Saturdays for the benefit of the Dundee Royal Infirmary, but no mention of them was made in any part of the institution's annual reports other than their inclusion in a general list of 'larger' donations. In contrast, Aberdeen Infirmary's 1899 annual report recorded the 'grateful acknowledgements' of the directors for the proceeds of £600 from the Hospital Saturday Fund.[29]

In their failure to publicly acknowledge their increasing reliance on working-class support, the governors of Dundee Royal Infirmary were not just turning a blind eye to the changing trends in charitable activity. They were also displaying a concern to protect at all costs the traditional image of charitable giving as an essentially respectable, middle-class activity. This concern extended not only to a lack of recognition for the significance of working-class money in sustaining the institution but also, more crucially, to a determination to avoid ceding positions of status or decision-making powers to their working-class benefactors. In this too, there was evidence of a hardening of resolve in the face of increasing working-class financial commitment to the Hospital. In the 1830s the governors had sought to encourage working-class donations with the introduction of a 'penny-a-week' scheme which entitled the 'workpeople who contribute among themselves to the requisite amount, to be permitted to elect from their number, persons to be entitled to the privileges of Governors for the year.'[30] Several groups of workers, including employees from Craigie Mill and Claverhouse, took advantage of this inducement.[31] By the end of the nineteenth century, however, working-class aspirations for a greater level of involvement in the running of the Infirmary were met with a determined resistance.

In March 1906 a letter was placed before the directors' monthly meeting from the secretary of the Dundee & District United Trades and Labour Council 'requesting that they be allowed a representative on the Board of Governors'. The response from the Infirmary was 'that the Directors had no power to grant the request'.[32] In 1910 a further appeal was made by the vice president of the Trades and Friendly Societies Benevolent Association for direct working-class representation on the Board of Directors. This time, information was sought from the infirmaries in Aberdeen, Glasgow and Newcastle on the subject of working-class representation, but again the appeal was rejected. The Infirmary directors did no more that express 'much sympathy' with the idea of direct working-class representation on the Board.[33] Unfortunately the minutes then become silent on this matter.

Attempts made to place working men and women on hospital boards were met with rather more success in Glasgow. There, the Royal Infirmary appears to have first considered the question of modifying representation on the board of management in 1891.[34] It was in 1899, however, that a resolution was put forward stating:

> That this Meeting, being of opinion that it is in the interests of the Infirmary that Women and Working-men Representatives should be on the Board of Management, request the Managers to take the question into consideration . . . and to report at the next Annual General Meeting.[35]

This resolution was unanimously agreed to, and by 1901 two women and two working men had been duly appointed. [36]

The directors of the Dundee Royal Infirmary, however, were not alone in their reluctance to see working men in middle-class board seats. Governors of the London hospitals resented the requests made for representation and the manner in which they were 'demanded', by the Metropolitan Hospital Saturday Fund.[37] The medical profession was also hostile to the idea of such involvement. The *British Medical Journal* [*BMJ*] was a particularly vocal opponent of the idea and was highly suspicious of the initiation of the penny-a-week scheme which it regarded as a 'dangerous precedent'. The *BMJ* complained that this system would be 'essentially provident' and that it would 'establish a moral if not a legal claim' to treatment by the hospitals.[38]

While some general hostility to working-class involvement was prevalent it can also be argued that local factors influenced hospital policy. The greater willingness of the directors of the Glasgow Royal to allow working-class men and women onto the Board of Management could have been the result of the greater competition for charitable funds in Glasgow. With the opening of several new hospitals in the city in this period, there was an element of competition for working-class support which may have made infirmary directors more amenable to the idea of ceding management powers. The situation in Dundee was somewhat different. As the Dundee Royal was the only charitable infirmary in the city it was the main focus for working-class support and the directors were not faced with the possibility that worker donations might be directed elsewhere if their petitions for management status were refused.

By the end of the nineteenth century the Dundee Royal Infirmary was a very different institution from the small charitable venture established in 1798. Throughout the nineteenth century it grew to become one of Scotland's premier infirmaries. A place on the board of management was a position of some importance and influence. Seats on the boards of such organisations were seen as important in terms of securing both position and prestige within the community. This was a privilege which the city's middle classes were reluctant to share. Charity was of considerable importance to the ways in which the Dundee middle classes continued to reinforce class divisions within the city and maintain their authority and influence. The attempts of ordinary working men to gain places on the Infirmary Board of Management threatened this social status. While Glasgow accepted and acceded to working-class pressures to become involved in the management of the city's hospitals which they so generously supported, Dundee stood firm in its refusal to do so. In Glasgow, the middle classes, perhaps through a greater confidence in their social status and as a result of their continuing financial importance to the Glasgow Royal, were prepared to acquiesce to the demands for working-class involvement in hospital management. In Dundee meanwhile, possibly as a result of a greater insecurity in their social standing and as a consequence of their decreasing financial importance to the support of the Infirmary in relation to that of the city's workers, the middle classes were determined to withstand working-class efforts to infringe traditional middle-class territory.

SIX

'An Insurrection of Maids': domestic servants and the agitation of 1872[1]

Jan Merchant

ON THE EVENING of 19 April 1872, a meeting of local maidservants was held in Mathers' Hotel, Dundee. Informal but animated, it was addressed by two girls arguing for changes in the working conditions of domestic servants, and concluded with the formation of the Dundee and District Domestic Servants' Association [DDDSA].[2]

The meeting was the culmination of a lively exchange of letters concerning the rights and wrongs of domestic service that, since January, had been filling the columns of a local newspaper.[3] The correspondence had developed after two maids had written to the newspaper expressing the desire to see their hours of labour reduced from over 100 a week and for a holiday once a month.[4] Replying, 'A Mistress' had accused them of laziness, arrogance and presumptuousness, advising them to 'have a little more regard for the truth' and 'not to forget that we are their superiors'.[5] Such a peremptory response provoked a flood of letters from indignant maidservants and by April, the maids had decided to hold a mass meeting to discuss their grievances.[6] These included their long hours of labour, irregular and little leisure time, the wearing of a uniform that they found degrading, and the degree of control of a mistress over her servant's career.[7] By the first week of June, the maidservants had held three further meetings and had clarified the aims of the DDDSA. They claimed that over 200 local maids wished to join the union. (This represented around 10% of Dundee's resident maidservant population.)[8] They had also won the support of the Dundee United Trades' Council.[9]

The agitation attracted considerable publicity from the British press, and even from further afield, including the *New York Herald* across the Atlantic.[10] The reaction in the editorials and correspondence columns of British newspapers was generally hostile. Employers were concerned because they assumed and demanded unquestioning subservience from domestic servants. The maids' agitation upset Victorian notions of propriety and respectability; a woman's place was in the home, 'creating a haven of peace, beauty and emotional security for their husbands and children'. They should certainly not be acting in public and stridently demanding change.[11] In Dundee, employers and working men were regularly tormented by an army of female textile workers, whose dominating presence earned the city its reputation of 'a woman's town', and whose frequently irreverent behaviour appeared to make a mockery of male authority.[12] Masters of the households in Dundee felt they could at least rest easy in their homes where, through the direction of their wives and daughters, domestic servants did their work quietly and unobtrusively. The agitation in 1872 rudely punctured such complacency.

At the centre of the furore lay issues relating to the maids' roles as employees and as women. Was domestic service a respectable occupation? What kind of social status should be granted to maidservants by their employers and other female workers? The maidservant agitation provides the opportunity to consider these questions, and by so doing, to examine indoor domestic service. There is also the pressing question of why the agitation occurred in Dundee. Analysis of female employees other than textile workers, who have tended to dominate the received image of Dundee, also provides an opportunity to broaden our under-standing of the city as a 'woman's town'.[13]

Domestic service had always generated some dissent among its recruits. The 'servant question', much debated by the Victorian middle classes, focused on the difficulties of finding and keeping respectable and intelligent maids. In their turn, servants highlighted the subservient nature of service.[14] In 1892, the long-standing debate re-surfaced in the correspondence columns of Dundee's *People's Journal*, threatening to reignite maidservant agitation.[15] During the First World War, girls left service in their thousands and found alternative employment.[16] Clearly, there were tensions associated with an occupation which was the single largest employer of women in Britain.[17]

In Scotland, domestic servants formed around a quarter of employed women in the second half of the nineteenth century. The peak year was 1881, when they represented 27% of the female workforce.[18] This matched the number of females employed in textiles, and outnumbered those employed in the clothing, food and drink industries or in the white-collar sector. Their employment was often a necessity in middle-class Victorian homes which, with their rudimentary ame-nities, were highly labour intensive. Social status also played its part in the recruitment of maids, as the presence of a servant conferred respectability upon the household.[19]

The ethos of respectability was an important element of Victorian society.[20] It underpinned the attitudes and values that pervaded the worlds of home and work and particularly affected the role of women in society. A keystone of respectability was the home and its management. The master of the household should be able to afford to keep his wife and daughters free from the necessity of engaging in any paid occupation. In its ideal form it also sought to keep the mistress free from household drudgery.[21] Her household duties were to be no more than the supervision of an army of maidservants who scrubbed and polished, swept and dusted, laundered clothes, emptied slops, laid fires, heated water, ran messages, prepared elaborate meals and cared for her children.

This ideal was not always attainable, and respectability was seen in slightly different ways at different levels of society. For instance, many middle-class wives had too small an income or too large a family to retreat into a completely leisured existence.[22] Skilled workers sought to maintain the trappings of a respectable lifestyle through their subscriptions to clubs, societies, unions and dissenting churches. They and other groups, the lower middle classes and less well-off workers, maintained standards through principles of punctuality, discipline and cleanliness.[23] For the working classes, respectability was also denoted by the ability of the male breadwinner to provide for his dependants and keep his wife free of paid employment, hence the struggle for a 'family wage' by the male-led labour movement.[24] Where working-class women were not formally employed, respectability centred on their housewifery skills; what counted was the cleanliness and order of the house, their management of the family budget and ability to feed their family nutritiously.[25] Even in Dundee, where women quite commonly returned to work after marriage, it was found that many females condemned the practice – 'wives working made idle husbands and miserable homes'.[26]

Notions of feminine respectability were not confined to the female's role as housewife, but also influenced her employment in the labour market. Acceptable female occupations tended to be ones which reflected their 'natural' feminine domestic talents, such as dressmaking, rather than in manufacturing and industry.[27] In Dundee, the traditions of married women's employment and of single women living in lodgings, removed from a mother's instruction, caused many to fear that their feminine skills were being neglected.[28] There were worries that the mill girl could not 'make or mend, wash or clean, bake or cook a dinner', and that her lack of domestic know-how would have dire consequences for the family and community.[29] At the turn of the century one social investigator commented that:

> a large proportion of the women in Dundee are artizans, not housekeepers, a circumstance which has a most important bearing on the social and physical conditions of working class life in the city.[30]

However, other than the textile industries, there was a limited range of occupations for the women of Dundee, particularly ones that were appropriately feminine. In 1911, women represented half of the city's labour force, and over 65% of occupied females were employed in textile mills and factories. The two other largest groups of workers, those in retailing and indoor domestic service, each employed only around 6% of the occupied female population. By the end of the nineteenth century, food processing, the clothing and printing trades, teaching and nursing were all well established in Dundee. However, none of them employed more than 3% of the occupied female population.[31]

Despite the relatively narrow range of employment opportunities for women in

Dundee, there was nevertheless, a clear, albeit unofficial, hierarchy of employment, one created by wage rates, the nature of the working environment, the cleanliness of the job, whether it involved heavy labour or special skills, and finally, the degree to which it reflected feminine attributes. Retail work was popular because it was light, despite long hours spent on foot and the lack of sanitary provision. Office work was so attractive, that one position was reported to have attracted 150 applicants.[32] Clerical work was considered to be one of the most respectable occupations for working-class women and was near the top of the hierarchy, whereas manufacturing was at the bottom.[33]

Indoor domestic service was considered to be one of the more respectable occupations for working-class girls, particularly by the middle classes. The current belief was that by finding employment within a household, girls would not only be working in their proper sphere, but they would also be learning skills that would ensure the comfort of themselves and their future husbands and families. Domestic service also appeared to keep females firmly under male authority. When a girl left her own home, her father's authority was passed on to the master of the household, or to his deputy, his wife. Once married, mastery then shifted to her husband.[34] The middle classes also viewed service as a means of maintaining society's social order and cohesion. As members of the working classes, maids would be serving their betters and keeping their place; either during her career, or later when she married, a maid would also serve as a cipher through which respectable middle-class mores and manners would pass into the wider community.[35]

Both middle-class commentators and female workers broadly subscribed to the hierarchy of employment in Dundee.[36] Middle-class views of domestic service, however, were not necessarily those held by the working classes. For many of those who worked in factories, shops and offices, the term domestic servant 'had sunk in connotation as being associated with lack of independence, subservience and servility'.[37] Mill-girls particularly viewed domestic servants as 'skivvies', because the maids lived in their employers' homes and were subject to their rules and regulations.[38] They were also denied the 'monkey parades' of the mill-girls when 'in the evenings you would walk down to the town, see somebody you would talk to – have a walk around and a talk'.[39] The mill-girls considered this a perfectly normal form of social intercourse, although others viewed it as unseemly.[40] While the middle classes considered domestic service more respectable than retail employment, lower-ranking women themselves frequently 'preferred employment in shops where a better style of dressing, &c., is allowed, even though the wages are much less'.[41]

Dress was an important symbol of feminine respectability. The 'frowsy haired, bare-armed, short petticoated, shawlied lassie' of the mill was disdained.[42] Such an image served to foster the perception that millwork lacked esteem compared to the factory which, as it was a relatively cleaner environment, encouraged the weaver's more refined way of dressing.[43] As one operative noted, 'Oh ye, the weavers were toffs . . . still wore their hats and gloves going tae . . . their work as if they were going tae a party'.[44] While middle-class observers approved of the maidservant's neat uniform, other workers saw it as a symbol of her lack of personal freedom, a view shared by the majority of the agitators in 1872.[45]

Among the working classes, notions of hierarchy in formal occupations served to strengthen self-esteem. The Dundee Social Union noted that the daughters of skilled workers were likely to be 'occupied as shop assistants, dressmakers, typewriters, etc.', and that they were less likely to enter the mill or factory.[46] The daughters of working-class families who were encouraged to enter domestic service did so by mothers who 'thought we were a better class' than their neighbours.[47] Although textile work offered more independence, 'it was hard work and it was dirty work', and even some textile workers left the industry to find employment as maidservants.[48] Girls frequently recognised the opportunity service could provide for social advancement by learning to speak 'properly' and to live in a more elegant or comfortable manner.[49] At the very least, domestic service provided board and lodging, an important consideration for girls from poverty-stricken families who sought relief by respectable means.[50]

The relative independence of the female textile worker has served to promote a belief that the women of Dundee rejected the ethos of respectability. It has been argued that the mill workers 'were paid enough to resist the authority of husband and father, but never enough to coax them into respectability'.[51] There are numerous examples of the textile-women's irreverent behaviour, but the conclusions drawn from these can be over-stated.[52] Textile workers did have middle-class supporters who argued that there were 'thousands of mill-girls superior in religious and moral character to many of a higher station'.[53] Despite their reputation for intemperate behaviour, spinners were aware of the stigma attaching to women who entered public houses and indulged in displays of drunkenness.[54] Such women might be criticised for their lack of domestic skills, but amongst their ranks were those who secured praise for the cleanliness and order of their homes.[55] Even classes in domestic economy could boast some success; the YWCA counted over a thousand women on their roll in 1909 and had to find bigger accommodation.[56] Despite their struggle with poverty, the budgets of working girls could include money spent on the motifs of respectability such as chapel and funeral societies.[57] Personal appearance was important to weavers, shop assistants and domestic servants alike, who were all inclined to withdraw from the workplace once they married. For the weaver to have to return to the factory 'was an awful slur'.[58]

Evidently, the working women of Dundee could and did subscribe to the ethos of respectability, if not on quite the same terms as their middle-class employers. Even in textiles, individual works were ranked, the few firms that provided the best facilities and working conditions being considered the more reputable. They were therefore more popular with the workers, sometimes employing generations of employees from the same families. Similarly, when electricity was being installed in some factories, the women frequently requested a transfer to the flats where it was used.[59] Self-esteem was an important consideration for Dundee's female workers, especially for the city's maidservants who could be dismissed by other workers as lackeys. In 1872, by campaigning for improvement in their working conditions, the maidservants sought to improve their sense of self-worth and challenge the view that they were inferior to the more independent textile worker or shop assistant.

Indoor domestic service was not a uniform occupation. The number of maidservants and the terms on which they were employed helped define a household's status in the community. To employ a team of residential servants who lived and worked within the household conferred a higher status than a casual or a daily maid. From the maidservants' perspective, a housemaid who was one of five or six servants employed in a wealthy household, was likely to be viewed as more respectable than the lowly maid-of-all-work working alone for someone who ran the local corner shop.[60]

Maidservants also judged their employers. No matter what her social standing, the most reputable mistress was one who kept a well-run household, had good management skills and who treated her staff with respect. The least reputable was one who expected one maid to do the work of two, or who harried and bullied those who worked for her. Maids condemned those mistresses who 'never [felt] satisfied with the work they get out of their servants,[and] let them toil and sweat as hard as they can'.[61]

Servants could be treated kindly, and the workload, demands and expectations of the family would have obviously varied between households.[62] However, there were rules and rituals of domestic service which, when they were closely followed, promoted minimal interaction between maid and mistress, and were used to emphasise the employer's distinct and superior social status. In the first place, maidservants were on call twenty-four hours a day, had limited free time away from the household, and were certainly not permitted any 'followers'. These rules kept the maid isolated and under the firm authority of her employer. Isolation was further promoted in large houses where servant quarters and backstairs kept the maidservant out of sight from family members. In smaller homes, the servant was confined to the kitchen except when executing her duties. Deference to the mistress, psychological and physical distance from the family was encouraged not only by the demand that maids be obedient, but also through certain rituals. For example, the domestic servant was always formally summoned to the mistress's presence when given her orders for the day. She had to address her mistress as 'ma'am', but in return, was addressed simply by her forename or surname. Experienced maids would 'drum it in well to a youngster that they *must not*, whatever happened, join in the conversation when waiting at table'.[63]

Maidservants who preferred to remain aloof from their employers accepted many of these customs. They viewed such conventions as a way of ensuring that they were treated as hired labour, rather than as dependants of the household. Problems arose, however, when the maid and the mistress differed in their views about precisely which customs should govern service. These problems bubbled over in 1872.

The agitators were agreed that 'if one is to go to serve she must serve'. Service was, nevertheless, not to be equated with servility, so they also declared that 'if we are to go to service, we might perform it in as reasonable a way as possible'.[64] They did not, therefore, see the importance of always having to wear a uniform, which distinguished maids from their employers and also from other workers. An apron was necessary as protection from dirt, but wearing a gingham dress in the morning and a black afternoon dress was simply unreasonable. The maids saw the uniform as a degrading symbol of their subservience. The cap (Plate 26) was considered to be particularly demeaning. As one agitator wrote:

['A Mistress'] tells us above everything not to forget that mistresses are our superiors. Mistresses in general don't let us forget that. I remember once of a mistress telling me to get on my cap before she would give me orders for dinner. I suppose she thought I did not look inferior enough without my flag.[65]

The DDDSA demanded that 'Full and fair latitude [should] be accorded to servants as to the style of apparel which they may think it not improper for them to wear'.[66]

Tensions were also created when a mistress was perceived to be undermining or crossing the normal boundaries between employer and employed, or when an employer was intruding into areas which were the maid's special preserve. Constant interference in the maid's work and locking up food and other necessities were interpreted as being 'suspiciously watched'.[67] One servant commented that, 'a servant who knows her work requires no more than the order for the day, and no lady who gives a wage for an experienced servant troubles herself farther than to do the former'.[68]

Mistresses could and did abuse their authority, and observers frequently commented when they took advantage of their position to mistreat employees. Reports of insufficient or inferior food and accommodation were common, as were complaints of overwork.[69] During the 1872 agitation, it was noted that some mistresses 'had no less than three different servants since Martinmas last, on account of their petty tyranny'.[70] Maidservants complained that, owing to their leisured position, many mistresses had lost the art of housekeeping; it was their ignorance which caused them to overwork servants who, when they spoiled a meal or failed to finish the housework, were treated to 'a good scolding'.[71]

The employer's authority also extended to influencing the later course of a servant's career. Demand for domestic servants was consistently strong, but servants could be dismissed at a moment's notice, sometimes leaving them destitute and 'no longer [able to] obtain a situation through not having a character'.[72] The question of character references was a vexed one for maid-servants. It underlined their dependence on the mistress and the importance of their having a good relationship with them. A favourable testimonial was vital if the maid wished to find a new situation, especially if she sought one in a grander household. It was recognised that unlike the female textile workers, who could move easily from firm to firm, 'a servant has tae stand mony a snash undeservedly for the sake o' her ain reputation'. She could not just 'dicht her neb an' flee up'.[73]

References were usually written, although verbal testimonials were also common. They focused not just on the standard of work, but also on the maid's personality, a further source of resentment. Many maidservants related tales about false or misleading reports on them, and how outright refusals to give a reference had cost them employment.[74] The problem was seen to be so pervasive that in 1919, a government enquiry into British domestic service recommended that written testimonials should always be given and 'restricted to definite statements [dealing] as little as possible with matters of opinion'. Neither should a mistress be able to enquire informally about another one's maid.[75]

At the height of the agitation, the maids of Dundee proposed another solution: to have an equal right to enquire into the characters of potential mistresses. Thus, they declared their intention to establish their own servant registry. It would make all the engagements for the members of the DDDSA and provide a medium through which they could investigate the character of potential employers.[76] The agitators argued that 'a good mistress would have no objection to the servants knowing as much as possible about her before they engaged with her, as she would like to see her servants as comfortable as herself'.[77] They were convinced that 'a mistress that knows the important and responsible position of her trust will be led to treat her servants with kindness and respect, and will have nothing to fear from having her character placed alongside of ours'.[78]

The agitators in 1872 were not seeking to undermine the position of the mistress – they were attempting to improve their own. Since the 1850s, other workers had benefited from legislation and practices that provided a degree of protection and rights, and which afforded them some respect in relation to their employers.[79] The maids did not seek legislation, but by resisting the authority of the mistress when it demeaned their status and self-respect, they were attempting to rid domestic service of its connotations and aspects of servility. As one maid wrote: 'A great deal could be done to make [us] less like slaves – sold to their employers to work at their will'.[80] The agitators also argued that to improve their situation would benefit their employers. By improving their working conditions, maidservants would gain more dignity and pride in their occupation while the mistress would gain by having more contented and productive employees.

The grievances which were articulated by the agitators in Dundee in 1872 were common throughout Britain. Why then, did the 'insurrection' occur in Dundee? Of the four main Scottish cities, Dundee consistently had the smallest maidservant population. In 1871, just over 41% of occupied females in Edinburgh were employed as indoor servants; in Aberdeen the proportion reached 25%; and in Glasgow, about 17%. In Dundee, by contrast, less than 8% of the occupied female population were employed as indoor domestic servants.[81] This low proportion reflected Dundee's small middle class compared to these other cities.

However, it was not only the middle classes that aspired to the employment of a maidservant. Table 13 demonstrates that in 1871, while over 80% of the maids' employers were from the middle classes, the proportion of working-class masters and mistresses reached nearly 13%. It also shows that, at just over 28%, the largest single group of employers of maidservants was retailers.

Table 13 Occupation of household heads employing resident maids in Dundee, 1871.

Occupation	%
Middle-classes	
Professional	15.03
Merchant/Manufacturer	15.41
Farmer/Proprietor of land or property	01.12
Retailer (including producers)	28.40
Managers/Administrators	09.02
Clerical	03.38
Retired/Annuitant/Private means	09.02
Working classes	
Foreman/Supervisor	00.37
Skilled workers (including small employers)	10.52
Semi-skilled workers	01.13
Unskilled workers	00.75
Unknown	05.26
Total number of households sampled	363

Sources: Dundee Resident Samples, 1871, Merchant, 'The Maidservant and the Female Labour Market', 140; G. Routh, *Occupations of the People of Great Britain 1801–1981 with a compendium of a paper (Occupations of the People of the United Kingdom 1801–81) by Charles Booth* (Basingstoke, 1987).

In Dundee, these ranged from the lone grocer and spirit dealer, living and working out of a couple of rooms in the Scouringburn, to the affluent draper, with business premises in Reform Street and living in the refined air of Constitution Road.[82] Many retailers' wives were enumerated by the 1871 census as 'shop-

1. Dundee Town House (the Pillars), by William Adam (RCAHMS).

2. *The Executive*, by Henry Harwood. Leading members of the Dundee Town Council and other notable citizens, gathered in the High Street to discuss public affairs. From left to right: Baillie Reid, merchant (*the powerful Executive*), John Baxter, writer (*Judas*), Deacon Cathro, dyer (*Set the Mills*), Robert Christie, shipping agent, coal merchant &c. (*Protests Ready Made*), Walter Thomson, shoemaker (*Ishmael, or the Solicitor's Jackall*), Robert Mudie, teacher and editor of the "Advertiser" (*The Highest Bidder*), David Brown, clothier, twice Provost of Dundee (*Rise to Order*), Thomas Bell, manufacturer, Provost from 1838 to 1841, Justice Blair, cloth inspector (*Faculty*), Patrick Anderson, Provost from 1818 to 1823 (*The Previous Question*), George Rough, glover (*Interdict or Man of the Breeches*), Thomas Spalding, manufacturer (*Not Competent*), John How, bootmaker, High Street (*A Potsherd*), Rev. James Thomson, fifty years Minister of the Steeple Church (*The Power that be*), Samuel Addison, deacon of the Flesher Incorporation (*Corporation in Hand*), George Clark, shipowner (*the Go Between*).

3. High Street looking east, by Joseph Swan, from Charles Mackie's *History of Dundee* (1836). It shows William Adam's Town House, Samuel Bell's 1776 Trades Hall closing the east end of the street and in the foreground, the corner of Reform Street (Dundee University Archives).

4. The Trades Hall, designed in 1776 by Samuel Bell, photographed by John Valentine just at the point when the Narrows of the Murraygate (to the left) are being widened under the 1871 Improvement Act. The widened Seagate opens to the right and the Clydesdale Bank, which replaced the Trades Hall, is already built to its rear (RCAHMS).

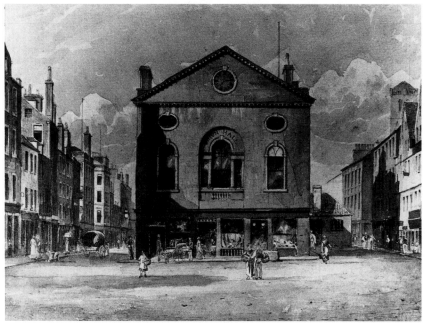

5. The Union Hall, designed in 1782 by Samuel Bell, with the Nethergate opening to the left. From Lamb's *Dundee* (McKean).

6. View of the High Street from the east, by William Young in 1822 for *Dundee Delineated*. The Town House is on the left and Samuel Bell's English Chapel (later Union Hall) closes the west entrance into the Nethergate. The Overgate curves away to the right of St Mary's tower (McKean).

7. Detail of view of the town and harbour from the river, drawn by William Crawford, junior, and published in 1793.

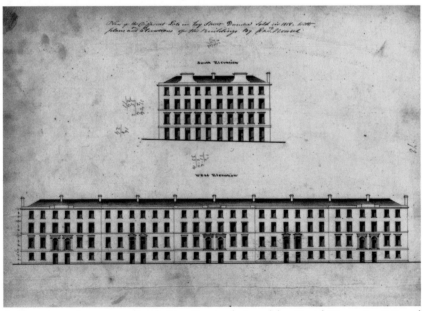

8. Elevation of nos 1-27, South Tay Street, designed by David Neave in 1818 and possibly feued by Alexander Riddoch. It is the only substantial palace-fronted block of terraced houses in Dundee (RIAS collection).

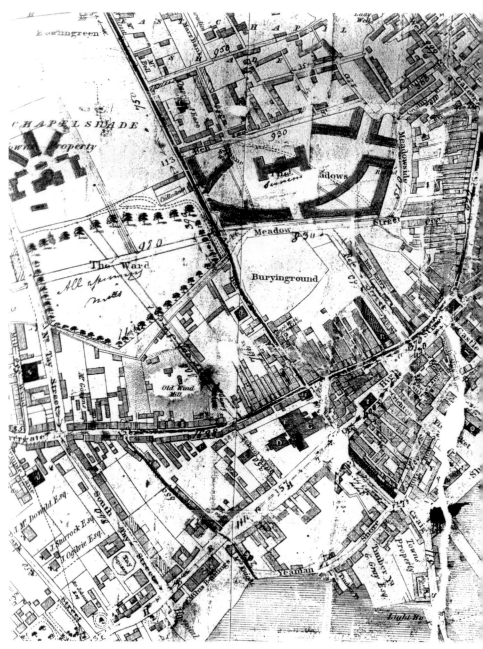

9. Extract from John Wood's 1822 plan of Dundee onto which someone unknown has scratched new streets, the proposed prison (top left), the new Exchange Street (centre, beside the dock), Union Street – and above all, a plan for elliptical streets about the Seminaries or High School (upper centre). The form implies that this was either James Brewster's or George Mathewson's plan. The drawing illustrates just how much of an opportunity for the town lay in the Meadowlands and the Ward.

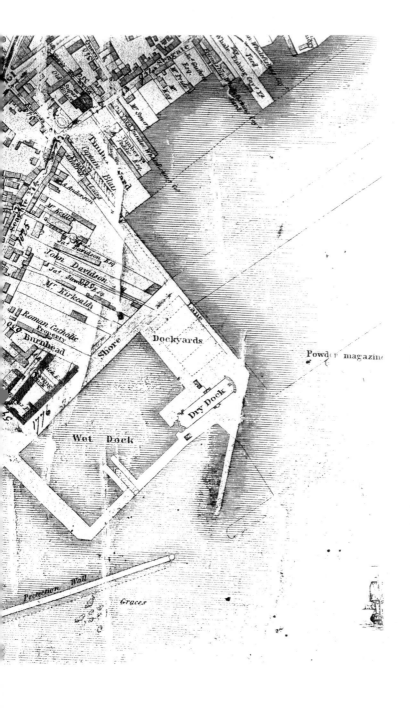

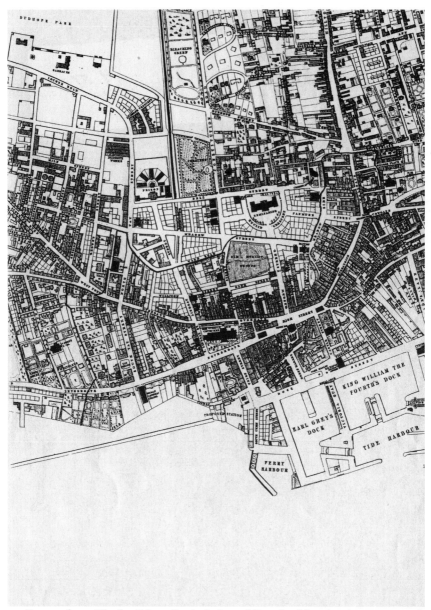

10. Extract from Charles Edward's 1846 plan of Dundee 'showing improvements'. The hollow squares indicate unbuilt properties. It is particularly valuable in depicting another plan of terraced buildings for the Meadowside surrounding the Seminaries, and how Euclid Crescent was originally intended to be completed.

11. Dundee Courthouse, designed by George Angus, from 1832, and completed by William Scott, to face down North Lindsay Street (Dundee Public Libraries).

12. Camperdown House, designed by William Burn in 1824, is one of Dundee's 'glories', and was originally the home of Admiral Duncan, Viscount Camperdown (McKean).

13. The Albert Institute (now McManus Galleries) by George Gilbert Scott, 1865–1867. It was built to house a working-men's library and from 1889 accommodated the town's permanent art collection (McKean).

14. New Public Seminaries, or High School, Dundee. Albert Square remains a meadow. Drawn by Joseph Swan in 1836 for Charles Mackie's *History of Dundee* (Dundee University Archives).

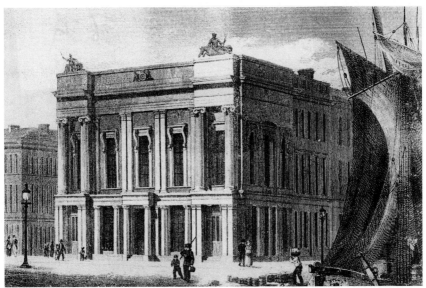

15. The Exchange Coffee House, designed in 1828 by George Smith on an older site overlooking Dundee's new docks. Taken from the 1832 *Dundee Directory* (Dundee University Archives).

16. Dundee Customs House, designed in 1842 by James Leslie, the architect-trained harbour engineeer, and John Taylor. It was the largest customs house in Scotland (Dundee Public Libraries).

17. The Royal Exchange. Designed by David Bryce in 1854 in the style of a Flemish Cloth Hall, it was built as new premises for Dundee's Chamber of Commerce.

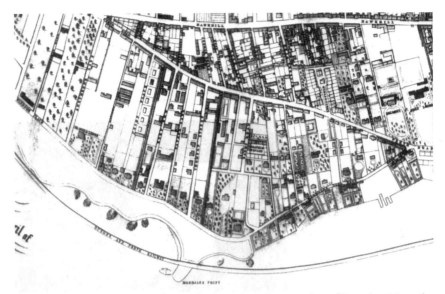

18. Magdalen Green suburb, from Charles Edward's 1846 plan of Dundee. Note the route of the Dundee to Perth railway line along the riverside.

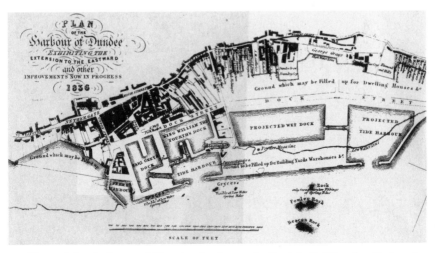

19. Plan of the harbour of Dundee by James Leslie (1836) (Dundee University Archives).

20. Dundee's Earl Grey Dock *c.*1836.

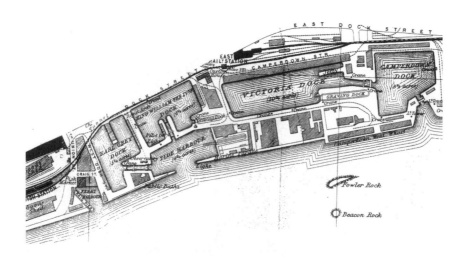

21. Dundee harbour in 1892, from a survey by John Bartholomew for the *Ordnance Gazetteer of Scotland*. Note the proliferation of railway lines around the new docks.

22. Joseph Grimond of Bowbridge Jute Works, partner in one of Dundee's biggest textile firms, but absent from the Town Council.

23. Frank Henderson, leather merchant and manufacturer. Elected to the newly reformed Town Council in 1868 and later chairman of the improvement committee.

24. The opening of Baxter Park, 1863. Massive crowds participated in this major civic occasion. Note the great variety of people mingling there, from all classes (*Illustrated London News*).

25. Dens Works, 1869. Detail of an idealised drawing of Baxters' enormous linen works, including works' school and some workers' housing. Note the semi-rural location, the clean lines of the buildings, the Italianate cupolas and the obelisk-like chimneys (Dundee University Archives).

26. Two Dundee maidservants wearing the despised 'flag' (cap) as part of their uniform (Dundee City Council, Arts and Heritage).

27. Mary Lily Walker, warden of Dundee's Grey Lodge settlement house, dressed in the distinctive attire of the 'Grey Ladies' (Dundee University Archives).

THE
EVERGREEN

A NORTHERN SEASONAL

THE BOOK OF WINTER

PUBLISHED
IN THE LAWNMARKET OF EDINBURGH
BY PATRICK GEDDES AND COLLEAGUES
IN LONDON BY T. FISHER UNWIN, AND IN
PHILADELPHIA BY J. B. LIPPINCOTT CO.
1896-7

28. Title page for *The Evergreen: The Book of Winter*, with decoration by John Duncan.

29. The Principal and professoriate, University College Dundee, 1889. Patrick Geddes is standing second from the left (Dundee University Archives).

30. Evidence of the disruption caused by the entry of the Left's more combative style of politics in the Council: David Buttar grapples with Prohibitionist and Labour councillor Edwin Scrymgeour. *City Echo*, Oct. 1907.

31. James Thomson, Dundee city architect (1904-24) and engineer (1906-22).

32. Photograph showing Crichton Street as it existed in 1910.

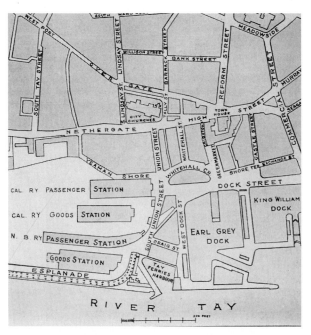

33. Plan of existing site of Thomson's proposed central improvement scheme, 1910.

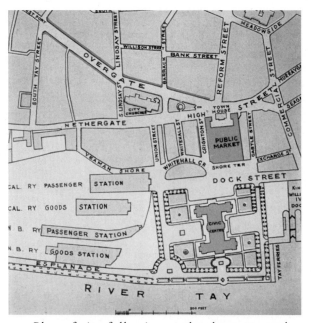

34. Plan of site following re-development under Thomson's scheme, 1910.

35. Watercolour painting of how the view down the realigned Crichton Street would, in Thomson's scheme, terminate at the grand civic hall, the centrepiece of his central redevelopment plan, 1910. A major goal of Thomson's scheme was to create a civic centre of wide, straight streets and arresting vistas.

36. Watercolour painting of Thomson's proposed new civic hall. Several other major features of his scheme are also illustrated here, notably the covered market with roof garden, seen in the background, a major public space in front of the city hall (left), and a monument (bottom left) which would terminate the view from down the re-aligned Union Street.

37. Photograph of dilapidated tenement housing in the Vault, behind the old William Adam town house. The clearance of these tenements was one of the few elements of Thomson's scheme to be proceeded with.

38. Watercolour painting of the Caird Hall, including the famous North Portico, *c.* 1915. Note the dome of the proposed monumental city hall of 1910 appearing above the roof of the Caird Hall. Even in 1914-15, Thomson had not given up dreaming of his grand civic centre.

keeper' or as someone who 'helps in the business', a further indication of their ambiguous social status.[83]

The line between the middle classes and sections of the working classes could be confused, and there were householders on the lower rungs of the middle-class ladder who sought to stress their social status by the employment of a maid, even though it was not always justified by their income. It was alleged by the Dundee maidservants that many mistresses were 'would be's' (as in 'would be a lady'), who had 'not the means to keep a servant and do justice to themselves, let alone a servant'.[84] 'Would be's' were mistresses of households where 'much was sacrificed . . . to provide the domestic help necessary to achieve a certain degree of gentility'.[85]

One of the major reasons for the autocratic behaviour among mistresses appears to have been the uncertainty about their social standing. Their insecurity was taken out on the maidservant who suffered when employers stuck rigidly to the conventions of domestic service. Such employers were said to have been 'in a state all the time because their superiority as a mistress is not more obvious'.[86] It was not unusual, in this context, for maids to be employed by someone who was 'just a step above [the maid] in the social order'.[87] For example, the mother of Elizabeth Ross, the wife of a grocer and spirit dealer, had herself been a domestic servant.[88] The majority of maidservants came from lower working-class families, with their parents being employed in semi-skilled or unskilled occupations. Nevertheless, based on what is an admittedly small sample, somewhere around a quarter of maids came from the families of skilled workers, half as many had fathers who were retailers, while approaching a tenth were the daughters of manufacturers.[89] The employers of domestic servants were merchants, doctors, solicitors and ministers but they also included grocers and spirit dealers, joiners, shopmen and masons – the very same occupations as many of the maids' fathers.[90] Thus, in Dundee, with its significant proportion of working-class employers of servants, and where middle-class status could be precarious, resentment of mistresses determined to impress their superior status upon the maid must have been fiercely felt. This is also suggested by the fact that the majority of households employing lone maids in 1871 were valued at between £15 and £20 *per annum*, well below the average valuation of £36.[91] These households are unlikely to have been able to provide the space necessary to keep the family and maid apart; close proximity would be more likely to promote interference from the mistress and invite antagonism. Neither were they as likely to provide as comfortable an environment as the villas and small mansions of the city's elite masters and mistresses.

The opportunity for Dundee maids to 'better themselves' and find households which could offer them more dignified employment was for most only feasible if they moved and looked for work in service elsewhere.[92] Only a small minority of 7% of Dundee's households employed three or more maidservants in 1871 whilst over 70% employed a single maid-of-all-work.[93] Although maids from house-holds with several servants were involved in the agitation, the single maid-of-all-work was likely to be employed in a less wealthy household and thus have more to complain of.[94]

The agitators of 1872 expressed contempt and frustration towards those households which had pretensions above their formal social status, arguing that, 'it is not very easy to find [our superiors] in this quarter. There are many servants obliged to serve their inferiors, just because they have not got money', and remarked that, 'some of them [mistresses] are just set up with a little authority, and they think they have the ball at their own feet, and that they can kick it any way they like'.[95]

It seems likely therefore, that the maidservant insurrection of 1872 occurred in Dundee because the relationship between the maid and mistress was particularly fraught and antagonistic. On the other hand, the nature of domestic service in Dundee was by no means unique. Other industrial towns, such as Rochdale in Lancashire, had similar social and economic structures and were likely to experience similar problems. Like Dundee, Rochdale had an economy based on the textile industry; like Dundee it also lacked a substantial professional stratum, and was characterised by a small elite of manufacturers and a large working-class population. It was also a town whose maidservant labour force was tiny in relation to the numbers of women employed in the textile industries.[96] Nevertheless, there is no evidence to show that Rochdale was ever the scene of maidservant agitation. Clearly, it was more than the circumstances of Dundee's household structures that led the city's maids to insurrection.

The agitators' discussions had an irreverent tone that reflected that of much of the popular press in Dundee. The local press frequently prided itself on pricking the bubbles of complacency that could surround sections of the city's population. Common targets were those subscribing to 'suburban snobocracy', including 'dandified clerks' and significantly, 'the west-end mama and her useless daughters'.[97] For example, *The Wasp*, published in the 1890s, concentrated on lampooning the great and the good. It criticised the jute lord who was 'allowed to do very much as he pleases', compared to those earning 'a poor, but honest living' who certainly could not.[98] Even the more restrained newspapers could take delight in deflating the pompous and ostentatious. Through the guise of a letter from a 'maidservant', supposedly employed by 'ane o' yer Jute Lords – a little stumpin' hedie wi' a wife an' some brats o' bairns', the *People's Journal* drew a picture of an elite society which was outwardly grandiose, yet inwardly vulnerable and shallow. It presented a picture of triumphant businessmen who teetered on the edge of bankruptcy and of wives who were thoroughly idle and spoiled.[99]

Such criticisms were attempts to promote a sense of social justice in Dundee, a city of marked inequalities in wealth, but also to divert discontent from taking a more dangerous direction. The newspaper empire of John Leng was particularly eager in championing the working classes. Under Leng's leadership, the *Dundee Advertiser* was revived as a paper, 'firmly and sincerely attached to the cause of the people in the most liberal sense of the term'.[100] Thus, whilst rejecting the socialist solution as a means of advancing the working classes, the *Advertiser* supported issues such as the working-man's vote and municipalisation.[101] It rejected egalitarianism, but nevertheless sought to alleviate the poor social conditions of the workers. For example, the genesis of Baxter Park was apparently the result of Leng's criticism of William Baxter. After Baxter's death, Leng had highlighted how little the workers had been rewarded for helping make his fortune, thus prompting the Baxter family to purchase and donate the park to the city.[102]

In 1858, Leng also founded the *People's Journal*, a weekly paper that paraded its support of 'the intelligence and character of the respectable portion of the working classes'.[103] Its news content was mixed with editorials of a strong paternalistic slant, literary competitions that celebrated the respectable working man and woman, and stories that had a high moral tone. It featured characters like Tammas Bodkin, Matilda Towhead and Sarah Snawdrop, who commented on local events through couthy letters and articles written in a broad Dundee dialect.[104] Leng appointed William Latto as editor, a man who was praised as a pioneer of the 'kailyard' school of literature and someone who could be held up as an example of working-class progress and probity. Born illegitimately in rural poverty, Latto had been an enthusiastic Chartist, was self-taught and had eventually trained and been employed as a schoolteacher.[105]

The *People's Journal* played a vital role in the agitation, as we saw at the beginning of this chapter. In addition to publishing the maids' correspondence, the newspaper also published an encouraging letter by Matilda Towhead. As 'an' auld servant mysel'', she argued that as regards the 'puir servant lasses', there was 'no a mair traichilt class o' bein's on the face o' this earth'. Detailing her own experiences, she recognised that the desirability of the employer lay largely in the treatment of her maidservant: 'Miss Lovelace, as douce a weel-livin' an' respectable a woman as onybody . . . found nae fault wi' onything ever I did, whilk encouraged me the mair aye tae dae my utmost'.[106]

However, the confidence and zeal for unionisation amongst the maidservants soon became the target of the *People's Journal*'s sardonic humour. An editorial praised the DDDSA and would 'be glad to see it successful', arguing that 'much good might flow if it was prudently conducted'. But at the same time it voiced concern about the maids' demand for a regular half-holiday, arguing that, 'there are girls whom . . . set free from wholesome restraint . . . would be almost certain to get into mischief'.[107] Latto, writing under the alias of Tammas Bodkin, openly mocked the aspirations of the DDDSA. One of his tales portrayed uppity, dirty and lazy servants who 'had to consult the Union first' before they could agree to take a job.[108]

Latto's condemnation reflected the response of most of the British press. This included the *Dundee Advertiser* which openly criticised the maidservants' demands.[109] Apart from the newspapers of other industrial towns like Bradford and Manchester, which were quite supportive and sympathetic, the response was uniformly hostile.[110] This was especially true of papers based in London, such as the *Daily Telegraph*, the *Pall Mall Gazette* and the *Illustrated London News*. Their editorials, articles and poems mocked the maids and voiced incredulity at their audacity of complaining in such a public manner. The maidservants of Dundee were 'a more ill-conditioned and impertinent set of persons [who] have seldom made themselves ridiculous', wrote one commentator.[111]

Dundee's press may well have inadvertently encouraged the maids' frustrations to boil over into open criticism, but they also fervently promoted ideals of respectability and domesticity. Columns of newsprint, in the form of articles, stories and competition essays, were devoted to the subject of the proper role of women. It was a situation that was ultimately bound to lead to disapproval of the agitation. Despite the initial publication of the maidservants' letters and lukewarm editorial support, the *People's Journal* had attempted to stifle their dissent. Concurrently with the maids' correspondence campaign, the seamen of Dundee began to conduct a newspaper debate about their wage levels. Latto urged the seamen to call a meeting to 'bring their grievances under the notice of their employers'.[112] But he had no such advice for the maids and in April declared that their 'discussion' would be closed.[113] He was too late: a notice calling the maids to a meeting appeared the following week.[114]

As the householders of Dundee aspired to domestic respectability, working men also sought to improve their working conditions. By the early 1870s, helped by a buoyant economy that encouraged collective industrial action, the labour movement had been making some headway. There had been the extension of the franchise in 1868, some legal protection under the 1871 Trades Union Act and the inauguration of the Trades Union Congress.[115] In early 1871, the Nine Hours Movement, which sought a shorter working week, had reached Dundee and had gained the support of the Trades' Council.[116] The maids' insurrection had been incited in the first instance by the invective of the anonymous mistress, but was also encouraged by the success of a strike staged by the local engineers. The first maidservant's letter had directly compared the two groups of workers, writing that 'we would never think of seeking fifty-one hours, like the "black squad". We would be thankful if we could only get our hours of labour reduced to eighty hours a week.'[117]

In the early months of 1872, groups of painters, sailors and joiners all threatened strike action in support of the Nine Hours Movement.[118] Thus the climate of industrial unrest almost certainly encouraged the maidservants to hold their own meetings, to make demands and to form their own union.[119] What it cannot do, however, is explain why Dundee was the focus of servant agitation. The Nine Hours Movement was a national demonstration of labour cooperation that saw unrest throughout Scotland and the North of England. Despite letters of support and sympathy with the Dundee maids, there was little evidence that domestic servants elsewhere felt as confident in demanding change.[120] Neither Edinburgh, with its massive domestic-service sector, nor Glasgow with its stronger trade-union tradition, witnessed public agitation amongst its servant classes. It was only from the south of England that reports spread of some maidservants, laundresses and dressmakers who had followed the example of the maids of Dundee and formed small associations.[121] In March 1872, maidservants in Perth had held a meeting to discuss their hours and wages.[122] Although they were credited with 'giving birth to the revolt against kitchen tyranny', the meeting was held in secret and nothing came of it.[123] It was not until the 1890s that domestic servants elsewhere in Britain began to unionise and actively seek improvement in their working conditions.[124]

It has been suggested that one reason for the unruly behaviour of the mill-girls in Dundee is that the majority were under twenty years old and subject to youthful high spirits.[125] Maidservants also tended to be aged between fifteen and twenty years old, so the fact of their youth might be another factor behind the Dundee maids' dissension.[126] However, if anything, Dundee's domestic servants tended to be older than maidservants elsewhere in Scotland.[127] As elsewhere, the vast majority of recruits were also from the countryside. (The lack of work available for women in rural areas forced them into towns where there were relatively abundant employment opportunities.) Employers believed that, far from family and friends, they would be more tractable and thus welcomed country girls. In contrast, their urban-born sisters were more likely to be able to easily draw upon a network of support.[128] Certainly, in 1912 when Jessie Stephens attempted to start a union for maidservants in Glasgow, she blamed its failure on the large numbers of girls from Ireland and the Highlands who, far from home, were too afraid to take a stand.[129] Domestic servants who had been born in Dundee were not unusual, but as Table 14 demonstrates, between 1861 and 1871, their proportion had shrunk by 11% and never quite recovered their previous numbers.

However, what may have encouraged the maidservants' daring stance was the dominant presence of Dundee's female textile workers. The contribution to the city's economy of the mill and factory women and their ability to achieve economic independence served to reformulate conceptions of domesticity, feminine dependence and respectability. As we have seen, the women did subscribe to these ideals, but they were frequently modified by economic realities that saw the city dependent on a female labour force who were likely to be the main breadwinners of the family. Unlike Lancashire, Dundee had no familial workplace structure whereby male weavers restrained the actions of their wives and daughters, thereby replicating and reinforcing masculine authority within the home.[130] So, particularly within the walls of the mills and factories, we find the women of Dundee's textile industry inclined to promote their own values and aspirations in the face of masculine censure. This frequently took the form of spontaneous strike action that culminated in their parading through the streets of the city, hooting and yelling at employers.[131]

Table 14 Birthplace of resident maids employed in Dundee, 1861–1891.

	1861 %	1871 %	1891 %
Dundee	28.32	17.22	18.23
Twenty mile radius	47.81	48.07	42.16
Eastern lowlands	10.23	12.33	11.11
Western lowlands	00.34	01.28	01.42
Highlands and Islands	04.77	11.56	16.80
Borders	00.68	00.25	00.56
Other Scottish cities	03.07	02.82	03.70
Ireland	01.70	01.79	01.42
England and Wales	00.68	01.79	02.56
Abroad	00.34		01.42
Unknown	02.04	02.82	00.56
Total no. of sampled maids	293	389	351

Sources: *Scottish Population History*, ed. M. Flinn (Cambridge, 1977), Map 3, xxxiii; *Gazetteer of Scotland*, ed. R. Munro (Edinburgh and London, 1973); W. Chalmers, *The Gazetteer of Scotland* (Dundee, 1803); Merchant, 'The Maidservant and the Female Labour Market', 218. The regions of Scotland all contained towns with populations of 5,000 and over, but few of the sampled maidservants clearly originated from them. For instance, only two maids in 1871 specified an urban birthplace. In view of this, it was felt justified to include them with the nearest city.

Such independent behaviour at work was mirrored in their domestic and social lives. One perceptive (male) observer noted that household dependence on the women's income meant that 'the father sinks into a position of insignificance and disrespect which is detrimental to his authority'.[132] Female economic independence on the other hand was something to be relished, so we find delayed marriage and a high proportion of households in Dundee headed by females, as well as a propensity for women to live in lodgings away from restraining family influence.[133] Of all the Scottish towns, Dundee also had the highest proportion of married women in its workforce.[134] It is possible, therefore, that occupied women in Dundee enjoyed a less restrained social climate than existed elsewhere. In Glasgow, by contrast, the economy was dominated by heavy industry where a strong male ethos prevailed. In Edinburgh, because the majority of women worked in the domestic-service sector, masculine authority was underpinned and less likely to be challenged. Despite its similarities to Dundee, Rochdale did not perhaps witness maidservant agitation because the familial structure in the mills and factories reinforced masculine supremacy.

Dundee's female textile workers may have influenced their sisters in domestic service by the very public example they set by their strident industrial actions and boisterous behaviour outside the workplace. This is also supported by the fact that women quite often were, at different times, employed in both the textile and service sectors.[135] One agitator commented that 'a great many servants leave their situations every six months and go to the public works'.[136] Both fields of employment were open to casual workers, particularly at a time of economic boom as occurred between the mid 1860s and 1873. Unskilled women could find work within the preparing departments of the mills, while the continual demand for maidservants was practically a guarantee of finding some kind of work in service, if not in the most superior households.[137] Thus we find spinners like Margaret Thompson and Helen Thomson who were employed as maids after leaving the mill.[138] It is likely therefore, that Dundee's maids were not only familiar with the relatively liberated lifestyle of the female textile worker, but might also have personally experienced the spontaneous industrial action of the mill and factory environment.

While further research into female employment patterns is needed to ascertain the extent of mobility between the two occupations, there are clear similarities in the behaviour of the agitators and the striking textile workers. In its attempt to be taken seriously, the DDDSA was clearly modelled along the lines of established male trade unions. However, by taking advantage of the general industrial unrest to present their case, the maids also reflected the spontaneity of striking textile women. Instead of spreading the word on the factory floor, the maids used the press to incite action. Their meetings lacked any formal structure. Individuals took the opportunity of running an errand to take part, and even at the third meeting, as the chairwoman attempted to ascertain views on each of the rules of the DDDSA, there was a free flow of comments and stories about their employers' misdeeds. There was also a stream of maids who left the floor to join the officials on the platform. Their speeches, which were mainly reported verbatim, were constantly interrupted by laughter and enthu-siastic applause, and were reminiscent of the atmosphere of ribaldry that characterised the parades of the female textile workers.[139] They were also extremely scathing about Dundee's male workforce, reflecting the textile women's disdain for trade unions governed by male structures and demands. The maidservants appear to have been as capable as the female textile workers in organising themselves. Certainly, when it was suggested that they should marry striking engineers instead of trying to emulate them, the Secretary of the DDDSA wrote:

> had they come forward to assist us there might have been some fear of us being captivated with their manliness; but as it is, there is no fear of any such thing. But we have done pretty well so far, without their help: and if they mean to hold back like cowards and see the weaker sex fight it out for themselves, let us hope we will still be successful.[140]

Although never quite as brazen as the textile workers, the maids of Dundee were surely not the docile and modest females they were expected to be.

The Dundee insurrection of maids was a short-lived affair and, despite the support of the Trades' Council, no further activity was reported after November of 1872.[141] But what is nevertheless remarkable is that the maidservants, the majority of whom worked alone, found it possible to overcome their relative isolation and take part in this striking instance of collective action.[142] Although domestic-servant societies existed, these were benefit societies, dependent on middle-class patronage, and only concerned with providing aid and succour in times of illness and unemployment.[143] The meetings of the Dundee maids made it quite clear that the DDDSA intended actively to improve the terms and conditions of employment in indoor domestic service.[144] Nor were the Dundee maids dependent on others to fight their cause. They had initially and ineffectively called for 'some of the stronger sex [to] enlist in our cause and give us a start', but the DDDSA was instigated and, until the Trades' Council gesture of support, sustained by the women themselves.[145] It appears that the DDDSA was the first domestic-servants' association in Scotland open to women, and unlike later London-based unions, its membership remained purely fe-male.[146] It is also notable that the maidservants' attempts at unionisation anticipated the involvement of women in textile trade unions. Women were recruited into the short-lived Dundee Mill and Factory Workers' Association, but this was not inaugurated until 1875, while Henry Williamson did not establish the Dundee and District Mill and Factory Operatives' Union until 1885.[147]

The agitation in Dundee was a unique event in Britain and captured attention world-wide, but the maidservants were articulating grievances felt by female domestic servants throughout the nation. In 1872, the Dundee maids had sought to improve the conditions of their employment and prevent the supercilious treatment meted out by many of their employers. Despite the aspects of service that sought to keep her humble and isolated, the maid felt she deserved the respect of her mistress and of other groups of workers. The agitators were demanding to be treated like other groups of workers who benefited from various protective rights.

The agitation also, finally, serves to teach us that the legendary chutzpah of Dundee's women was not solely confined to the city's textile workers. Service could be fraught with tensions and maidservants were not always the docile and contented inhabitants of the domestic world. There was a mood and set of attitudes present in Dundee which was moulded by a media that encouraged moderate working-class improvement, and which was overlaid by the presence of a vigorous and relatively independent female workforce. They helped to create a culture marked by relative freedom of expression amongst the working classes, particularly towards those who were deserving of criticism. The maids of Dundee were very much a part of that culture and, exasperated with many of the households where they worked, and their mistresses, they boldly seized the opportunity of industrial unrest in 1872 to campaign for change.

SEVEN

The Grey Lady: Mary Lily Walker of Dundee

Myra Baillie

THERE IS MUCH in the historical literature about the appalling living conditions of Dundee's working-class folk in the nineteenth and early twentieth centuries.[1] Indeed, one eminent historian recently referred to Dundee as a 'notorious black spot' where conditions were among the worst in Britain.[2] However, little has been written about the enterprising middle-class social reforming elite in Dundee who sparked a number of exciting innovations and placed their city at the forefront of social reform developments in Scotland. It was owing to their efforts that Dundee had, at the beginning of the twentieth century, the most advanced programme of maternal and child welfare in Scotland. Given the 'gender apartheid'[3] of early twentieth-century Scotland, it is quite remarkable that the driving force behind Dundee's reforming initiative was a woman. At the beginning of the twentieth century, Mary Lily Walker (1863–1913) was Dundee's leading social welfare activist, breaking into the public sphere in both the voluntary and the statutory arenas. As the warden of Grey Lodge settlement house and the honorary superintendent of the Dundee Social Union [DSU], she introduced a number of social services for Dundee's working-class women and children; and as a member of the Parish Council, the Distress Committee, and the Insurance Committee she worked hard to implement new social welfare legislation. In Dundee, social reformers with a highly developed sense of civic responsibility sought new ways to combat the debilitating effects of industrial life. And in Dundee, more than in any other Scottish city, a woman operated in positions of civic authority, and moved freely in the highest levels of the town's social reforming circles.

Walker's career spanned a crucial period in the development of social work and social reform, illustrating the changing views and practices from the late nineteenth-century reliance on private philanthropy to the early twentieth-century realisation that increasing state intervention in the lives of its poorer citizens was necessary. Since 1869, the social philosophy of the Charity Organisation Society [COS] had dominated middle-class charitable action, with its emphasis on self-reliance and its encouragement of the habits of industry, sobriety and thrift among the poor. By the 1880s, however, some reformers were starting to question the validity of COS doctrine and the value of its methods.[4] There was a growing awareness of urban living conditions due mainly to the social investigations of Charles Booth and Seebohm Rowntree which revealed that destitution was more widespread and complex than had been realised.[5] The South African War (1899–1902) focused national attention on the pitiful physical condition of many working-class recruits, and the subsequent reports of the Royal Commission on Physical Training (Scotland) (1903) and the Interdepartmental Committee on Physical Deterioration (1904) provided further evidence of the relationship between poverty and physical decline. The well being of the working class became a matter of national concern and the tone of public discussion increasingly shifted from the character of the individual to the condition of his environment. Some 'New' Liberal and Socialist thinkers, recognising that poverty and unemployment were features of the economic system and not manifestations of an individual's character defects, called for the intervention and resources of the state. The COS, on the other hand, adamantly rejected the idea of extending state intervention, claiming that it would undermine personal responsibility and lead to social dependency. The COS held that each individual was responsible for his own betterment, whereas the New Liberals viewed the state as a collection of individuals where betterment was a matter for collective action.[6] The notion of citizenship was central to Walker's idea of social reform. In 1896, she addressed the DSU:

> It is difficult to state what I believe to be the underlying principle of the [Social Union] . . . It is not charity, nor . . . an aimless attempt to do good in a general way. It is an attempt to set forth in quiet action the conviction . . . that this busy town of Dundee does not consist of a mass of individual units, each at war with his neighbour, but of a large community whose members are bound to each other by indissoluble ties, by common interest, and to whom each member has duties and responsibilities.[7]

Walker believed that Dundee's middle class had both a civic and a moral duty to intervene in the lives of their poorer townsfolk.

Lily Walker was at the forefront of social reform initiative in Scotland. Among the Scottish witnesses to the Royal Commission on the Poor Laws in 1907, Walker stands out. She performed more functions and held more civic positions than the other six Scottish women giving evidence.[8] In addition, her testimony is remarkable for its professionalism. While some women's evidence was narrow, opinionated and generally ill-informed, Walker's testimony, based on factory inspectors' reports, census reports and her own research in the DSU report, was factual and authoritative. More than any of the other women, Walker exhibited a thorough knowledge of the social and industrial conditions of her home town. There was also a marked contrast in attitude. Many of the women, who were associated with COS district offices, had a cold, administrative approach, regarding the poor as a race apart, to be controlled and contained. In their opinion, drink was the primary cause of poverty, and the shocking condition of working-class housing was due to the 'ignorance' and 'thriftlessness' of working-class mothers. They believed that the condition of sickly, undernourished children was due not to a lack of food, but to 'badly cooked, innutritious food', and their solution lay in the teaching of domestic economy.[9] By contrast, Walker never talked in terms of drink and domestic economy, nor did she ever use the discriminatory catchwords of 'intemperance', 'thriftlessness', or 'ignorance'. Instead, she believed that the peculiar industrial conditions of Dundee created distress and unemployment. She once wrote, 'We are repeatedly told that drink is at the root of these miserable homes, but in many cases it is the miserable conditions of life that send husband and wife to the public house'.[10] Walker saw poverty in terms of environmental conditions rather than character defects. She embraced the new ideas of social reform and pushed Dundee's middle-class reformers ahead of their more conservative counterparts in Edinburgh and Glasgow. An examination of her work reveals the degree of progressive civic initiative in Dundee.

Mary Lily Walker was born on 3 July 1863, the elder child of Thomas Walker, a well-established Dundonian solicitor and his second wife, Mary Allen. Lily Walker enjoyed a comfortable middle-class childhood, living in a large Victorian villa at 61 Magdalen Green, and attending Tayside House, a private school for girls. She was very fortunate to have lived in Dundee when University College, Dundee [UCD] opened in 1883. For, at the age of twenty, she was granted a privilege denied to young women in all other Scottish cities: she was allowed to attend the same university classes as men.[11] Lily Walker had a brilliant university career. Every year between 1884–88, she won first prize in subjects ranging from Latin, literature and history to botany, zoology and physiology.[12]

Although busy with her studies and scientific research, Walker nevertheless found time to take an active interest in the DSU when it was founded in May 1888 by the new UCD professoriate who were shocked by the conditions they encountered in Dundee. Although previous accounts have attributed the founding of the DSU to Professors J. A. Ewing, J. E. A. Steggall and D. W. Thompson,[13] it is highly likely that Patrick Geddes played a major role as the DSU was inaugurated on 24 May 1888, six weeks after Geddes took up his appointment at UCD, and was largely modelled on the Edinburgh Social Union [ESU] which Geddes had formed in January 1885. The DSU, following the 'give not money, but yourselves' school of philanthropy, did not propose to relieve the poor by dispensing handouts but by enlisting middle-class volunteers to carry out 'improving schemes'. Its housing committee adopted Octavia Hill's celebrated method of philanthropic rent collecting whereby middle-class 'lady rent collectors' acted as housing factors for the owners of slum properties. Once a week they visited working-class tenants in their homes to collect rents, arrange repairs and give advice on hygiene and house management. In 1891, Walker became the superintendent of housing, responsible for directing the work of the rent collectors. Philanthropic rent collecting, however, never became a successful DSU venture. The Union factored only 102 houses, which, as one member acknowledged, 'were not a large proportion of the 10,000 single-roomed dwellings in the city'.[14] Every annual report of the 1890s carried complaints about the lack of volunteers willing to do the work and rent collecting remained 'in the hands of three or four harassed driven workers, who have to overtake the work of ten'.[15] The large number of Dundee women who worked in the mills during the week required that rent collecting take place on Saturday afternoons when working-class mothers were too busy to listen to lectures from middle-class 'visitors'. Walker was fully aware of this problem:

> The most ardent enthusiast would find it discouraging to discourse on ventilation on a Saturday afternoon with Tommy scrubbing his face at the sink, Jeanie blacking the grate, the harassed mother with baby wrapped in her shawl, evidently eager to get off to her shopping, and the father of the family, the only one who can take life easily, reading his paper, or perhaps stretched on the bed.[16]

By the late 1890s, the housing committee, despite having 'capital waiting to be invested', was unable to assume the factorship of additional properties.

Although housing was its main focus, the DSU dabbled in other late Victorian philanthropic practices aimed at befriending the poor and elevating their condition. In the early 1890s, some members formed a recreation committee which held concerts, magic-lantern shows, and other 'simple entertainments' for DSU tenants. The audience turn-out, however, was not encouraging. In 1890, only eighty out of a possible 350 tenants attended a New Year's Day tea party, and a few years later, the average attendance at concerts had dropped to fifty-two, most of whom were children. By 1896, the committee resolved to arrange 'no more entertainments' as 'those held last winter had not been attended by those for whom they were principally provided, namely, the grown-up tenants'.[17] It required rather more than concerts and condescension to surmount Dundee's class barriers.

Throughout the 1890s, the DSU was a small, insignificant philanthropic society in a state of steady decline. The recreation committee had disbanded, the work of the housing committee did not expand, and the number of members dropped from ninety-eight in 1892, to seventy-five in 1895, and to a low of sixty-six in 1899.[18] Yet in the early years of the twentieth century, the DSU became a vibrant organisation, branching into new areas of welfare work and rapidly increasing its membership. In 1905, there were 168 members; the following year, 197; and by 1913, there were 300 members, including '120 visitors, helpers and rent collectors'.[19] What can account for the sudden upsurge of interest in the DSU? The root of the transformation lies with Lily Walker. Between 1900 and 1913, she increasingly steered the direction of the DSU, her ideas and efforts determining the nature of its activities.

Lily Walker never married and both her parents died when she was quite young. She was, therefore, a highly intelligent woman with an acute social conscience and no family obligations, looking for a sense of purpose in her life. The death of a close friend at the end of 1897 served as a catalyst. She made a conscious decision to deepen her commitment to social work in Dundee and prepared herself by spending a year, from May 1898 to May 1899, with the Grey Ladies, a religious settlement house in London. She consulted her minister, the Reverend Simpson of St Paul's Episcopal Church, who advised her:

> It [is] good for you to go away for a while before appearing in your new character . . . a break with the past is good: you will come back to a certain extent as a different person . . . Something like a discipline and training is essential, if the enthusiasm of the amateur is to be tempered with the wisdom of the professional worker.[20]

The Grey Ladies gave Walker not just social work training but, more importantly, emotional support and spiritual sustenance. As part of the Grey Ladies organisation, she felt 'much less isolated' when working in Dundee, as she had 'a centre to be in touch with' where she could seek 'advice or a little consolation if too much worried'.[21] Walker thoroughly enjoyed her year with the Grey Ladies and continued to wear the distinctive grey and black Grey Lady uniform for the rest of her life.

In May 1899, Walker returned to Dundee determined to inject life into the DSU. She addressed the annual meeting that year, assailing her audience with a mixture of Marx and Carlyle:

> A thoughtful writer remarks that . . . we may be divided into workers and parasites, the former class comprising those who in any way add by their activity to the output of the manifold life . . . and the latter, those who live on the labour, that is, the life of others. Amiable and cultured lives though they may be, they are the lives of parasites . . . It is the merest truism to say that we women of leisure are living on the labour of others. The food we eat, the frocks we wear, are literally so much of the life of others – for ten hours a day, week in, week out, is the bigger part of life . . . Work is the only legitimate end of all culture, all sensibility . . . And at this present time the outlet which is the nearest and which presents the strongest claim is undoubtedly social work.[22]

Walker stimulated interest in the DSU by a flurry of activity. She invited guest speakers to deliver lectures which 'resulted in the growth of a wider interest in . . . social work, and . . . induced volunteers to come forward'.[23] She hosted public conferences on social issues, where 'papers were passed around which might be signed by all willing to become members of the Social Union'.[24] She also introduced new areas of philanthropic activity that she had experienced in London. Walker had recognised the limitations of rent collecting, writing to her friend Anna Geddes, 'I know you will agree with me that we cannot change the fate of a man entirely by improving his dwelling! At least I have found it so!'.[25] Increasingly she re-directed the focus of DSU activity to maternal and child welfare, and annual reports started to carry news of the DSU's 'progressive and encouraging' work.[26]

The most important factor in the revitalisation of the DSU, however, was the foundation of Grey Lodge Settlement House. Fully aware of the pitfalls of part-time voluntary help, Walker knew that she needed a core of professional, full-time social workers to implement her welfare schemes. She bought a solid, stone Victorian villa situated high on a steep hill at 9 Wellington Street and called it Grey Lodge. She presented a proposal to the DSU, setting forward her vision of Grey Lodge, and asking them to provide the salaries for the social workers:

> I am quite willing to undertake the responsibility of this as a social settlement if the Social Union agree to find the salaries for two paid workers – at a salary of £100 each, that is £50 to Grey Lodge for residence and £50 beyond; so that each lady would be offered board and residence and £50.
>
> Excluding rent I find that the house can be managed for £200 with four residents. I would contribute the £100 and have a student, who would come for training if she had board and residence . . . In this way we would really be four workers and I would be able to give my time to supervision and training instead of being overburdened with detail . . . Without some such support and response I cannot continue.[27]

The DSU agreed to Walker's proposal and within a few years Grey Lodge accommodated six residents, some of whom were full-time workers while others were students-in-training.[28] With her nucleus of workers in Grey Lodge and aided by the financial support and volunteer help of the DSU, Walker forged ahead with innovative plans for social work in Dundee.

Grey Lodge was the fourth settlement house to be established in Scotland and the only one not connected to a university. In 1889, male students of both Glasgow and Edinburgh Universities had founded settlement houses, and in 1897, the women of Queen Margaret College of Glasgow University had founded the Queen Margaret Settlement.[29] Marion Rutherford, the warden, and Kay Bannatyne, a prominent member, had both, like Walker, received training in women's settlement houses in London. Rutherford's role as warden, however, was circumscribed by the administrative council of the Queen Margaret Settlement, which insisted that she take part only in services which had a direct bearing on the work of the settlement. Indeed, in 1904, they vetoed her candidature for the Parish Council as they believed that it would interfere with her work as warden.[30] Walker, by contrast, had ensured that she would retain control over Grey Lodge affairs by including in her proposal to the DSU that 'no work should be undertaken, no class started without my consultation and permission'.[31] Walker, therefore, had much more autonomy to develop her social welfare initiatives than Rutherford had. Certainly, in her evidence to the Royal Commission on Housing in Scotland, Rutherford, although familiar with the area of Glasgow immediately surrounding the settlement, did not exhibit Walker's firm grasp of conditions in Dundee.[32] In addition, the two Scottish women's settlements differed in the nature of their social work activities. The Queen Margaret Settlement, which was greatly influenced by the COS, promoted lightweight reforms such as savings banks, girls' clubs and scout troops, in contrast to Walker's more complex and ambitious schemes of maternal and child welfare. In addition, the Queen Margaret Settlement closed down in the summer months when Glasgow's middle class vacated the city.[33] The Queen Margaret Settlement did not form an integral part of the social reforming fabric of Glasgow to the extent that Grey Lodge did in Dundee.

In 1904, Walker undertook an ambitious, large-scale social investigation of Dundee, which was published the following year as the DSU *Report on Housing and Industrial Conditions and Medical Inspection of School Children.* Although the DSU had formed a social-enquiry committee to act in an advisory capacity, the committee took no part in the research and writing, entrusting 'the direction and oversight of the whole enquiry . . . to two ladies', Walker and Mona Wilson, a former secretary of the Women's Trade Union League in London who had been hired specifically for the task of the investigation.[34] Wilson later remembered 'the strenuous year of the Dundee Social Union Enquiry [and] the various crises and perplexities which assailed us'.[35] Considerable tension developed between the women and the committee over the scope and interpretation of the report. Walker vented her frustration to D'Arcy Thompson:

> I do not think you realise the difficulty of the job – we have understaffed [sic] all along . . . were told distinctly by the Committee that we must simply curtail our work. This means that the last month Miss Wilson and I have been wrestling through tabulations etc. when we ought to have been quite free for the writing. Our directions were *no* opinion only above statement of fact – and give numbers . . . It seems to me that the most we can hope under these conditions is to present results in a form that cannot be discredited [StAUA, DWT, MS 14722].

Despite the difficulties, Walker and Wilson produced an impressive document which provided empirical information on Dundee's insanitary housing, ill-nourished children, overworked women, and shockingly high infant mortality rate.

The aim of the report was to shake middle-class complacency and to act as a catalyst for social reform. The report certainly shook Dundee's citizenry and became a point of heated discussion in the local press. While some criticised the DSU for producing 'an opprobrium upon the city',[36] others were plainly shocked by its contents. One person wrote on the flyleaf of his/her copy: 'An admirable

Report. It is astonishing to find such deplorable conditions existing in *Scotland* in the twentieth century. e.g. 215 persons, *one* privy'.[37] The report also caused a stir on the Town Council, where the public health committee agreed that it 'should lose no time in investigating the matters dealt with in the Report', and undertook a number of ameliorative measures, including the installation of water-closets, wash-houses and ashpits.[38] The report also attracted attention at the national level. In 1907, Ramsay MacDonald, the secretary of the Labour Party, speaking in the House of Commons in support of a bill permitting local authorities in Scotland to feed school children, said, 'so far as Dundee was concerned, the report issued by the Dundee Social Union on housing and social conditions furnished sufficient evidence for the application of this measure'.[39] The report also contributed towards a change in attitude towards poverty. Its tone and approach differed considerably from contemporaneous COS-based social investigations which pointed to working-class intemperance, thriftlessness, and ignorance as the root causes of poverty. For example, the City of Edinburgh COS 1906 *Report on the Physical Condition of Fourteen Hundred School Children in the City*, which is a listing of Edinburgh families in receipt of charitable aid, heavily underscores the drinking habits of the parents, and lacks the analytical approach, depth, and objectivity of the DSU report.[40]

A few weeks after its publication, Walker set about tackling one of the most disturbing revelations of the DSU report: Dundee's infant mortality rate, which was the highest of all the principal towns in Scotland. Walker attributed this fact to insanitary living conditions, poor nutrition and the necessity for mothers to work ten-hour days in the jute mills one month after childbirth.[41] After reading an article in *The Times* in December 1905 entitled 'How they fight infant mortality in Paris', Walker travelled to France to meet Mme. Henri Coullet, who had established a restaurant to provide meals for nursing mothers.[42] On her return, she submitted a proposal for a similar restaurant to the DSU executive,[43] and in May 1906, Scotland's first two restaurants for nursing mothers opened in Hilltown and Maxwelltown, Dundee.[44] The restaurants provided a three-course dinner (for 2*d.* to mothers who could afford to pay, and at no charge to those who could not) on the condition that the mothers brought their babies to be weighed and did not return to work. Walker appealed to the Town Council to open additional restaurants, and in 1908, they agreed to finance two new municipal restaurants and to contribute towards the maintenance of the DSU restaurants.[45] In conjunction with Dundee's Medical Officer of Health, the DSU expanded the restaurants into baby clinics where staff kept charts, dispensed advice and made follow-up visits to the mothers' homes.[46] Dr Leslie MacKenzie's 1917 report on maternal and infant welfare, *Scottish Mothers and Children*, contains a number of references to the pioneering work of the DSU and includes a chapter on 'The Dundee Scheme'.[47] Walker had laid the foundation for an advanced scheme of infant welfare in Dundee which, according to one of her contemporaries, was the first city in Scotland to possess an organised municipal infant-welfare service.[48]

Walker's enterprise in Dundee stands in direct comparison to historian Hilary Marland's account of Huddersfield's nationally renowned infant-welfare scheme at the beginning of the twentieth century. In Huddersfield, two municipal leaders, the Mayor and the Medical Officer of Health, devised a plan of infant visiting and then enlisted the help of 'committees of ladies' (of which the Mayor was president) to implement their scheme.[49] In Dundee, the initiative came from a private citizen who operated through a voluntary society and later incorporated the municipal authorities. Walker had originally envisaged Grey Lodge working alongside the local authorities, believing that its objective was 'to strengthen the hands of existing agencies . . . to work with the Public Health, the School Board, the Poor-law'.[50] Increasingly, however, Grey Lodge performed a leadership, rather than a supportive, role in the provision of social services in Dundee.

This pattern of voluntary initiative preceding official municipal action is also evident in the founding of Dundee's first school for handicapped children. In 1902, Walker had introduced to the DSU an invalid-children's-aid committee which quickly progressed from its initial function of organising lessons for housebound children to campaigning for 'a properly equipped invalid school'.[51] In 1904, Walker suggested a collaborative enterprise with the Dundee School Board, whereby the DSU would provide the bus and the classroom if the Board would provide the teacher. When the Board rejected the offer, the DSU set up its own school. They rented a hall, hired a teacher, arranged transportation, and returned to the Board requesting a contribution towards the teacher's salary. Over a number of years, the management of the school gradually transferred from the DSU to the education authorities, and by 1912, the Board had assumed complete control and was planning a new school to accommodate 200 children.[52] The genesis of the school, however, lay entirely in voluntary initiative and action.

Walker's dealings with the Dundee School Board were not always successful. Since the DSU report had drawn attention to the 'large numbers of badly nourished and undersized children' in the poorer schools of Dundee,[53] Walker agitated persistently, but unsuccessfully, for the School Board to feed necessitous school children. After the 1908 Education (Scotland) Act which permitted the rate-supported feeding of Scottish school children, Walker expressed her hope that the 'School Board, with its new powers, would provide feeding centres for school children'.[54] In 1912, when a series of strikes led to 'a great deal of distress and privation in the city' and many were 'on the borders of starvation',[55] Walker organised a large civic conference with prestigious guest speakers to publicise the benefits of a school-feeding system.[56] Despite Walker's tenacity, however, the Board persisted in its refusal to use public money to feed hungry children.

While the School Board often baulked at extra responsibility, Walker speedily undertook any scheme which might benefit Dundee's children. When a philanthropic organisation, Pearson's Fresh Air Fund, offered the Board a substantial sum of money to pay for day excursions for school children, the elected officials 'could not see their way to recommending the Board to undertake and carry out the arrangements for the school-children's holidays during the summer months on account of the great responsibility involved'.[57] Walker, on the other hand, willingly accepted what the School Board had rejected and formed a sub-committee 'for the administration of Pearson's Fund'. Within a month they had selected schools, set dates, arranged boat sailings and organised food purveys for 3,000 children. In subsequent years, Pearson's Fund continued to provide the money and the DSU the organisation to give thousands of Dundee children a short respite from the slums and the great excitement of a summer day's outing.[58] Dundee provides us with an excellent example of the importance of voluntary initiative at the municipal level. In many instances, the impetus for reform in Dundee came not from elected civic officials, but from middle-class reformers in voluntary societies.

Walker did not confine her activity to the comfortable environment of voluntary societies, but branched out into positions of public accountability. As a member of the Dundee Parish Council, the Dundee Distress Committee, and the Dundee Insurance Committee she extended her sphere of welfare work into the wider community. Parish councils in Scotland were popularly elected local bodies which administered the poor law by dispensing small sums of money to the 'outdoor poor' and by overseeing the management of the poorhouse. Under the terms of the 1894 Local Government (Scotland) Act, women householders were eligible to vote and to stand for election. In 1901, Walker and Agnes Husband became the first women elected to Dundee Parish Council. The Parish Council was the only committee on which Walker encountered gender dis-crimination. During the women's first term in office the male councillors limited their activities to gender specific tasks such as investigating the quality of food in the poorhouse, and arranging a Coronation Day tea for the poorhouse inmates. Walker had not become a parish councillor to make tea and inspect the quality of oatmeal. She had hoped that the Council, with its legal powers and large amount of public money, would be an effective vehicle for reform, but time and again she was disappointed. Throughout her twelve-year tenure on the Council, Walker tried to push through a number of reforms such as the establishment of a fixed rate of aliment, and the appointment of a woman inspector to supervise the care of pauper women and children. Although she managed to introduce some small improvements, like the teaching of handicrafts to poorhouse inmates, in most instances, the majority of male councillors banded together to block the reforming agenda of Walker and her female colleagues. Leah Leneman has pointed out that at this time Dundee was an active centre of female-suffrage agitation, and that two parish councillors, Agnes Husband and Elizabeth Scotland, were prominent members of the Women's Freedom League. It is likely that some male councillors, outraged at the suffragists' actions, used the Parish Council as a battleground to keep the women firmly in their place. Certainly, in the Parish Council minute books and local press reports, one senses a determined male resistance to middle-class women muscling their way into prominent public positions.[59]

In contrast to her experience on the Parish Council, Walker became a valued member and assumed a leadership position on other local governing bodies. In 1905, the Dundee Distress Committee was formed to deal with the growing problem of unemployment by establishing a labour exchange and providing relief work for the unemployed. Walker, one of the committee's most energetic members, quickly took a leadership role. Within a month of its formation, she was chairing meetings, signing the minutes 'M. L. Walker, Chairwoman', and exercising 'the power . . . to abstract from the register the most necessitous and urgent cases'.[60] In 1910, when high-ranking civic officials formed a children's welfare committee, they asked Walker to join their executive. Again, Walker became one of the committee's most active members, conducting investigations, writing reports, and gathering funds for the construction of a summer camp for boys in Largo Bay.[61] Walker also took a leadership position on the Dundee Insurance Committee which had been constituted under the terms of the National Health Insurance Act of 1911 to administer unemployment and sickness insurance. As convenor of the medical-benefit sub-committee, she had the responsibility of administering and explaining the new maternity benefit to women workers and the wives of insured workers.[62] Walker became a recognised authority on conditions in Dundee. In the *Handbook to Dundee and District,* produced to mark the British Association's 1912 meeting in Dundee, there are seventy-four articles, only two of which were written by women, one of whom was M. L. Walker.

Walker's leadership position was most evident in the DSU. The only female member of the executive committee, she controlled and directed the entire organisation. Its minute book bristles with phrases indicating her agency: 'Miss Walker recommended . . . it was approved', 'Miss Walker submitted a proposal . . . it was agreed'. Always alert to new ideas, she often suggested that the DSU adopt a new scheme 'as an experiment'. The DSU was by no means a harmonious, friction-free organisation. Walker often argued with vice-president J. E. A. Steggal, but they differed over approaches to social work and not over gender power struggles. Her gender in no sense hampered her work within the DSU. Walker, however, did not receive full public recognition for her role in the DSU. Newspaper reports of annual meetings conveyed the impression that men were the DSU leaders and women the tag-along followers. While the introductory paragraphs of newspaper articles were top-heavy with the names, titles, qualifications and civic positions of the men present, typically a brief, perfunctory sentence at the bottom of the page recorded 'a cordial vote of thanks to Miss Walker and her staff'.[63] But while men were the figureheads in the DSU, Walker was undoubtedly its driving force. In fact, she had considerably more opportunity to develop her plans in the mixed-gender environment of the DSU than Marion Rutherford had in the Queen Margaret Settlement's company of women.

By commanding a firm leadership position in the DSU and on local governing bodies (with the exception of the Parish Council), Walker contradicts the findings of some prominent historians of social welfare. For example, Martha Vicinus found that settlement-house women in London were 'only peripherally active in sexually mixed political and social organisations'.[64] Michael Moore's study of the Guild of Help movement in Bradford showed that women

> did not initiate the formation of social service agencies . . . In the Guilds . . . and other such agencies, women held positions commensurate with what were thought to be female interests and abilities: lesser administrative posts such as depute secretaries [and] visitors to the poor.[65]

Walker, as we have seen, was the central point of the DSU with her finger on the pulse of the entire organisation, and a highly regarded and valued member of a number of important local governing bodies.

Given the difficulties of Scottish women breaking into the public sphere, Walker's ability to surmount the gender barriers of late nineteenth-century Scotland is impressive. What can account for her remarkable position in Dundee? Of central importance is the close connection between the DSU and Dundee's new University College. We cannot underestimate the influence on Walker of the group of young university professors, particularly Alfred Ewing, Patrick Geddes and D'Arcy Thompson, who provided the initial stimulus for the DSU. As one of the first, and most brilliant, UCD students, Walker benefited from their teaching and encouragement and gained from them the confidence to stand on public platforms and to pursue her goal of a career in social work. She admired both Geddes and Ewing and stayed in contact with them after they had left Dundee.[66] She was particularly close to Thompson who remained an active member of the DSU executive and a staunch supporter of her plans after his appointment to St Andrews University. Walker was godmother to Thompson's second daughter who was christened Mary Lily, but called 'Molly'.[67] In setting the tone of the DSU, the enlightened views of the university men also helped to lift Dundee out of the narrow, closed-minded approach to social welfare of the COS. The Dundee COS was an ineffectual, stagnant organisation, whose work through the years never progressed from its initial objective which was 'to discover and repress mendicity' and 'to distinguish the deserving poor from imposters and sharpers'. The same agent served the Dundee COS for over thirty years from its founding in 1886 to his death in 1918, and its annual reports became progressively flimsier and sparser. Furthermore, it is noteworthy that very few women (and in some years, no women) served on its committee or functioned as district visitors.[68] This was unusual as most COS district offices depended on the services of middle-class women to compile exhaustive files on applicants for relief. In Dundee, it was the DSU with its progressive approach and highly developed sense of community, which set the pace and tone for social reform.

We must not, however, discount the personal contribution of Walker. The extent of her influence on the DSU may be gauged from a brief comparison between the DSU and its sister organisation, the Edinburgh Social Union [ESU]. In the mid- to late 1880s, Patrick Geddes had been involved in the inauguration of both the DSU and the ESU with his scheme of lady rent collectors. By 1912, the DSU was spearheading an expanding system of social work programmes for women and children. As well as the restaurants, baby clinics, school-feeding schemes and invalid school, the DSU organised playgrounds and vacation schools, and owned and operated convalescent homes for children. By contrast, in 1912, rent collecting remained the principal concern of the ESU, whose contribution to maternal and child welfare consisted of lectures from a lady doctor, and the distribution of leaflets on 'Temperance' and 'The Training of the Young' to working-class women.[69] It was Walker, responsive to the needs of working-class women and children, who directed the DSU along its more ambitious and distinctive path.

A study of Walker does not contradict the image of Dundee as a 'notorious black spot'. Indeed, it is largely due to her work as co-author of the DSU report that historians know as much as they do about the appalling living conditions and plight of Dundee's working-class folk at the beginning of the twentieth century. A study of Walker does, however, show another side to this gloomy picture of Dundee. In Dundee, an active group of progressive middle-class reformers instigated an ambitious programme of welfare measures geared to the needs of working-class women and children. And in Dundee, a woman was at the centre of social reform initiative and administration, providing the city with what was arguably the most dynamic social welfare programme in Scotland.

Mary Lily Walker died on 1 July 1913, a few days before her fiftieth birthday. Her will included a trust disposition leaving Grey Lodge in the hands of trustees 'to be used and employed by them as a Settlement House so as to provide a focus for social work, and a place of training for ladies engaged in such work'. The work of the DSU and Grey Lodge settlement continued until the 1930s when they were formally amalgamated into the Grey Lodge Settlement Association 'to ensure the continuance of the work so well founded by Miss Walker'.[70] Walker's legacy included another institution for the promotion of social work in Dundee. In the autumn of 1920, Grey Lodge, the DSU and the University joined forces to form the Dundee School of Social Study and Training which had the power to grant students a diploma or a certificate in Social Study. The curriculum was divided between theoretical lectures from university faculty and practical training which was directed from Grey Lodge with Miss Batting, the current warden, as Director of Studies. The first annual report, while acknowledging that many universities in England and the universities of Glasgow and Edinburgh had established similar schools of social study, noted that 'probably in no case is the association with the University so intimate as between the Dundee school and the university'.[71] The close connection between the DSU, Grey Lodge and the University continued to form an important part of social work initiative in Dundee.[72]

EIGHT

The Patron, the Professor and the Painter: cultural activity in Dundee at the close of the nineteenth century

Murdo Macdonald

AN AWARENESS OF the industrial and economic strengths of Dundee has tended to obscure the consideration of the artistic and academic life of the city. The purpose of this chapter is to give a sense of such activity as it flourished in the late nineteenth and early twentieth centuries. In order to do this I will give specific consideration to the artistic and intellectual activities of three figures whose careers were interlinked, James Martin White, Patrick Geddes and John Duncan. White was the inheritor of industrial wealth and an imaginative and informed patron both in his home city of Dundee and, subsequently, in London. Patrick Geddes was a remarkable polymath – among other things a pioneer of ecologically and culturally-based town planning – who, thanks to White's financial support, was appointed professor of botany at University College, Dundee, in the early years of that institution. John Duncan, born and trained in Dundee, was the leading artist of the Celtic revival in Scotland. He was, during the period in question, a close colleague of Geddes, whose thinking had a profound influence on the direction of his work. He numbered both White and Geddes among his patrons.

On 9 February 1881, the textile-mill manager Peter Carmichael (of Baxter Brothers) attended a meeting of the Dundee Naturalists' Society.[1] This society had been founded in 1874[2] and it quickly built up a membership which included as associates not only Peter Carmichael, but his fellow industrialists James Guthrie Orchar and James Farquhar White.[3] Speakers to the society addressed a range of topics from those of local geographical interest to explorations of developing technologies. The subject of the meeting of 9 February falls into the latter category; it was an exhibition of Swan's increasingly successful experiments to establish practical electric lighting. This had been a matter of keen interest in Dundee since 1835, the year in which James Bowman Lindsay's demonstration of sustained electric light had been reported in the *Dundee Advertiser*.[4]

It must be stressed here that the 1880s was a decade in which there was an almost tangible shift in the view of electricity as a matter of research interest, to the consideration of it as a practical form of domestic and industrial power. Revealing here are the contrasting treatments of the subject in different editions of the *Encylopaedia Britannica*. In 1879 George Chrystal's article on 'Electricity' was published in volume VIII of the ninth edition. Chrystal was professor of Mathematics at the University of Edinburgh working in the wake of James Clerk Maxwell's insights. (Maxwell had himself been science editor of the same edition and died in the very year Chrystal's article was published.) For Chrystal the issue was still the theory of electro-magnetism, not its practical application. By the time the equivalent volume of the next fully re-edited edition of the *Britannica* (the eleventh) was published in 1910, the emphasis had changed, and an entire article was devoted to 'Electricity Supply'. The author of the 'commercial aspects' section of the article[5] provides a context for the activities in Dundee in 1881. He writes:

> Edison's British master-patent was only filed in Great Britain in November 1879. In 1881 and 1882 electrical exhibitions were held in Paris and at the Crystal Palace, London, where the improved electric incandescent lamp was brought before the general public. In 1882 parliament passed the first Electric Lighting Act.[6]

The Dundee Naturalists' Society thus played a significant role in the dissemination of scientific knowledge. In a letter of 10 February 1881 Carmichael noted that 'on the whole it seems as if one difficulty after another is being conquered'. He went on to mention that 'Mr White who purchased the Balruddery property lately is extending the mansion house and has arranged to light it with Swan. The motion is to be got from water power driving a turbine wheel'. [7] The 'Mr White' to whom Carmichael referred was James Farquhar White, father of James Martin White. It is likely that both father and son attended the Naturalists' Society meeting along with Carmichael. As has been noted White, senior, was, like Carmichael, an associate of the Society. His son Martin White (as he is normally known) was by this time a member of the council of the Society. Later in the same year, on 30 November, the society heard the latter's account of the state of the art demonstrations given at the Paris Electrical Exhibition. His talk was entitled 'Notes on the Paris Electrical Exhibition – with experiments' and this subject gives insight into his character as an active amateur, well aware of contemporary scientific advances.[8]

Further evidence of the forward-looking nature of the Society is clear from a lecture given only a month later. On 27 December 1881 an extra meeting of the Dundee Naturalists' Society was held on the subject of 'The Classification of Statistics'. The lecturer was Patrick Geddes, twenty-seven years old at the time and demonstrator in botany at the University of Edinburgh. From a modern viewpoint his topic might seem somewhat dry and specialist for a generalist body with a significant lay membership, such as the Dundee Naturalists' Society. But in the 1880s the nature and use of statistics and their wider implications for the structure of the social sciences were matters of intense debate, not least with respect to their potential for providing the scientific foundation for the nascent discipline of sociology. Geddes's talk was based on a three-part presentation he had made to the Royal Society of Edinburgh, earlier in the year. In his own words 'it was probably the first [paper] which has attempted to organise the whole body of our recorded social knowledge into a form presentable to the cultivators of the preliminary sciences'.[9] The ideas that Geddes discussed at that meeting were to have a major influence not only on his own eventual career path, but on the direction of Martin White's patronage, for White was to become a key source of finance for the development of sociology in the United Kingdom. Indeed Philip Abrams in his classic account, *The Origins of British Sociology*, notes that White's 'interest in sociology was largely formed by his early friendship with Geddes'.[10] That early friendship, forged in Dundee, led some thirty years later to White endowing both of the first two chairs of sociology at the University of London.

It is likely that Geddes's invitation to speak at the Dundee Naturalists' Society was initiated either by Martin White himself or by the honorary secretary of the society, Frank Young, for both men had, according to Geddes's biographers, known Geddes since his youth.[11] It should be remembered here that Geddes had spent the formative years of his life in Perth, a mere twenty miles up the Tay from Dundee, and well connected to Dundee by steamer and rail links, as well as by road.

Perhaps the invitation came from Frank Young, for he may well have attended Geddes's lectures at the Royal Society of Edinburgh. Geddes had been elected as a Fellow on 7 June 1880[12] and Young was elected on 1 May 1882. His proposers included Geddes himself, Geddes's friend and teacher the geologist James Geikie, and George Chrystal, whom we have already encountered through his *Encyclopaedia Britannica* contribution on electricity.[13] Geddes again lectured to the Dundee Naturalists' Society on 8 February 1882 on the subject of the occurrence of chlorophyll in animals.[14] This biological topic is at first sight in marked contrast to the sociological subject of Geddes's previous paper on the classification of statistics, yet it shares two important features with that paper. First of all it was a highly-original piece of thinking, an account of the then little understood symbiotic relationship of plant and animal functioning together within one body.[15] Secondly it tackled an area which required insights from both botany and zoology. Thus both papers were pioneering and both had an interdisciplinary slant. As such they were typical of Geddes, however different the subject matter may have been. He was elected an Honorary Member of the Dundee Naturalists' Society later that same year.[16]

Dundee's industrial growth in textile manufacturing and shipbuilding had been driven by engineering innovation and financial expertise. But the strength of this pragmatic culture had not been fully echoed in the development of institutions of education. In December 1881 the situation changed completely with the signing of the Deed of Endowment of University College Dundee by Mary Ann Baxter and John Boyd Baxter. In 1883 the new University College enrolled its first students. Towards the end of 1884, applications were invited for the chair of biology and Geddes applied. In the light of some of the letters sent to him at the time from members of the Dundee Naturalists' Society and others it seems reasonable to regard him as the front runner. He had the strong support of Frank Young; he had the ear of the College Principal, William Peterson. But in the event the chair went to D'Arcy Wentworth Thompson. That was an inspired choice on the part of University College, reclaiming a native of Edinburgh from Cambridge, to give Dundee (and more than thirty years later, St Andrews) the benefit of the teaching and research of one of the great zoologists of the twentieth century. But whatever the benefits of Thompson's appointment, the issue which must be addressed here is why Geddes, with his influential local support, failed to get the chair for which he was such an obvious candidate.

A factor may have been that Geddes, although he had studied with Huxley in London, and had even come into direct contact with Darwin, had never taken a formal degree. This could have counted against him at a time when the sort of codification of achievement in qualifications which we take for granted today was becoming more important. But it is unlikely that this was a factor of significance, indeed Geddes's friends in the Dundee Naturalists' Society while not regarding his appointment as a foregone conclusion, were at first both confident and enthusiastic in their support. One alternative factor has been noted by Paddy Kitchen.[17] The suggestion is that Geddes's failure to be appointed was at least in part due to doubts raised about his religious orthodoxy. This suggestion bears further examination.

On 30 November 1884 Frank Young found himself having to write to Geddes about rumours that were circulating about his religious tendencies, specifically his 'seeking to eliminate the spiritual element from the natural world'.[18] This sense of uneasiness about Geddes's less-than-conventional religious views, is the more intriguing when one sees it in the context of the Deed of Endowment of University College Dundee. A 'fundamental condition' of that deed is 'that no student, professor, teacher or other officer shall be required to make any declaration as to his or her religious opinions or submit to any test of [them] and that nothing shall be introduced in the manner or mode of education in reference to any religious or theological subject which can reasonably be considered offensive to the conscience'. [19]

Geddes was well aware of this 'fundamental condition' and consequently of the irony of finding his own hopes of appointment undermined on grounds specifically excluded from the formal process of appointment. He responded with bitter humour to a letter from one of his Dundee supporters, James Cunningham, who had requested 'a short statement of your philosophical and theological standpoint, that I might use or not at discretion'.[20] The question that must be asked is why were Geddes's religious views an issue with respect to this appointment? It may be naïve to think that they would have no bearing at all in any circumstances, even in the light of the Deed of Endowment. But Geddes himself was not making an issue out of them, so why should anyone else have been? The answer to this conundrum, which saw a major appointment to a newly established institution of higher education made in a way which on the face of it seems quite contrary at least to the spirit of the Deed of Endowment of that institution, lies not in Dundee, but in Aberdeen, and not in biology, but in the study of the Bible.

In the late 1870s and early 1880s the religious and academic structures of the Free Church of Scotland, at that time a major cultural force in the land, had been shaken and split by the controversial writings of William Robertson Smith (1846-1894). In 1881 he had been removed from his post as professor of Hebrew and Old Testament Exegesis at the Free Church College of Aberdeen, on grounds of heterodoxy. The issue in question was the higher criticism, described, in the words of Robertson Smith's own inaugural lecture, as 'the fair and honest looking at the Bible as a historical record, and the effort everywhere to reach the real meaning and historical setting, not of individual passages of the Scripture, but of the Scripture records as a whole'. He goes on to say 'This process can be dangerous to faith only when it is begun without faith – when we forget that the Bible history is no profane history, but the story of God's saving self-manifestation'.[21] G. F. Barbour has pointed out that

> for over five years after his appointment in 1870 Smith quietly pursued his scholar's way in Aberdeen. General statements as to the need for unfettered historical study of the books of the Bible themselves, rather than of traditions regarding them, did not unduly alarm the orthodox, although the more thoughtful might have seen that the postulates of such a critical study were radically opposed to the traditional view of the Bible as of equal historical value in every part. Criticism and a theology based on the idea of literal inspiration could not long exist together.[22]

The split began to become clear on the publication of Robertson Smith's article, 'Bible', published in December 1875 in volume III of the ninth edition of the *Encylopaedia Britannica*. To be aware of how this might have affected Geddes one should note Barbour's emphasis on the public and indeed popular dimensions of the debate which took place from 1876-1881:

> As the range of the dispute became clear, the whole mind of the Scottish people was stirred to activity and interest. The debates of Presbyteries or Assemblies on the views of Robertson Smith were followed and reproduced in railway carriages and workshops and country smithies.[23]

It is important to note that far from being an anomaly within the Free Church, Robertson Smith was part of a tradition of investigative intellectualism which had been strong since the Church's foundation.[24] The Free Church had been formed a little under forty years previously on a point of principle which asserted the independence of religion and state, a principle guaranteed by the Acts of Union in 1707 but subsequently ignored by the Westminster parliament. Those who had supported the formation of the Free Church had been agreed on this principle but were otherwise of diverse view, for example a substantial number of members of the new church had come from academic and artistic circles, not least among these the physicist David Brewster and the painter and photographer D. O. Hill.[25] Thus the Free Church had from its foundation, attracted radical thinkers. This was no less true in theology than in science or in art. Robertson Smith, although challenging the idea of the literal truth of the Bible, had a great deal of support in this project within the church itself, both in terms of his right to 'follow his scholarly way' and with respect to his conclusions. Indeed, he nearly survived the challenge to his academic role, and remained a minister of the Free Church for the rest of his life. Nevertheless what the Robertson Smith case had done was to make issues of the relationship of religion to academia salient at the time that Geddes's application for the chair of biology was being considered. It might seem unlikely that such considerations would spill over into an appointment in the sciences in a new university established as a secular institution. Yet it is clear from Geddes's correspondence that that is exactly what, at least in his view, had happened.

In his reply to Cunningham, Geddes not only made clear his awareness of the conditions of the Deed of Endowment of University College Dundee but also of a direct link between his own predicament and that of Robertson Smith. What at first sight seems to be an obscure aside in which Geddes writes of 'the illustration of the beautiful uniformity of cause and effect offered by the association of Britannica articles with heresy-hunts',[26] is in fact a direct reference to the Robertson Smith case. It has been mentioned that the heart of the case against Robertson Smith was based on his writings for the ninth edition of the *Britannica*. Geddes had himself contributed to the same edition and one must conclude from his comment that this, at least in his view, was an element in the undermining of his position, even though one might have expected contributions to such an eminent publication to bolster rather than hinder his application.

Geddes's direct reference to the Robertson Smith case does not seem to have been clear to previous commentators. However attention has been drawn to a further element which Geddes's supporters feared would count against him. This was his friendship with Annie Besant and his disinclination to conceal the fact.[27] Mrs Besant was at that time a major figure in the Secularist Movement, and in that role had been prosecuted in 1877 on grounds of obscenity for the publication of a pamphlet on contraception.[28] She was also a figure of scandal due to her separation in 1873 from her husband, the Church of England cleric Frank Besant. Part of the background to that separation was Annie Besant's ceasing to believe in the divinity of Christ, and consequent refusal to take the sacrament with her husband.[29] Thus Patrick Geddes through his academic and personal contacts both north and south of the Border was, at the time of his application for the chair of biology at University College Dundee, associated not only with a heresy case but also with an obscenity trial. In addition, the defendant in the latter had recently declared herself to be at odds with a fundamental aspect of Christian doctrine. This was precisely the sort of free-thinking academic and cultural climate in which Geddes thrived, but that can have been of little comfort to him as he saw his hopes of a chair at University College Dundee slipping away.

It is, of course, tempting to conclude that had Geddes's position not been brought into question on the issue of religion, he would have been appointed to the chair of biology. Had that chair gone to anyone other than the chosen candidate, D'Arcy Wentworth Thompson, one might feel more confident in such a conclusion. But Thompson, though younger even than Geddes, was no light-weight candidate. He was a biologist of brilliance, and as such was well capable of gaining the appointment on merit alone, merit which Geddes himself recognised. Indeed, despite his own disappointment, Geddes offered to accommodate Thompson while the latter was transferring from Cambridge to Dundee and in the light of this (and the Edinburgh connections of both men) it seems likely that the two were already friends. In subsequent years they certainly became so, indeed in a moving letter to Geddes's daughter Nora Mears, written some years after Geddes's death in 1932, Thompson referred to his 'lifelong friendship' with her father and to his happy memories of Nora herself from her childhood onwards. The occasion of this letter is Nora's desire to have D'Arcy's comments on a collection of poetry she was proposing to publish, and in which the letter in due course took its place as a kind of informal preface.[30] Nora seemed to regard Thompson as a kind of unofficial uncle, a role he clearly reciprocated. This evidence of closeness between Geddes's family and Thompson adds an interesting personal dimension to an appreciation of Thompson's high regard for Geddes as a thinker.[31]

Whatever the initial disappointment that their candidate had not been appointed, the members of the Dundee Naturalists' Society took to D'Arcy Thompson soon enough. Not long after taking up his appointment in early 1885 he gave his first lecture to the Society on 'Modern Methods of Biological Study'.[32] That year he was also elected to the council. Martin White by this time had taken on the duties of honorary secretary, sharing them with Frank Young.[33] Never-theless, whatever Thompson's qualities, Frank Young and Martin White must have been concerned by the way in which Geddes had been treated. However, on a positive and unifying note for all concerned, the scientific standing of the Dundee Naturalists' Society itself was underlined that same year of 1885 by the election to Fellowship of the British Association for the Advancement of Science of three of its members, James Martin White, Patrick Geddes and D'Arcy Wentworth Thompson.

Geddes's failure to gain the Dundee chair in biology in 1884 seems to have put his career advancement on hold. He had already failed, in 1882, to be appointed to the chair of natural history at Edinburgh University. In 1888 he failed again to be appointed to an Edinburgh chair, for the regius chair of botany had fallen vacant on the death of his friend Alexander Dickson in 1887. Geddes's problems were compounded by the fact that he was now showing himself to be a generalist thinker at a time when narrow expertise was beginning to be the index of academic recognition that it still is today. The effective nature of this generalism is indicated by a recent description of Geddes as 'a seminal influence on sociology and planning and the father of environmentalism'.[34] But his pioneering and wide-ranging thinking, frequently in areas which have only been properly defined as academic disciplines in the wake of his exploratory work, was to confuse his more conventional colleagues for the rest of his career. He was capable both of presenting an expert view, and of understanding and valuing the wider cultural context of such expertise. One of his aims was to develop the academic discipline of sociology to give structure and method to the scientific study of such wider cultural contexts, issues and sympathies. His papers to the Dundee Naturalists' Society in 1881 and 1882 already illuminate this breadth for they reflect both his specialist knowledge of biology and his desire to situate all knowledges within a wider sociological framework. His commitment to such a generalist approach enabled him to develop a holistic, ecological approach. However this same generalism opened him to accusations of lack of focus[35] and such comments, sometimes justified, did not help him in his academic career.

In this situation of uncertainty for Geddes the patronage of Martin White was of all the more importance. White had come to control the family wealth on the death of his father in 1884. By 1886 the relationship of patronage as well as of friendship between Geddes and White had begun to assume a pattern which was to continue for more than thirty years. This pattern consisted on the one hand of Geddes asking White for money for various schemes, and on the other of White attempting to finance Geddes in a way which was both controlled and creative. Not surprisingly, there were tensions between the two men. For example in a letter of 27 January 1886 White writes from Dundee to Geddes with reference to the terms of a £200 loan requested by Geddes for some unspecified purpose. The tone of the letter is very much that of a close friend, indeed part of the letter refers to a trip to Greece which the two men were about to make. However this intended journey also draws attention to the stresses consequent on disparity of wealth, for Geddes's participation in the trip was made possible because he was being employed as a tutor. White continues

> now regarding going away I assure you I wish you not to feel, and I shall not, the rich and poor sentiment you expressed. If I can put a good scientific man in 'real good shape' consciousness of accomplished duty is my reward, for I advance science. And you must in this instance remember the pleasure I have in scientific company and in yours especially. You are to be cashier and we are to travel unrestrained and joyously . . . Hurrah for Greece – I wish I were off.[36]

The main body of the letter is full of suggestions about Geddes's future which show White's concern that Geddes's work should not be lost to academia, and the fact that White even mentions the possibility of such loss, suggests Geddes's uncertainty of academic direction at this time. It is clear that White sees himself both as a personal and as an academic advisor to Geddes (quite apart from his role as a patron). For example, without even starting a new paragraph, White shifts from loan repayment details to considering Geddes's future:

> I think you want some true stimulus to take you out of the in some respects, unproductive speculative and give the world some of your matured thoughts or conclusions. Your publications would be valuable in themselves, and their loss must not be risked.

White goes on to write of introducing Geddes more fully to the public where he would 'gain an enlarged sphere of usefulness, beneficial influence and enlarged aims towards further work . . . And all this you could do without much sacrifice to your pursuits'. Here White seems to be sounding out Geddes with respect to some sort of stable employment. In due course, after Geddes had failed to be appointed professor of botany at Edinburgh University (1888), White and his siblings financed a part-time chair of botany, named in memory of their father James Farquhar White, for Geddes at University College Dundee, a post that allowed Geddes the freedom to engage with his other interests for most of the year. It is by no means clear that this scheme was in his mind when he wrote to Geddes in 1886 but from the tone of the letter it seems likely that White was at least beginning to consider some such idea. One wonders how much an awareness of the injustice done to Geddes in the treatment of his application for the chair of biology was a factor in White's suggestion to University College Dundee that such a chair, specifically for Geddes, might be appropriate. Whatever the case, in 1888 Geddes was appointed and University College Dundee found itself with two remarkable biologists (both also outstanding visual thinkers) on its professoriate. They were to remain so for the next three decades.

The correspondence between Geddes and White over the next decades repeats a familiar pattern of loans and friendship, the loans often now directly related to Geddes's Dundee chair, but also to other projects such as the finishing of Geddes's Ramsay Garden project in Edinburgh.[37] This remarkable building was at the heart of an informal college, which comprised, along with flats for academics, a network of student residences and the teaching materials of the Outlook Tower. Along with associated civic activities, architectural conservation and renewal projects, and gap-site gardens this comprises one of the most extraordinary educational experiments of this period. Geddes's civic activities in Dundee were also notable. As noted elsewhere in this volume,[38] it is highly likely that it was Geddes's appointment in 1888 that stimulated the professoriate of University College to establish the Dundee Social Union on 24 May of that year, six weeks after Geddes took up his post. Another notable, but unsuccessful project was Geddes's proposal to establish a botanical garden at the eastern end of Magdalen Green.[39]

Geddes's part-time role and growing involvement with sociology, cultural revivals and town planning, left him open to criticisms of neglecting his role in Dundee. For example, Martin White himself wrote in 1904 of hearing 'various rumblings at the little attention Dundee gets from you'.[40] There may have been some justice in White's comment, for at the best of times Geddes was not a conventional academic, but it must be stressed that by 1904 Geddes had made possible a remarkable contribution to botanical research in Dundee, inspiring work of the highest quality from one student in particular, the brilliant but short-lived Robert Smith. Alexander Mather has made clear the quality of Geddes's academic leadership during his years in Dundee:

> The golden age of vegetation mapping in Scotland can be attributed to a remarkable coincidence of several factors: the inspirational genius of Geddes and his European connections, the industry and enthusiasm of Robert Smith, the cartographic innovations of John Bartholomew in producing the maps and of the (Royal) Scottish Geographical Society in publishing them.[41]

The author goes on to suggest that this vegetation survey project:

> can be seen as a metaphor for, and flagship of, the greater Geddes project. For a few years around 1900, there was a real prospect that a distinctive Geddesian geography could emerge that was international in outlook, conceptually aware but empirically grounded, holistic, and practical in orientation. Given the setting in a period that was critical in the evolution of geography (and other disciplines), the significance of the enterprise could have been profound and fundamental: in essence Geddesian geography was human ecology.

But the enterprise was not sustained, for at the time there was no critical mass of like-minded botanist-geographers in Scotland to support Geddes's initiative. Robert Smith's tragic death made things worse. What is clear with hindsight is the high quality of research made possible by Geddes. The point made about the importance of John Bartholomew's mapping to the project leads one to note also the high production values of the *Scottish Geographical Magazine* in which these Geddes-inspired botanical surveys were published. In volume 16 in 1900, Robert Smith published the first two parts of his 'Botanical Survey of Scotland', those for Edinburgh and for North Perthshire.[42] In a sad irony, this volume also includes Smith's obituary, written, of course, by Geddes.[43] Robert Smith's work was continued by his brother, William. Further valuable papers were written for volumes 18, 20 and 21 of the *Scottish Geographical Magazine*.[44] Geddes maintained his close links with the magazine, and notable is another obituary, that of the French anarchist geographer, Elysée Reclus.[45] Along with William Smith's 'Botanical survey of Forfar and Fife', this lengthy obituary occurs in two parts in volume 21.

Further insight into Geddes's wider activities while he held the chair of botany at University College Dundee is afforded by other papers in volumes 20 and 21, specifically those reporting the work of another Geddes student, this time an Edinburgh one, the polar explorer William Speirs Bruce. Bruce had earlier laid out his ambitious scientific plans for his Scottish National Antarctic Expedition in the pages of the magazine. His voyages were a significant scientific success. It can be noted in the context of the present chapter that Bruce's first taste of Antarctic exploration had a direct link with Dundee, for he had sailed as scientific and medical officer on the whaler *Balaena* on its first foray to explore the possibilities of Antarctic whaling in 1892–93.[46] Although this Dundee expedition was primarily commercial rather than scientific the writings and lectures given by Bruce and his colleague W. G. Burn Murdoch on their return 'started an interest and led to Bruce's further and purely scientific voyages which placed him in the forefront of naturalist navigators and explorers'.[47] Peter Speak, whose scholarship has done a great deal to re-awaken interest in Bruce's work, has credited this Dundee expedition with the reopening of Antarctic research after a break of some fifty years.[48]

In 1904 White was writing to Geddes not in Dundee or in Edinburgh but at a new address, Low Valleyfield, Dunfermline. This was Geddes's temporary residence while employed on the making of a report, which was to become recognised as a classic statement of the principles of urban conservation and renewal.[49] This report was Geddes's proposed plan for the area around Pittencrieff Park in Dunfermline, which he had undertaken in response to a request for proposals from the Carnegie Dunfermline Trust. By the time Geddes was ready to publish this copiously illustrated report of over 200 pages, White appeared distinctly unenthusiastic about reading yet another ideas-packed document by his old friend. He wrote from London on 15 June 1904: 'I shall be glad to see the Dunfermline report but hope it is not too long'.[50] Too long it may well have been for the long-suffering White, but it was nevertheless one of the most important early twentieth-century documents on town planning and city development. It had a significant impact on twentieth-century thinking, on the one hand through the work of Geddes's American disciple, the theorist of cities Lewis Mumford,[51] and on the other through its influence on British planners such as Patrick Abercrombie.[52]

It is an irony that having helped to set up Geddes in a career with a degree of security White's enthusiasm for Geddes's schemes was showing signs of waning at the very time when his support for Geddes was beginning to bear fruit. The essential creativity of the relationship between these two men is indicated by the fact that thanks in large part to Geddes's inspiration as far back as 1881, White was increasingly conscious of the possibilities of the new discipline of sociology, and was by this time firmly committed, as a patron, to establishing sociology on the academic map. Geddes was still very much involved in this project but White was beginning to view the subject with a different emphasis. For example, although both were involved in the foundation of the Sociological Society in London (in due course a key port of call for the young Lewis Mumford), White criticised a circular by Geddes relating to the foundation of the Society as 'too purely scientific'. Instead he advocated more emphasis on philosophy, and this in turn should correspond to two distinct sections of the Society.[53] Where once White might have deferred to Geddes on academic matters, it is clear that he no longer did so. At the end of the letter White introduced a topic which was to have major ramifications: he mentioned his anxiety to establish a chair of social and political philosophy at St Andrews. It seems that nothing came of this scheme at St Andrews, or indeed in Scotland, but it did bear fruit in London, for, as already noted, White went on to endow the first two chairs of sociology at the University of London. From 1905 he had given money for 'temporary endowments of Teacherships in Sociology, including Ethnology' and on 21 September 1907 he gave £10,000 for the foundation of a permanent chair in sociology, in due course held by Hobhouse. One can note, in the light of White's injunction to Geddes in 1903 to pay more heed to philosophy, that Hobhouse was by training a philosopher. In 1911 he made money available for a second chair, to which Edward Westermarck was appointed.[54] It is, perhaps, something of a surprise to realise that the University of London owes its early pre-eminence in social science, at least in part, to the wealth created by the Dundee textile industry.

While White was hoping that the Dunfermline report was not too long, another Dundee figure had contributed to it. This was the painter John Duncan who made five illustrations for the report, including proposals for an allegorical statue *Time and the Fates: the Dial of History*, and other statues of *St Columba* and *Ossian*. He also contributed a mural design of one of the key events in the history of Dunfermline, *The Marriage of Malcolm and Margaret*. However his contribution was not limited to illustration, for in his text Geddes invoked the example of Duncan's murals in Ramsay Lodge in Edinburgh to demonstrate the practicality of revitalising cultural history through the visual arts.[55]

John Duncan was more than a decade younger than Patrick Geddes. He had been born in Dundee in 1866, the son of a grocer father and weaver mother.[56] He was a talented illustrator and from an early age contributed to the burgeoning journalistic culture of Dundee. Like many Scottish artists of the day he was also well travelled having studied in Antwerp and Italy. It is unlikely that he met Geddes before his return from Italy in 1891,[57] but that meeting was almost certainly in Dundee, perhaps at the Dundee Art Society. By 1893 the two were working closely together. In due course Duncan was to become the leading artist of the Celtic revival in Scotland, and he owed much to the opportunities afforded him by his links with Geddes. It is easy to assume that it was Geddes with his interest in cultural revival in general who inspired Duncan to Celtic revival work.

In fact Duncan showed clear interest in things Celtic at least six years before he is thought to have met Geddes, for he signs himself in a Gaelicised version of his name, 'Eoin Donnchadh', in a letter to his friend William Craigie written on 3 August 1885.[58] It thus seems that the meeting between Duncan and Geddes was very much a meeting of minds, it may even be that it was at least in part Duncan's influence that guided Geddes in the direction of specifically Celtic – as well as general Scots – revival. It can be noted that Geddes's other main collaborator in the Celtic revival aspect of his activities, William Sharp, did not even meet him until the autumn of 1894.[59]

In another letter to Craigie, Duncan made reference to his earliest project for Geddes.[60] In this letter he asked for Craigie's help with ideas for a series of murals showing the history of the bagpipes which he had agreed to paint for Geddes's new flat in Ramsay Garden. He introduced Geddes as 'Professor Geddes whose name you may have heard – who occupies the chair of Botany at Dundee'. The mural scheme was carried out, but has been since destroyed, so its precise composition is not known. As Duncan outlines it the original proposal proceeded from an image of reeds blown in the wind, to Pan teaching Apollo, the first musician, to play the pan-pipes, thence to pipes played before Moses parting the Red Sea. Then followed a Bacchanalian scene with satyrs and maenads; the Pied Piper of Hamelyn; a medieval Celtic piper (Duncan asks Craigie for a suitable incident to illustrate), and as a final image the body of the early Jacobite leader Claverhouse being carried from the field of Killiecrankie 'with the pipes of the highland clans that fought with him marching beside their slain chief'.[61]

Soon afterward Duncan was closely involved in Geddes's magazine, *The Evergreen: A Northern Seasonal,* which was published by Geddes and Colleagues from the Lawnmarket (that is to say, the Ramsay Garden/Outlook Tower/Halls of Residence complex) in Edinburgh. A number of his designs for the magazine echo the subjects of the murals, for example *Apollo's Schooldays,* from the *Book of Spring* published in Spring 1895, and *Bacchanalian Revel,* published in the *Book of Summer,* in 1896. The close relationship between these murals and the *Evergreen* images is demonstrated by Duncan's request to Geddes to send his watercolour sketch of his Bacchanalian procession because he is 'about to do my drawing for *The Evergreen,* and I can't get along without having that sketch by me'.[62] Writing in July 1895 Duncan requests two copies of the first issue of *The Evergreen* (the aforementioned *Book of Spring*), one for himself and one for a fellow artist in Dundee, Stewart Carmichael.[63] The latter contributed in due course in 1903 to a student magazine, *The Meal Poke,* which shows every sign of being inspired in its design, by *The Evergreen.*[64] There were certainly copies of *The Evergreen* within the student body, for Geddes used this first issue as a prize in his Dundee botany classes.[65]

John Duncan had the leading role in Geddes's Old Edinburgh School of Art, a key part of his Old Town renewal activities in Edinburgh. As ever, Geddes was short of money for the project and, as John Kemplay has noted, this led to friction with Duncan.[66] But as with White, any friction was within a context of creative collaboration based on mutual respect, and Duncan remained faithful to Geddes's ideas for the rest of his life. This is not the place to explore this relationship in depth, but a letter from Duncan to Geddes, written in 1898 can illuminate it for the purposes of this chapter. There Duncan makes a very polite request for money for work done, which shows just how far he had, by this time, come to evolve a *modus operandi* with Geddes. Duncan wrote from his studio in Dundee and referred to having the services of a talented assistant, presumably the able but short-lived George Dutch Davidson (1879–1901). He also referred to Tayport-based Miss Nell Baxter. Along with Duncan she had made a substantial contribution to *The Evergreen* and had been one of the several women whom he had trained at the Old Edinburgh School of Art.[67] The letter ends with reference to an Arts and Crafts society 'forming in Glasgow at the present moment', and Duncan was clearly delighted to have been asked to become one of its twenty founder members. He listed the others in full, and it is indeed an impressive list. The two foremost architects of the day, Rowand Anderson and John James Burnet were included as were Duncan's *Evergreen* colleague Robert Burns and the foremost sculptor of the day Pittendrigh MacGillivray (also an *Evergreen* contributor, both of graphic work and poetry). Also listed were a number of key proponents of the Glasgow style associated with Charles Rennie Mackintosh, including Mackintosh himself, his wife-to-be Margaret Macdonald and his key supporter, the director of Glasgow School of Art, Francis Newbery. Newbery's talented wife Jessie was also included as were David Gauld, George Walton, and the outstanding all-round craftswoman and artist Phoebe Anna Traquair. All in all a list that allows one to appreciate Duncan in the wider context of his peers.[68]

Over the next fifteen years or so both Geddes and Duncan further developed friendships with a number of these artists, not least Margaret Macdonald and Charles Rennie Mackintosh. One finds this reflected in an affectionate note, written not later than 1914, from Margaret to Geddes's wife Anna. Margaret referred to seeing that Geddes had been lecturing in the Outlook Tower and regretted not having 'someone like him here'. She went on to mention visiting John Duncan and his wife in their new house in Edinburgh.[69] Patrick Geddes was an admirer of Mackintosh's architecture, and a few years later commissioned him to produce designs which almost certainly relate to planning work in India.

It was now over thirty years since Patrick Geddes had given his first papers to the Dundee Naturalists' Society. Soon, in 1914, in his sixtieth year, he would begin to develop a new phase of his work, in India, Palestine and France, departing his Dundee chair for the new chair of civics and sociology at the University of Bombay in 1919. But there was one last great event in the history of the city of Dundee in which Geddes's influence was felt and in which James Martin White and John Duncan also played a part. This was the meeting of the British Association for the Advancement of Science in September 1912.[70]

It has been mentioned that Martin White, Patrick Geddes and D'Arcy Thompson had all been elected as fellows of the British Association in 1885. By 1912 Thompson had become a key figure in the organisation, not least as president of Section D (zoology) at the 1911 meeting of the Association. Although this chapter has not dealt with Thompson's contribution to the intellectual and cultural life of Dundee, it will be clear from those references that have been made that his contribution was immense. He was a key figure in the local organising committee for the British Association meeting in 1912, and was also a vice-president of Section D.

Among the contributors to Section D was W. S. Bruce, speaking on 'Zoological Results of the Scottish National Antarctic Expedition'. Both Geddes and Thompson had supported Bruce in this venture, and one might at first sight suppose that Bruce's results would have been one of the highlights of this Dundee meeting. Geddes himself, reflecting his growing role as a sociologist, was a vice-president of Section F (economic science and statistics). He contributed a paper entitled 'Regional and Civic Surveys: the needed Co-operation of the Sciences towards the Town Planning Movement'. Among other contributors to this section was Ramsay MacDonald MP, speaking on 'The Minimum Wage'. Geddes's former student, William Smith, building on his botanical survey work at University College Dundee, gave a paper (jointly with C. B. Crampton) on 'The Influence and Origin of Grasslands'. This was presented to the newly formed Section M (agriculture) which had developed out of Section F.

Geddes may well have been present to hear Bruce speak in the session of Section E (geography) devoted to Antarctica. It is, however, notable that Bruce is not even listed as a contributor. This gives a clue to a dramatic aspect of polar research during this period. A vice-president of Section E was Sir Clements Markham, who contributed a paper on 'Antarctic Discovery' that was noted in the proceedings as opening a discussion on the Antarctic. The full discussion is reported in the *Geographical Journal,*[71] and there one finds that Markham's paper was directly followed by a shorter, but substantial, contribution by Bruce. Reported also is discussion from Bruce's supporter (and later biographer) Rudmose Brown, and others. In recent years Markham's complex character has become a subject of some interest,[72] and his attempts to thwart Bruce's careful scientific explorations in favour of the more heroic style of his own protégé, Robert Falcon Scott, have been noted.[73] Certainly the fact that Bruce's paper to the British Association in Dundee is not recorded in the proceedings is consistent with this. The tragedy of Markham's contribution is that part of his agenda seems to be to make of Scott a legend in his own lifetime, yet by that date, unbeknown to Markham, Scott had lain dead and undiscovered for several months. An irony is that, in his selective account of Antarctic exploration, Markham not only ignores Bruce, he also makes no mention of Amundsen. The latter had by this time not only reached the South Pole in advance of Scott, but had also survived to tell the tale, although the tale had not yet been told. By contrast in the discussion reported in the *Geographical Journal,* Rudmose Brown made sure that Amundsen's previous explorations are given due credit.[74] A final, sad, critique of Markham comes from another discussant, T. V. Hodgson, who describes Markham's advocacy of human rather than animal traction in polar exploration as 'a serious mistake'.[75] Whether Scott's death can be attributed to this 'serious mistake' is a moot point but the comment illustrates the clash in the ideologies which surrounded Antarctic research. For many years such controversy was obscured by the myth of Scott that Markham so assiduously created. While one cannot be sure that Patrick Geddes and D'Arcy Thompson managed to attend this session, their sympathies would have been with Bruce's science rather than Markham's mythologising.

Martin White had no active role in the meeting but had written to Geddes on 6 September hoping to see him there.[76] He did, however, make a less obvious contribution to the event for he had presented a work by John Duncan to Dundee Corporation in 1912. This work, *The Riders of the Sidhe,* had been displayed at the Royal Scottish Academy the previous year, and shows Duncan at the height of his skill as a Celtic revival symbolist. It was exhibited as part of the major loan exhibition mounted in the Victoria Galleries to mark the visit of the British Association.[77] This exhibition was notable both for its scale and its quality. International in scope, it had Scottish art at its heart, including a large number of works by Raeburn. Among much else there was a previously unexhibited late work by William McTaggart who had died in 1910. Through the patronage of McTaggart's friend James Guthrie Orchar, Dundee had developed a close link with this artist.

By this time John Duncan was resident in Edinburgh, Martin White was ever more closely involved in affairs in London, not least through his advocacy of sociology, and Geddes would soon embark on the final international phase of his career. The British Association meeting of 1912 is thus as good a point as any to conclude this glimpse of the interplay of patronage, academia and artistic culture in Dundee. Its programme, participants and associated events are symbolic of the achievement of University College Dundee in little more than three decades.[78]

NINE

Red Tayside? Political change in early twentieth-century Dundee

John Kemp

CHANGE CAME SWIFTLY to Dundee's politics at the beginning of the twentieth century. In no other Scottish city did Liberalism decline so rapidly or from such a seemingly unassailable position. Dundee had been Liberal since the creation of its parliamentary seat in 1832. The Unionist gains of 1895 and 1900, which wiped out all of the Liberals in Glasgow, had little effect on their dominance in Dundee.[1] And yet in 1906 Dundee was one of the first places in Scotland to elect a Labour MP; one of only two seats the party won in that year in Scotland, one of only three the party held before the First World War in Scotland. While the rest of Scotland was returning to Liberalism, Dundee was turning against it. By 1910 Dundee was the 'least Liberal city in Scotland'.[2] By 1922, the year of Labour's electoral breakthrough across Scotland, Dundee was far more left wing than any other city, a deeper, and more vivid, red than even Clydeside. In Glasgow that year just over one-third of the registered electorate voted for a Labour or Communist candidate. In Dundee nearly half voted Labour, Prohibitionist or Communist.[3]

Dundee's precocity in turning against Liberalism is matched by a paradoxical lateness in recognising the importance of independent Labour representation. The Scottish Labour Party's James Macdonald gained only 354 votes in the parliamentary election in 1892 and 1,313 as an Independent Labour Party [ILP] candidate in 1895: over 8,000 away from victory in 1892, 6,000 away in 1885. Of the 1892 contest his election agent wrote that it 'was hopeless from the start: his ideas were new to the multitude and unwelcome to all classes'.[4] Labour politics came late to Dundee municipal elections. Glasgow had had Labour councillors since 1889, though their numbers and profile only became significant after 1896.[5] Aberdeen had had five ILP members on the Council in 1893.[6] In Dundee it was not until 1905 that the first official Labour candidate stood, though there had been Labour councillors on the School Board and Parish Council before then. Dundee in the 1890s was almost entirely free of class-based politics. As Walker has argued, Dundee was not politically backward if one measures this by the presence of bodies espousing radical ideas.[7] Dundee had branches of all of the usual socialist or labour bodies at one time or another. But support for these bodies did not exist in sufficient numbers to make any significant impact.

It is not the intention here to rehearse the whole 'strange death' of Liberalism debate. But there are lessons to be learned from Dundee. In part these lessons are important simply because Dundee is not Glasgow. Perhaps naturally, given the size of Glasgow and the number of Labour MPs elected from the West in the 1920s, much of the literature on Labour's breakthrough in Scotland has tended to concentrate on that city. But knowing what happened in Glasgow does not tell us what happened in Scotland, nor even in urban Scotland. Red Tayside is as important as Red Clydeside to the bigger picture of political change in Scotland.

Scotland as a whole was not in the vanguard of Labour electoral success. The conventional view expressed by I. G. C. Hutchison is that the 'breakthrough achieved by the Labour Party in Scotland after the First World War was sudden and emphatic' and that little happened before 1914.[8] In this he is widely supported.[9] While acknowledging the fact that the scale of the breakthrough after the war would tend to point to origins before the war, Hutchison casts doubt on whether the pre-war stirrings amounted to much.[10] Some have seen important developments before the war in both support for and organisation of the left, some seeing the period of industrial unrest between 1910 and 1914 as important.[11] Sometimes Labour's progress before 1914 has been seen as being at the expense of the revolutionary left rather than the Liberals.[12]

Dundee was different. The evidence from Dundee is that a substantial change in the political mood had taken place well before 1914. The cross-class alliance that had allowed Liberal dominance was in serious trouble in Dundee by 1906. Support for Labour was substantial and that support was at the expense of the Liberals. There is a nervousness about using the word 'class' in connection with popular politics in the wake of recent critiques of the concept. What happened in Dundee supports Patrick Joyce's contention (though he was, of course, writing about England) that a feeling of class came late to politics, if at all.[13] But when it did come to Dundee, it came quickly and transformed political life.

The two Labour victories in Scotland in 1906 had little in common. George Barnes' victory in Hutchestown and Blackfriars in 1906 was against the general trend in Glasgow politics, happening at the same time as reverses for Labour in municipal elections,[14] and has been attributed to a switch in the Irish vote rather than a wider change in political mood.[15] Alexander Wilkie in Dundee received no such help. The Dundee Irish were advised by the United Irish League to vote against him as an enemy of Ireland.[16] Wilkie's success in Dundee has been seen as the voters of Dundee imposing a Lib-Lab pact, of the kind that existed in many English two-member seats as a result of the Gladstone-MacDonald pact, on a reluctant Liberal party.[17] Wilkie may himself have been a natural Lib-Lab (as was Barnes), but his election came at a time when fundamental change was underway in Dundee politics. This was far more than just a squabble about who should have been the second Liberal candidate. Because Dundee was a two-member seat we know something about where his votes came from. Many of those who voted for Wilkie also voted for the winning Liberal – 3,183 of the 6,833 – but nearly a thousand also voted for one or other of the Unionist candidates and 2,553 did not use their second votes at all.

Because there was such a profound shift in Dundee politics around 1906 there is a danger that Wilkie's election may seem more important than it actually was. His election was one – but by no means the only signal of change. On its own Wilkie's election could be dismissed as an aberration or a fluke. It was not. In a fairly short period in the years before Wilkie's election there was a transformation in Dundee politics. Labour began preparing itself for a parliamentary challenge in 1901. It is only by looking at the municipal politics of the town that we can see why that challenge was much stronger than previous ones. Until the early years of the twentieth century Dundee municipal government had been remarkably free of class politics. After the turn of the century this changed. In order to understand just how sudden and momentous this change was it is worth describing the pattern of municipal politics before then in some detail.

Until the advent of Labour and Prohibitionist candidates in the early 1900s, party politics were formally absent from Dundee municipal affairs. Candidates did not usually stand with explicit party or faction labels attached. Fitness for office, probity and the business acumen to run the city finances, were all more important than party or affiliation. Party politics got in the way of running the city well. There was no desire for a council that reflected the political views or social composition of the population. It was, ideally, a board of directors that was wanted. Councillors were judged on the talents, usually business talents, they brought to the council table.

The electorate that desired this council was by no means completely representative of the population. However, it was far from being dominated by the middle classes. The municipal electorate in 1901 totalled around 23,000 – 18,000 males and just under 5,000 females out of populations of 70,000 and 90,000 respectively. Women could not, of course, vote in parliamentary elections. Probably less than half of the adult male population and around one in twelve of the adult female population had the vote. Despite this, it is probable that the working classes constituted a majority of the electors, given Dundee's unusually small middle class.[18]

The electorate was, at least at first glance, an active one. Election meetings were generally well attended. It is tempting to think that this indicated a serious interest in politics on the part of the public. Entertainment was often an equally likely motive. The young men at one meeting who amused themselves by pushing each other off the platform until the speaker arrived may have been as common as the earnest worrier about public expenditure.[19] Newspapers were well aware of the entertainment value of election meetings. Coverage did not edit out the ridiculous. When a candidate in 1904 was asked his views on a crematorium and replied by saying how much he liked cream, the newspaper account reported the exchange in full.[20]

Between 1875 and 1910 just under half of the seats on the Council were filled without the need for a contested election. This is probably not an indication of apathy on the part of the electorate or potential candidates. In a system where there were no formal party structures organising automatic opposition to candidates of different parties, a candidate who, after taking soundings, realised he was unlikely to win had little to gain by pushing things as far as a ballot. Sometimes a body of acceptable candidates would 'emerge' across the whole city, as in 1901 when there were no contested elections at all. Wards which could not organise a councillor without recourse to a poll were sometimes criticised for burdening the city with the unnecessary expense of elections.[21]

Figure 5: Occupations of Dundee Town Councillors, 1875–1910.

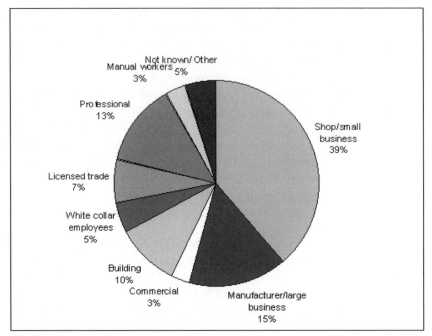

Source: Dundee Town Council Minutes, 1875–1910. From 1893 candidates' occupations were listed in the election return presented to the Council each November. Prior to this, the occupations listed in the *Dundee Directories* have been used.

Uncontested elections did not necessarily reflect satisfaction with the Council. There was a persistent level of unhappiness with the kind of people who sought to become councillors. The commonly shared view was that the Council was, as Southgate has said, 'an object of contempt among men of goodwill'.[22] Its members were seen as incompetent, sometimes corrupt and usually profligate with the public purse. A great deal of this was attributed to the background of the councillors. In 1871, a magazine of the (mainly working-class) temperance organisation, the Good Templars, bemoaned the fact that Dundee citizens, 'after getting easy in their circumstances and in a position to do good service to the community, prefer their own ease to the public good, leaving municipal matters to be attended to by any so inclined'.[23] Those so inclined were, another contemporary magazine commented, 'Miserable vendors of baps, beer and penny dreadfuls [who] may be excellent men in their own way, but they are scarcely justified in posing as the men best fitted to run the town's affairs successfully'.[24]

The shopkeeper and the small businessman dominated membership of the Council. An examination of the occupations of the 128 men who served on Dundee Town Council between 1875 and 1910 shows that nearly 39% owned shops or small businesses (see Figure 5). A further 17% were from the licensed or building trades, most of whom owned small businesses in that sector, making a total of 56% from that group.

Those from the licensed or building trades are worth counting separately for, in the eyes of many of the public, they were a different breed from the ordinary businessman. They were seen to be more interested in business advantage rather than the public good. A vendor of beer, though he may have been every bit as miserable in financial terms as a vendor of baps, was considerably less welcome on the Council. 'Dealers in whisky, property speculators and such like should be kept out of the Council by all means. They are there for their own interests and not for that of the ratepayers', wrote a typical newspaper correspondent in 1890.[25]

Figure 6: Dundee Town Council, 1875–1910. Percentage of candidatures successful by occupation.

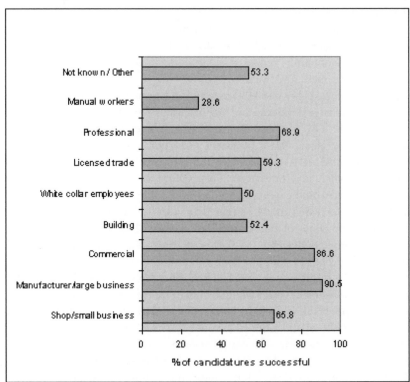

Source: Dundee Town Council Minutes, 1875–1910.

The public expressed their dislike of such candidates at the polls. On the face of it, Figure 6 suggests that candidates who were members of the licensed trade were only slightly less likely than average to be successful at the polls than others (59% as against an average for all candidates of 64% in the 1875–1910 period). But this figure is deceptive. Two substantial brewers, Hugh Ballingall and Peter Storrie, between them had a 94% success rate in their many elections. If they are removed, the success rate for the retail side of the drink trade drops to 43%, compared to an average for the general shopkeeper/small businessman class of 66%. It is difficult to assess how far this mistrust was justified and what licensees or builders obtained from being on the Council. Councillors who sought office in order to benefit themselves were unlikely to display their ambitions too openly. We can, however, find some examples of the kind of behaviour that ensured the Council was held in low esteem. In 1876 one councillor, William Blair, the proprietor of flats in Lochee, found himself in front of one of his Council colleagues, who was sitting as a magistrate, for failing to comply with a sanitary inspector's order that he install water into some of his properties. He protested that as the sanitary committee was dealing with the matter, it was not an issue for the court. He knew this because he was member of the committee.[26] This did not impress the bailie. Blair, feeling hard done by, is alleged to have financed a candidate against the bailie at the elections a few months later, ensuring his defeat.[27] Blair himself faced election the year after his court case and won, albeit narrowly, in a campaign in which the treatment of his tenants was raised but at which votes were allegedly available for 3*d.* worth of whisky.[28]

The most commonly proposed solution to conduct of this sort was the involvement of men who were well above this squalid level and who could bring vision, impartiality and efficiency to the Council. Over the period 1875–1910 owners of large businesses and manufacturers provided 15% of the members of the Council. This was seen as insufficient. The complaint that the wealthy shunned public affairs was a persistent one. This was not because they were under-represented. It is certainly not the case that one in six of the Dundee population owned large businesses. Their failure to serve in sufficient numbers was partly blamed on the inhospitable nature of public life. One Liberal suggested in 1886 that the reason might be that 'The vulgarities and personalities that are indulged in by some of our councillors in their deliberations of the town's business is simply disgraceful . . . they waste time, disgrace the community and take especial delight in exposing each others shortcomings'.[29] The triviality of much Council business was also blamed. The *Piper O' Dundee* was perhaps correct in its assessment that it would be unfair to 'expect gentlemen whose time, talents and opportunities could be better employed to listen to the humdrum and vaporous twaddle of the Council boards'.[30] The Dundee electors shared this desire for the involvement of more substantial members of the community and expressed it at the ballot box. There were few barriers to membership of the Council for men of this rank. Of the candidatures from owners of large businesses over 90% were successful compared with an overall figure of 64% for all occupations. Even more illustrative is the figure for unopposed elections. 57% of candidatures from this group were unopposed, compared to an overall average of 29% – they were almost twice as likely to be given a free run (see Figure 7).

The aim of a less corrupt, less wasteful Council was one shared by all. If there was a class element to local politics, it was in the mistrust of the small business class, particularly if their business involved drink or buildings. The working class and the wealthy were seen as allies against those in between. The membership of the Citizens' Association, a pressure group formed in 1895 to pursue stricter enforcement of the current licensing laws, better scrutiny of public expenditure and to oppose candidates who had an interest, direct or indirect, in licensed premises was one of the bodies that filled the gap caused by the lack of party

Figure 7: Dundee Town Council, 1875–1910. Percentage of candidatures unopposed by occupation.

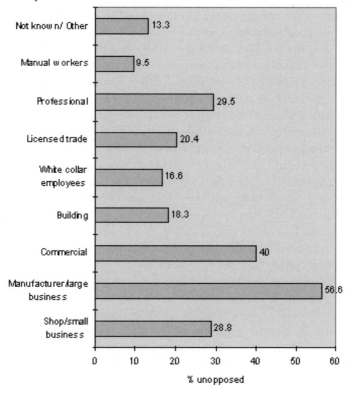

Source: Dundee Town Council Minutes, 1875–1910.

political organisation in municipal politics and illustrated the broad coalition. Peter Reid of the Trades Council who spoke at one of the first meetings, the Lochee Temperance Electors' Association, which wanted to join *en masse*, was worried about the level of subscription as its members included a large number of working men.[31] A list of office-bearers included the secretary of the Trades Council, eight manufacturers or owners of large businesses, at least four manual workers, eight members of the Liberal Party and at least two Unionists.[32] In 1896 the Trades Council, in discussing their attitude to the municipal elections, agreed to cooperate with the Citizens' Association in finding suitable candidates, believing that such a combination would be able to 'prevail upon a number of excellent men to offer their services' and lead to important changes in the composition of the Council.[33]

In this coalition of interests between the classes it was, of course, usually assumed that the role of the working class was to *support* the approved candidate rather than to *provide* that candidate. The Citizens' Association had working-class involvement and support, but its honorary chairmen tended to be manufacturers. Active campaigning for working-class councillors – on the few occasions that it happened – tended to come from elsewhere. The Trades Council had not always been content to prevail upon excellent men. In 1887 and 1890 they supported their own candidates. In doing so they were following the lead of other towns. Aberdeen had two Trades Council councillors as early as 1884,[34] while Edinburgh Trades Council ran two candidates in 1889, one of them successfully.[35]

The Trades Council's 1887 campaign ended in a narrow defeat in Eighth ward for their sole candidate, a ship's carpenter called John Wishart. However, it is worth looking in more detail at their successful 1890 campaign for what it tells us about the relationship of organised labour, in the form of the Trades Council, to the then existing system of municipal politics. That year they selected Robert Bruce, their president, and Robert Ritchie, their secretary, to stand. If successful they were to receive two guineas a week from the Trades Council while they served on the Council. (This was twice the wage of an adult male jute worker,[36] but less than the £2.10s that John Burns was being paid for service on the London County Council by the Trades Council there.) The payment of wages was intended to enable the candidates to attend the daytime council meetings and to counter any allegation that they were in the pocket of any richer member of the Council. This was not the dawn of socialism in Dundee. Bruce and Ritchie stood as labour (with a small 'l') candidates. They were not socialists and were at pains to stress that, while the Trades Council would be paying their wages, they would be there to serve their constituents, not the Trades Council. Bruce told his electors that municipal elections here were not fought on political grounds and that it would be unwise on their part if they fought them on Trades Unionist grounds.[37] The issues they stood on were the usual ones: council economy; the high level of rates; a reduction in the number of drink licences. The desire for working-class membership of the Council was the main motivation for their candidatures. But there was no whiff of revolution in the air. For most, labour representation was simply a way of reducing the number of councillors who were on the Council to further their own interests. The main specific proposal was that the candidates should campaign for a reduction in the rates. Working people would be happy to pay out money to provide wages for working-class members of the Council if they got more back in reduced taxation, one supporter argued.[38] The Trades Council were allying themselves with already existing themes in council politics, not offering a departure.

William Hunter, the retiring provost, who had been contemplating continuing on the Council, may well have stood aside to give Bruce a free run in the Fifth ward. In the Ninth ward, Ritchie received one of the largest votes ever polled in a local election, despite fairly strong opposition from supporters of an experienced sitting councillor. The Liberal establishment in Dundee was not at all perturbed by the two candidates and there was no reason why they should have been. That Labour's first attempt at winning a parliamentary seat in Dundee happened during their term of office – when James Macdonald stood in 1892 – was purely coincidental. Neither Bruce nor Ritchie was connected with the independent Labour movement in Dundee. David Lowe, one of the early Scottish Labour Party members in Dundee, who later joined the Independent Labour Party, and election agent for Macdonald, was not at all keen on the Trades Council, describing them as 'a feckless body'.[39] Ritchie and Bruce did not support Macdonald in 1892. In 1889 Ritchie had been present at the Liberal meeting which selected John Leng, owner of the *Advertiser*, to stand at the by-election caused by the death of one of the sitting members, J. F. B. Firth, rather than at the meetings organised by the Dundee Radical Association and the Scottish Labour Party called to encourage John Burns, the trade-union leader from London, and later MP, to stand.[40] An extract from a song written by a Labour supporter in the largely Tory *Piper O' Dundee*, expresses some of the growing doubts on the left about the worth of the two Trades Council councillors:

> Time wore on and brought cause to fear;
> We looked each other to our neighbour,
> For we heard folks at the babies jeer,
> And the SLP at our Bobbies leer,
> Even sending down their champion, Keir,
> To ask if we *meant* Labour.[41]

The election of the two had held out no great promise of change and none happened. When Bruce died part of the way through his term of office, the Council (which at that time filled vacancies itself without the need for a by-election) replaced him with former provost, William Hunter. The deputation from the Trades Council which asked for one of their nominees to be elected was ignored.[42] The following year the remaining Trades Council councillor, Ritchie, was defeated by the William Blair whose failure to repair his flats was mentioned above.

There were occasional attempts by other members of the working class to enter the Council. Care is required in looking at these. Many were not all they seemed. In several cases it was alleged that working-class candidates were financed by publicans or others in order to oppose councillors who had refused licenses or been obstructive in other ways. One working man who stood several times, John Aimer, was allegedly backed by a licensee who had had trouble at the licensing court from one of the councillors whom he opposed.[43] It is, of course, impossible to be certain of the extent to which these claims are true. It is certainly the case that the Dundee Wine, Spirit and Beer Trade Protection Association [DWSBTPA] used its influence with members and customers to support favoured candidates. It is also the case that on some occasions they were prepared to contribute to the election expenses of candidates.[44] But this was usually done out of the public gaze. Candidates who were happy to receive help were less happy to have it known that they were in receipt of that aid.[45] Unfortunately we do not have the minutes of the DWSBTPA for the period before 1888 when many of these allegations were made against working-class candidates.

As late as 1904 this pattern of municipal politics was still in place. The *Advertiser* reported the result of the municipal election as a victory for the anti-drink movement against the publican rather than for one party or class against another.[46] Indeed the *Advertiser* sided with the Trades Council's criticism of the lack of working-class membership of the Council, suggesting it showed a resemblance to a Council of the era of the unextended franchise: 'It has not merely in its constitution been a body drawn from a single class but it has tended to forgetfulness of the fact that it should represent, without favour, all classes'.[47] But there were stirrings. The Scottish Prohibition Party [SPP], formed in Dundee in 1901, had started to contest municipal elections. The title of the SPP is misleading. Its candidatures were not simply a variation on the 'temperance against drink trade' theme. The party promised that under its influence the Council would issue no licences at all, but it was also a radical socialist party. It sought council office to solve the problems of Dundee's workers. For Edwin Scrymgeour, the inspiration behind the party, the city's problems were caused not just by drink but by capitalism.[48] John Reid, who stood with Prohibitionist and Trades Council support in the Fourth ward in 1904, talked of the evils and tyranny which the apathy of the working class had brought upon them.[49]

The mainstream Labour movement was also becoming more ambitious. The Scottish Workers' Parliamentary Election Committee, the Scottish arm of the Labour Representation Committee, in conjunction with an eager local branch, had begun to consider selecting a candidate for Dundee very soon after their creation in 1900.[50] Few seats were discussed as frequently or with as much optimism as Dundee. George Barnes, the leader of the engineers union and originally from Lochee, was the initial choice of the local party for the seat. Barnes eventually withdrew when the Dundee Liberals refused to support him as a Lib-Lab candidate.[51] It is significant that the response of the Trades and Labour Council to this setback was to immediately start seeking a new candidate. They did not share Barnes's reluctance to break with the Liberals, and some had been unhappy at his negotiations with them.[52] W. F. Black, a local ILP member who worked as a journalist for the *Advertiser* before leaving Dundee to work for the ILP's *Labour Leader*, was selected in his place. Black had many disadvantages as a candidate. He was a poor platform speaker and, more importantly, did not have the financial backing of a union. His selection was more popular with the Dundee ILP than with the trade-union wing of the party.[53] His performance as a prospective candidate did not win the doubters over and Black was told bluntly by the secretary of the Trades and Labour Council that he was 'killing the movement here'.[54] Black resigned leaving the way clear for Dundee to select a candidate who would come with enough backing to make the fight viable. Wilkie was not the unanimous choice of the Labour organisations. The ILP were furious. John Carnegie of the Dundee branch described him privately to Keir Hardie as 'less advanced than either [sic] of the candidates already before the constituency, Tory, Unionist or Liberal'.[55] The preference for Wilkie over Black, for a candidate who came with the finance to win a campaign over a socialist of the kind who was unlikely to make much impact at the polls, was an indication of a new realism and optimism. It was an indication that they were now fighting to win – it was more important to have a candidate who could afford to be an MP than to have one who pleased the ILP.

Suddenly even the non-working-class candidates wanted to be working class. The working-class vote had always been appealed to quite deliberately. But this now took on a new intensity. In 1904 Peter Girrity and David Buttar both described themselves as 'The Working Man's Popular Candidate' in their municipal election campaigns. Neither was by any means a working man. Girrity was in fact a substantial contractor much of his work having been with public bodies.[56] Though he described himself at one meeting as a retired working man, he was a well-off retired man. Buttar was a solicitor who described himself as having exactly the same interests as the working man[57] and having been persuaded to stand by a large number of working men.[58] Whatever his motives, he was certainly not an unqualified friend of all representatives of labour. Within a few years he enlivened one council meeting by attempting to strangle Edwin Scrymgeour.[59] Scrymgeour himself, in a direct reversal of the frequent election tactic of proclaiming oneself a substantial ratepayer whose business acumen would be an asset on the Council, declared prominently on his election leaflet, 'His only Property Interests, the Commonweal' and urged the electors to 'Give the Worker's Representative a Trial'.[60]

In 1905 Scrymgeour, on his second attempt, was elected to the Council. Also elected was Labour's John Carnegie, the first Labour member of Dundee Town Council. Worse was to come for the Liberals. Only two months after this municipal breakthrough the Dundee electorate made Wilkie their first Labour MP. Wilkie's victory was both a contribution to and a reflection of the change in climate. But it would be wrong to read too much into this event. Ideologically Wilkie was not someone who caused pre-war Liberals to lose much sleep. Some Liberal supporters saw the appropriate response as being to adopt Wilkie as a

Liberal candidate for subsequent elections, thus ensuring that the Liberals again held both seats.[61] The real irritation was that Wilkie had won in Dundee without their permission. In 1902 Sir John Leng, one of the sitting Liberal MPs, had dismissed the idea of a Labour member replacing him on his retirement as 'premature and uncalled for'.[62] By 1906 the Liberals were unable to stop one being elected. It was this powerlessness that caused so much pain.

Many tried to minimise the scale of the change by attributing Labour's victory in 1906 to electioneering technique, rather than anything more fundamental. The *Piper O'Dundee* concluded that the obvious lesson of the election was 'organise, organise and again organise'.[63] The *Advertiser* had claimed that the 'Labourists' had had the support of a large body of skilled election workers and more cars than the other parties. Wilkie had a committee of 400 working for him, led by people he had brought with him from Newcastle.[64] They used a system of polling cards to be handed in by voters to party staff on the gates of polling stations so that the party's efforts could be focused on those who had not voted, something that the *Advertiser* saw as an attempt to subvert the Ballot Act.[65] The voting results certainly show that Labour was well organised. Of their candidate's 6,833 votes 2,533 were plumpers (those who had used only one of their two votes for the Labour candidate), 3,183 were combined with the sitting Liberal and only 124 with the second Liberal candidate and nearly 1,000 with the Unionist candidates (see Figure 8). If more had given their second votes to the second Liberal then he would certainly have won.

Figure 8: Dundee Parliamentary Election 1906 – cross voting for Alex Wilkie.

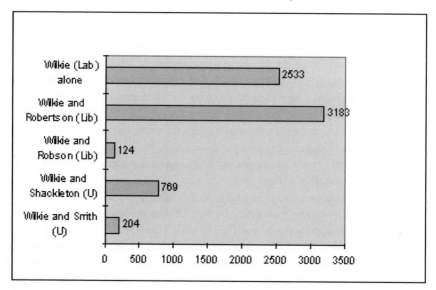

Source: *Dundee Year Book, 1906*, 15.

But this degree of organisation had existed before. In 1895 the Labour candidate Macdonald, despite coming a long way behind, had managed to ensure that only twenty-one of his second votes went to the second-placed Liberal. The difference was that whereas in 1895 party organisation had made the most effective use of 1,313 votes, in 1906 it had more than five times that number to work with.

Labour also had greater financial resources then ever before. In 1892 the Scottish Labour Party had stood a candidate 'with a splendid disregard of such minor details as ways and means'.[66] Labour in 1906, because they had selected a man whose union was prepared to back him, were able to spend as much on their candidate as was spent on the two Liberals combined.[67] The view from inside the Labour Party was not so sanguine about the skills of the Dundee party. The ILP organiser for the area thought the Dundee ILP one of his most difficult and ineffective charges.[68] One party member admitted that the Labour movement was unable to help one (successful) Labour candidate at all in one municipal election 'owing to a lack of organisation and a surfeit of work'.[69] The change in attitude in Dundee in the years before 1906 is indicative of something far deeper than a sharpening of the skills of the Dundee Labour Party. Other parties would have to improve their organisation – not because Labour had improved theirs, but because Dundee was suddenly no longer a one-party city.

This break with the past was not primarily based on ideology. Wilkie's selection as a candidate had been seen as a backward step by Carnegie and the ILP. For years he and others in the ILP had, he said, won over 'most thinking men in the town'. They found it difficult to support a man 'who seems to understand nothing of the causes of poverty, and whose sympathy is only for the trade unionist, and the extent of his political outlook to obviate the possibility of another Taff Vale decision'.[70] Several non-Labour councillors were happy to accept the LRC Council programme by 1908.[71] The real issue was not ideas, but the independence of Labour. Working-class political activists were no longer prepared to beg for favours from the Liberals. The suggestion that they should, now caused anger. When Barnes withdrew because the Liberals would not support him one Dundonian told Keir Hardie, that the more he thought about it 'the more I feel inclined to swear'.[72]

The full impact on the Liberals and the existing order on the Town Council of the change that had brought about Wilkie's election could be seen at the municipal elections of November 1906. The response of the Liberal *Advertiser* to a municipal election in that year, in which the first list of declared candidates suggested further breaking down of the single-class structure of the Council (that they had so deplored only two years before), was almost panic. Again the call for the leading citizens to enter municipal life was heard, but this time it was in a new context. It is worth quoting some of the coverage at length to get a flavour of their vehemence:

If the respectable citizens of Dundee do not quickly bestir themselves they are likely to regret that the representative principle was ever applied to municipal government . . . the very fact that some of the people named above [they had listed the candidates] think there is no impropriety in soliciting the confidence of the ratepayers shows that the general estimation of what is decent and proper is sadly at fault. If most of these candidates are fit to represent the city then the standard of fitness has fallen deplorably low. Should the misfortune fall upon us of seeing some of them elected it will be necessary for Dundee to make apologies to Tammany . . . this shunning of Council work by the true leaders of the city cannot longer continue . . . instead of a motley crowd of drink trade associates, insurance canvassers, loquacious lawyers and working class discontents we want a corporation formed of the best that the city has to show in talent, experience and character.[73]

In taking the action it did the *Advertiser* was consciously harking back to a campaign of forty years before when, in 1868, a similar call to the wealthy had been organised. On that occasion the call had been successful. It had been so, at least in part, because it was supported by the working class. James Cox, partner in one of the city's largest textile companies, one of the manufacturers who consented to stand, relates in his diary how he had refused a request to stand from a deputation of 'leading gentlemen' but had changed his mind after being asked by some working men.[74] Such working-class organisations as there were in 1868, the Dundee Working Men's Association and the Dundee United Trades Council, had fully supported the *Advertiser*'s campaign. In 1906 the attitude of the organised working class was very different. The ILP and the SPP turned up at the citizens' meeting organised by the *Advertiser*. But, far from supporting its aim, they heckled constantly, the ILP denouncing the meeting as 'a discreditable manoeuvre in the interests of the wealthy classes in Dundee'. The consensus behind the idea that encouraging the wealthy to become involved in municipal politics was the solution to all problems had now disappeared. A correspondent in the Glasgow-based Labour newspaper *Forward* noted that 'Never before in Dundee has such a platform as that which presented itself in the Kinnaird Hall received such a hostile reception from the workers, or so completely failed to impose its will upon them'.[75]

If the working class were no longer prepared to defer to the wealthy as the best people to run the town, then neither was the Liberal establishment prepared to doff its cap to the innate worth of the working class in the way it had done before. An article in the *Advertiser* by 'A Citizen' in 1906 explained why working-class candidates for the Council were suspect. Any wage earner concerned with fulfilling his responsibilities to his family and his home would not sacrifice the loss of wages necessary for council work, therefore any working-class man prepared to make this sacrifice was of the type who would sacrifice his home and family and so could not be trusted. 'You may run the 160,000 people of Dundee through a sieve without obtaining a suitable candidate from the real working class', the correspondent went on.[76] Not that all of the candidates who so worried the *Advertiser* were from the working class. Two of the Labour candidates were skilled manual or white collar workers, but the *Advertiser* was no more keen on Walter Walsh, the clergyman Labour candidate, or George Kiddie Smith, the business-owning Prohibitionist.

Some of the candidates in 1906 may have been less than ideal. James Reid, the ILP candidate (the others from the left were Labour Representation Committee or SPP candidates) was described privately by the ILP organiser on the east coast as 'vindictive and implacable, a man who often lost work because he irritated employers and aggravated workers'.[77] But there was no rational reason for the *Advertiser* campaign if, as stated, concern about the occupations of candidates was the reason for their anxiety. The Council of the first decade of the twentieth century was much improved in terms of its composition from that of the previous two decades if one uses the traditional measure of unsuitability: membership of either the licensed or building trades. In the 1880s over one-third of candidatures in Dundee were from the licensed or building trades. Between 1900 and 1910 these trades accounted for less than 13% of candidatures. It was the changed politics that caused their rage, not the standard of the candidates.

The air of change present in the years around 1906 was evident in a number of fields. 1906 was the year that saw the formation of the Jute and Flax Workers' Union, born out of a strike and dissatisfaction with the Mill and Factory Operatives' Union, which had been led by a local clergyman. Walker has pointed out some of the linkages between this and Labour's electoral success.[78] The SPP was growing fast. Its income quadrupled between 1905 and 1906 (from £90 to £373) and then nearly doubled the following year.[79] The ILP was, according to its own organiser, in less good shape in 1906.[80] But even this was soon changed. Just over a year later he reported a new spirit and fresh life in the branch, together with an influx of new members, many of them women.[81] The Council was changed too. In 1908 Scrymgeour proudly claimed that the 'coterie' system which saw the majority of members skip over council business while a small group of influential members took decisions outside the Council chamber was ended and that a number of councillors who preferred the quiet life that that system had given them had retired to their firesides.[82] Admitting much the same thing, but with less approval, the *Advertiser* had declared the year before that Scrymgeour 'creates an atmosphere from which good members retreat in disgust . . . and into which it becomes increasingly difficult to persuade desirable representatives of the solid sense of the community to enter'.[83]

The rapidity of change in Dundee is proof that unity is not always essential to strength. The ILP and the LRC were, as we have seen, divided over the selection of a parliamentary candidate. The Prohibitionists were always at war with everyone else. Scrymgeour's contribution to the election of Dundee's first Labour MP was to heckle at his meetings to the extent that he was threatened with ejection.[84] People flitted from organisation to organisation. John Reid left the SPP for the ILP. Scrymgeour had been in the ILP before the founding of the SPP. Walter Walsh went from the Liberals to the SPP, to Labour and then back to the Liberals again within the space of seven years. (Despite standing as a Labour candidate he was not a member of any Labour organisation and declined to join on the curious grounds that it would be better for Labour if he did not join as he could serve them best as an independent.[85])

The presence of someone like Walsh as a Labour candidate indicates one of the barriers the Labour movement had still to break. While middle-class men were describing themselves as 'working men's candidates' the Labour movement had trouble adapting to the idea that genuinely working-class candidates could win municipal elections. Candidates from the ILP, LRC and SPP in the first decade of the century included a clergyman (Walsh), one full-time politician (Scrymgeour), a manual worker who had graduated to owning his own business (he was described as a 'prominent businessman' rather than a politician in his 1928 obituary), and a shopkeeper, as well as a few manual and white-collar employees. Walker has suggested, convincingly, that the early Labour movement in Dundee sought a place in society which they were aware was beyond their usual station and which provoked disbelief and hostility from the electorate. Because of this they had adopted a seriousness of manner that made them ridiculous to Dundonians.[86] The appearance of respectability (as well as the substance) was still important to the Labour movement in the early twentieth century. The feeling that they were getting above their station had not completely gone. When the leading lights of the Labour movement in Dundee had portrait photographs taken they were in stiff formal poses with grim unsmiling faces.[87] Not for them the flat-capped appearance of, for example, The Working Man's Popular Candidate, Peter Girrity, in the 1904 election.[88] In selecting candidates from the middle classes, however, they probably made a mistake. The political mood had moved ahead of them. Status had become a distinctly double-edged electoral tool. Employers were now mistrusted for their status as employers, whatever their political views. The SPP candidate who owned his own business almost had to apologise for the fact – inviting the union that represented his workers along to his meetings to vouch for the fact that he was a good employer.[89] A despairing *Courier* noted that at one 1906 meeting 'many of those present seemed to have come with the sole idea of questioning the candidate on the wages he paid his employees'.[90] The *Advertiser*'s view in the 1870s that the way councillors treated their employees was irrelevant and should not even be mentioned may have been accurate then as far as most of the electorate was concerned.[91] By 1906 this was certainly not the case. Perhaps Walsh's vacillations between Labour and the Liberals were enough to cure Labour of this deference. In 1908 John Reid, elected a Labour councillor in 1907, was denouncing Walsh as someone who was not yet class conscious and so was unable to be a Labour member.[92]

On its own Wilkie's victory could be dismissed as an aberration that held no great portent. But taken together with the new heat that was displayed in municipal elections in the early years of the twentieth century it was an indicator of a fundamental shift in Dundee politics. A new politics, built on class, now existed. Patrick Joyce has written that popular Liberalism, and popular Toryism, were about the union of classes against class.[93] In Dundee that union had been strong until the early years of the twentieth century. By 1906 it was seriously breached. It took another fifteen years for the transformation of Dundee politics to be complete. At a by-election in 1908 when Labour, against the wishes of the party nationally, and of Wilkie (who sent an emissary to try to prevent the adoption of a candidate[94]), ran G. H. Stuart against the Liberal Winston Churchill, they were beaten. The reaction was to have far-reaching effects for Labour in Scotland. In retaliation the Labour Party nationally – annoyed at the risk that running two candidates in Dundee presented to agreements between Labour and the Liberals in many English two-members seats – decided it would affiliate branches in Scotland, ending the independence of the Scottish Workers' Representation Committee.[95] This ensured that there was no second Labour candidate for Dundee in 1910. Had the Labour Party nationally, and Alex Wilkie, been prepared to campaign against Churchill in 1908 and select a second candidate in 1910 then it is conceivable, though perhaps unlikely, that the Liberals would have been removed from Dundee even earlier. As it was each restricted themselves to a single candidate in 1910, in effect presenting a united front against the Unionists.

But by 1922 both of the city's parliamentary seats were in the hands of the left, one held by Labour's E. D. Morel, the other by Scrymgeour of the SPP – successful on his sixth attempt. Council elections were polarised between Labour and an alliance of anti-Labour forces under the name of the Municipal Electors' Association. In 1920 the *Advertiser* was asking the electors whether they wanted a town council or the 'soviet' that voting Labour would bring.[96] In Dundee at least this breakthrough was not caused by the war or its aftermath. The old political mould was cracked almost a decade before the war. It is then that the earnest, and hitherto ignored, activists of the ILP, the LRC and the SPP began to be electorally attractive in municipal and parliamentary politics. The change was not immediately obvious to all. Winston Churchill's belief, on accepting an offer to stand for Dundee in the 1908 by-election, that it would be a 'seat for life', turned out to be wrong. But, despite the presence of the Labour member who also sat for the seat, he cannot be blamed for thinking that way at the time. The peaceful co-existence of Wilkie and Churchill was deceptive and owed more to the unwillingness of the national Labour Party to fight for both seats than the aspirations of local activists. Walker has suggested that Wilkie's election was a confirmation of Dundee's Liberalism rather than a challenge to it.[97] There is truth in this to the extent that ideologically Wilkie differed little from his predecessors in the seat – and he was certainly less radical than the version of Winston Churchill which was current in 1908. Neither did Wilkie himself wish to further challenge the Dundee

Liberals, believing that Labour 'had no right' to ask for more than a share of the representation of the city, given their 'revealed vote'.[98] (A somewhat bizarre doctrine that would have meant a permanent *status quo* on the basis that the challenger had not won the previous election.) But, whatever his shortcomings in the eyes of Dundee socialists, Wilkie's election was a profound declaration of independence by the Dundee working class. Liberalism held on – but only at the whim of an electorate who could no longer be relied upon. Because Dundee was a two-member seat, continuity and change could live side by side for a while. With each party nominating only one candidate the final choice between Liberal and Labour could be delayed. 90% of those who voted for the Labour candidate in the December 1910 election also voted for the Liberal. How many did this willingly we do not know. In an election address for the earlier election of that year Churchill had welcomed the 'steady yet gradual development of Labour representation' as something that would change and improve the flexible British constitution. 'The people can be trusted. They are of age. They can act for themselves.'[99] A study of the changing municipal politics in Dundee would perhaps have indicated to him that once the people realised they could act for themselves the old cross-class alliance that was Liberalism was doomed.

TEN

'City of the future': James Thomson's vision of the city beautiful

Bob Harris

Cities were not merely emporiums for goods, centres for commerce and trade. They were something more than a mere cash nexus. They were places where utility, comfort and beauty could be and ought to be combined, so that the passer-by could have his or her artistic senses awakened and be made to feel better for having lived in and seen beautiful buildings every day.

(John Burns, address to the 1910 Royal Institute of British Architects [RIBA] Conference on Town Planning.)

THE EARLY TWENTIETH century saw a burgeoning confidence, amongst some at least, that, through the influence of town planning, the ugly, disordered and unhealthy city of the nineteenth century could be banished for ever.[1] Through their transformed urban fabric, the new cities would reflect a confidence in progress and new technologies, and in the progressiveness of their government. The disharmony and squalor which had disfigured the city in the previous century were to be removed; or rather, out of the disorder and misery of the nineteenth-century industrial city was to emerge a different, revitalised city – efficient, healthy, socially cohesive, and beautiful – in short, the 'city of the future'.

This chapter explores Dundee's participation in the early town-planning movement and the ways in which, under its influence, several individuals began, from the turn of the twentieth century, to imagine a new and radically different future for Dundee. A key figure in the story which will unfold is James Thomson. Born in Edinburgh in 1852, and after having served an apprenticeship to one of the capital's civil-engineering firms, Thomson arrived in the town in 1873 to join the staff of William Mackison, from 1868, the town's burgh engineer. For the next fifty years he was to work for the municipal authority. In 1904, he became city architect; two years later, he added to this the office of city engineer.[2] It was Thomson's singular achievement to absorb the most advanced, new currents of thinking about urban renewal and planning in the early twentieth century and to seek to apply them to his adopted home.

The gap between what was conceivable and what was actually achievable was, nevertheless, a large one, and there was a constant tension between what Thomson and others envisaged and what was done. In Dundee (as elsewhere) the major constraint was financial. If there was one constant in local politics in this period it was opposition, or potential opposition, to rising rates.[3] There were also well-placed conservative forces on the Council and its committees, and, increasingly, a new challenge in the form of the forces of organised labour and Socialist-influenced parties. Political support for costly municipal initiatives, especially those which did not offer the prospect of immediate, material improvements to the lives of the working classes, was before the Great War becoming more difficult to mould. Yet for all that this could be a chapter about impractical visions and much more limited achievement, the outlines of a different theme can begin to be discerned. This concerns how far Dundee, in significant measure through the actions of its municipal authorities, began after 1870 to recover from the problems of rapid surges of growth in the 1820s and again from the mid-century, and the way in which the authorities sought to construct a civic image in which improvement, progressiveness and modernity were essential elements. This was in line with developments in other major British cities at this time; nevertheless, it is an aspect of Dundee's history which has largely remained overshadowed by the emphasis which is often placed (not unreasonably) on the gravity and scale of social problems confronting the city and its population in the late Victorian and Edwardian eras.

Municipal efforts to control the development of the urban landscape in Dundee grew significantly from the 1870s. Although 1867 had seen new statutory powers conferred on the Council to undertake road improvements, it is 1871, the year in which the Dundee Police and Improvement Act was passed, which marks the crucial turning point in this context. Under this act, William Mackison directed a twenty-year programme of development of the central part of Dundee, excluding the Vault, the Overgate and parts of the High Street. Existing streets were either widened and gradients lessened (the Murraygate, Seagate, Nethergate) or extended (the High Street, Gellatly Street, Guthrie Street, Kincardine Street, and Victoria Street), and several new ones constructed (Commercial Street, Victoria Road, Whitehall Street and Whitehall Crescent).[4] Several motives lay behind the improvement programme, notably the clearance of insanitary areas, together with the 'slum dwellers' who inhabited them (over-crowding was directly linked in the contemporary mind to immorality, crime and disease), and the aggrandisement of the city's urban fabric and street architecture. Changing modes of transport also acted as a strong impetus to action. The 1870s saw the rise of tramways, which required straight, broad, unobstructed roads to run on.[5] In Dundee, the tramlines were – something which was relatively unusual at this date – publically built and owned, although they were initially leased by the police commissioners to a private company; it was not until 1893 that the operation of the trams came under direct municipal control. In the years which followed, tramlines were substantially extended to reach the more important working-class districts and outlying villages, such as Lochee, Downfield, Nine-wells, and Monifieth. In 1898, the city adopted overhead electric lines to power the trams; hitherto, they had been a combination of horse-drawn and steam-driven. There was even an abortive experiment before the Great War, the first in Scotland, with a trackless line along the Clepington Road.[6] A further stimulus behind municipal concern with roads and communications was the rise of motorised transport from the 1900s, and Thomson was, in his role as city engineer, to play a crucial role in this sphere. (Thomson's Kingsway, built after the Great War, was one of the first arterial roads to be constructed in the United Kingdom.)

Attempts were also made to regulate new building from the same period. Again, the 1871 Improvement Act was a milestone in this context. This act was designed to lapse after ten years, and was followed by a new act in 1882, which also contained important building regulations. How stringently these were enforced is much harder to say, and there were complaints in 1874 that the new powers were not being used.[7] Nevertheless, there were also other signs of increasing efforts on the part of the municipal authorities to create a more healthy, efficient and pleasant environment. The 1860s and 1870s saw a proliferation of new building types for public and semi-public use. These included bath and wash houses (the first district baths were erected in the 1890s); museums (the final stage of the Albert Institute, the Victoria Galleries, was opened in 1889) and libraries (the early 1900s saw, thanks to the generosity of the Scots-American steel magnate, Andrew Carnegie, several branch libraries built in different parts of the city – Blackness Library, Coldside Library – and new central reading rooms in Ward Road); schools (the school board was a major sponsor of new building, including the Technical Institute in Bell Street, opened in 1911); hospitals (a 'palatial' new poor-law hospital was opened in 1903); as well as cemeteries (the Eastern Necropolis and Western Necropolis) and markets of various kinds.[8] Following the gift of Baxter Park (1863), the increase of open space became a central plank in municipal policy, as in other large Scottish and British towns and cities. Balgay Park was acquired in 1870. In 1871, access to Magdalen Green, long a site of local recreation, was secured. The same decade also saw municipal control of the Esplanade between Craig Pier and Magdalen Green achieved. In 1886, a plan to extend the Esplanade up to Ninewells, through a programme of land reclamation was adopted. Dundee Law was acquired in 1878; Barrack Park (soon to be re-named Dudhope Park) in 1893; and Victoria Park in 1907. Municipal efforts were aided by substantial donations of land by wealthy Dundonians. Lochee Park was presented to the community by the Cox brothers in 1899. By 1912, the city boasted parks covering around 260 acres.[9] In the same year, Sir James Caird donated what was to become Caird Park to the city. Concerted efforts were also made after 1900 to improve their recreational value through provision of summer concerts, bowling greens, and finally, in 1915, tennis courts. The Law was improved as part of the work-relief scheme in 1908. Baxter Park had come into municipal control in 1903 after which it was extensively improved.[10] There were also open spaces dispersed throughout the town, on a number of which play facilities for children were erected. In 1907, the Council undertook measures to provide these in areas where there was no easy access to parks.[11] Trees were also planted along substantial stretches of road, for example, the Esplanade.

The municipal-led improvement and moulding of the townscape and urban environment extended still further. The general pattern is one common to many Scottish towns and cities in this period, encompassing municipal provision of water, gas, electricity, better cleansing, lighting and sanitary inspection, and greater efforts to control environmental pollution. In all these areas, the municipal record in Dundee would appear to be broadly comparable with other places, although this is a topic which requires systematic investigation.[12] On the other hand, there was a smaller increase in rates between 1890–1914 in Dundee compared to Glasgow, Edinburgh or indeed Aberdeen, the nearest to it in terms of population.[13] An important explanation for this may have been the strength of local opposition to increases in municipal expenditure, although this was also influential in other places. As Lord Provost Sir James Urquhart complained in 1914: 'One platform plank which seldom failed at election times was "capital expenditure" and the "rates are going up"'.[14]

Given the appalling incidence of overcrowding and prevalence of poor housing conditions in Dundee in this period – starkly revealed to contemporaries in the 1905 Dundee Social Union [DSU] report on housing and industrial conditions – it is perhaps surprising that there was no municipal provision of housing before 1914 in Dundee, unlike, say, Edinburgh, Glasgow, Aberdeen or even Perth. There were various possibilities open to the Council in this context, the most obvious being raising cheap loans to buy land and construct housing under the 1890 Housing of the Working Classes Act. There was considerable official and unofficial interest in this act in Dundee in the early 1890s and again in 1901.[15] Yet no action resulted. From 1905, there was a strong push to build model tenements in Blackscroft, and plans were prepared by Thomson.[16] Edwin Scrymgeour, the leader of the Scottish Prohibitionist Party, and other self-proclaimed representatives of Labour and the working classes, strongly supported the principle of municipal housing; however, they were opposed to the specific proposal as insufficiently generous in its provision of space. Other critics included the Reverend Walter Walsh, who was, as we will see later, to be a key ally of Thomson's in the cause of town planning. Walsh argued that the Blackscroft scheme was a 'bit of patchwork';[17] he was at this stage demanding a far more comprehensive approach to the housing question. Data was collected about municipal housing from other places, and this showed that almost none was profitable or even realised its annual charge on municipal finances.[18]

This was a period in which rates were climbing, and economy and financial management in local government were becoming extremely sensitive issues. The main attacks in Dundee came from Scrymgeour and his allies (dubbed the 'busy bodies' by the local Liberal press), ever anxious to assert the prevalence of cronyism and jobbery in council business. It was also, however, a trend which produced a movement amongst ratepayers for economy and probity on the

Council, one which came to a head in 1908.[19] Yet it was not just the financial implications which deterred the Council from financing tenement or cottage construction. Opinion was divided at the national level, and much of it hostile to the idea. One of the potential attractions of town planning, and the development of garden-city style suburbs, was that this appeared to provide a better, less financially burdensome, option. The theory was that artisans would move out of the city centre into the new houses, thus allowing movement into the now vacant, better properties amongst the unskilled and the poor. Both Walsh and Thomson cleaved to this view for most of the period. In some ways, the Logie scheme, opened in 1920 and the first proper example of municipal housing in Dundee, built under the terms of the 1919 Housing and Town Planning Act (Scotland), was an extension of the same underlying view.[20] Whether it was a realistic solution, given the composition and structure of the local labour force and levels of poverty in Dundee, is a moot point, as some argued at the time, and as Thomson may later have come to recognise.[21] Nevertheless, influential figures in the town-planning movement propounded it very vigorously, such as J. C. Nettlefold, who was responsible for Birmingham's housing and town-planning policy and who was an important voice in national debates given Birmingham's progressive record on these things.[22] Although there are signs that a shift in attitudes was taking place immediately before the war, it was to take the war, and the prospect of treasury subsidy, to induce the Dundee Council finally to embrace the option of municipal housing.

There was another alternative, which Dundee did adopt before 1914 – sanitary inspection and the forced improvement or demolition of buildings declared unfit for human habitation. There was no attempt, however, at wholesale purchase and clearing of unsanitary districts, except under the aegis of improvement schemes, for which specific parliamentary powers were necessary. Rather the Council utilised more limited powers created by the 1882 Police and Improvement Consolidation Act, referred to earlier. A major crusade against unfit buildings took place between 1890–97. In this period, 246 buildings were either demolished, their use changed to non-domestic, or improved. This policy was resumed in the mid-1900s, under the influence of Walsh and the Housing and Town Planning committee, when specific blackspots were identified and dwellings within them subject to more rigorous inspection and regulatory action. In the four years from the point at which the crusade was resumed, 298 houses were closed, while 800 others were improved.[23]

There were, therefore, important local precedents for the adoption of town planning in Dundee in the 1900s. To understand this development more fully, however, we need also to set it firmly against the background of national and indeed international debates about urban reform, and in particular the enthusiasm generated by the 1909 Housing and Town Planning Act. In retrospect, the huge stimulus to debates about town planning created by this act can appear odd; the legislation was actually very limited in scope as far as planning itself was concerned, and it attracted many critics. Its town planning clauses were permissive not mandatory – in other words, local authorities could adopt them at their discretion; they also only extended to areas of land which were unbuilt on or under development.[24] Notwithstanding such limitations, however, an architectural profession eager to strengthen its own credentials and public standing enthusiastically embraced it, or the possibilities it appeared to create. The architect was portrayed as the hero of urban renewal in periodicals such as the *Builder* and the *Town Planning Review* – founded in 1910, thanks to the generosity of William Lever, the great soap magnate, who also endowed a chair of town planning at Liverpool University to promote the new discipline. The architect was more than anything now a creative artist, someone who distilled pattern from disorder, who fashioned pleasant surroundings, and uplifting visions of a new urban world. It was a vision which encompassed new schemes of housing laid out on garden-city lines, zoning of land use, urban parkways, improved communications, and monumental civic centres.

That Dundee began at an early stage to embrace this new gospel owed a great deal to Thomson, but perhaps even more to the Reverend Walter Walsh, elected to the Council in 1906. Patrick Geddes, Professor of Botany at University College – a propagandist of international repute for town planning, albeit a very idiosyncratic one – appears to have exercised remarkably little influence, at least that is discernable.[25] He did propose the creation of botanic gardens to the Council in 1906, but this failed to win support from councillors largely on the too predictable grounds of cost; he also gave a series of lectures on town planning in the city in 1909, entitled 'Bonnie Dundee, a study of possible improvements'.[26] Perhaps his greatest contribution to the early town- planning movement was his emphasis on the importance of the civic survey as a prelude to any planning project. Interestingly, in 1912, as part of the response to Thomson's first major report on town planning, proposals for just such a survey were made.[27] These were dropped, although some photographs of the proposed improvements were included in the British Association exhibition mounted to accompany the body's visit to the city in 1912.[28]

Walsh's influence was much more direct and immediately apparent. From 1907, be became a forceful, passionate advocate of town planning as the solution to the city's social ills. He may well have embraced the new faith even earlier; he was one of several local personalities who were in 1901 members of the Dundee and District Housing Reform Council. The National Housing Reform Council [NHRC] was a propagandist body, founded by Henry Aldridge of Leicester, dedicated to popularising town planning, though a network of local committees and associations, and educating those in local government about it. It was the NHRC which can claim a great deal of the credit for the 1909 Housing and Town Planning Act.[29] What needs to be emphasised is just how enthusiastically Walsh promoted the cause of town planning in Dundee following his election to the Council as a representative of Labour, a step motivated in large part by his reaction to the problems and suffering revealed in the 1905 DSU report, referred to above.[30] His election to the Council marked a turning point in its approach to housing and interest in planning. In 1907, Walsh called on his fellow councillors to adopt the 1890 Housing of the Working Classes Act.[31] In the same year, he attended an International Housing Congress which organised visits to see recent housing developments in Sheffield, Liverpool, Port Sunlight, and Bournville. At this congress, Walsh cornered John Burns, ministerial architect of the 1909 act, and urged him to include Scotland in any new planning legislation.[32] Two years later (in 1909) Walsh and Thomson inspected recent examples of continental town planning in Germany and France as part of a continental town-planning tour organised by the NHRC.[33] In 1910, one newspaper printed a cartoon of Walsh, portraying him contemplating the city from a neighbouring hill laid out as a garden city. Walsh was a man driven by the intensity of his own imagination. He was also impatient with his fellow councillors for what he saw as their untimely economy and lack of vision. He was equally critical of 'institutionalism', by which he meant philanthropic measures and establishments, as a response to the city's social ills.[34] What was required was a fundamental transformation, and that transformation was to be effected by town planning.

It was Walsh who was also the principal mover behind the appointment of a special *ad hoc* committee on housing in 1907. In 1908, this committee produced a remarkable report, which fully reflected his influence as convenor.[35] It embodied all the key elements and thinking of the emergent town-planning movement – zoning, planning of unbuilt-on areas, creation of garden suburbs, erection of cottages rather than tenements, municipal purchase of land, municipal housing. It also contained the germs of Thomson's plan for the Kingsway, later contained in his 1918 comprehensive report on town planning and development. This was designed as an urban parkway, linking the city's major parks with a tree-lined arterial road. Walsh's report was, however, not adopted by the Council, according to him because of an unholy alliance of Scrymgeour and other Labour representatives and cheese-paring unimaginative councillors.[36]

One element, nevertheless, was: a permanent Housing and Town Planning Committee. It was this body, under the direction of Walsh until 1912, which was to provide Thomson with his opportunity. Walsh also claimed in 1908 that his report had been commended by Nettlefold and also by the Manchester housing reformer and propagandist for German town-extension planning, T. C. Horsfall.[37] Under Walsh's tutelage, the Council also began *before* 1909 exploring the possibility of laying out garden-city suburbs on land to be feued for that purpose by two separate individuals, at Clepington and on an area of the Craigie estate.[38]

To pursue Thomson through every turn, setback, and achievement of his planning activities from 1909 would be to follow a winding, tortuous path. The most important reports were produced in 1910 and 1918. There was a supplementary report to the 1910 report, which appeared in 1911; reports on the central improvement scheme made possible by the donation in 1914 of

£100,000 by Sir James Caird to build a town hall; reports on three town-planning schemes for garden-city suburbs prepared before the war; and further reports on housing schemes during the war, and another report after the war on the city's housing needs.[39] The 1918 report was the culmination or summation of work and thinking done in the previous decade. It was also the substantial work which had been done prior to 1914 that helped Thomson and Dundee win the 'municipal derby' to be the first authority in Scotland to build council housing (the Logie scheme) after 1918.[40]

The subject of the 1910 report and the 1911 supplementary one was a central improvement scheme. At its heart was a programme of street widening and realignment designed to open up a series of vistas and spaces; the construction of a new covered public market behind the old William Adam townhouse in the High Street; and the creation of a large area on the foreshore on which to build a new city hall and municipal buildings. (The basic elements of the re-development are shown on Plates 33 and 34, taken from the 1910 report.) The focus of the transformed civic centre would be the river, as well as the municipal buildings. Thomson showed this very clearly in a series of water-colour illustrations executed to accompany the report (Plates 35 and 36). The supplementary report concerned the exploitation of the reclaimed esplanade. Thomson also suggested the construction of a road bridge on the foundations of the old rail bridge. In both reports, he emphasised the utility of the plans, as well as their obvious aesthetic ambitions. The street widening and clearance of land necessitated by the plans would involve the destruction of several concentrations of slum properties left untouched by Mackison's improvements of the 1870s. He also argued that the cost could be recouped by an increase in land values and the product of the rents of business and retail properties on new streets.

What was the significance of these plans? The first thing which needs to be explained is why begin with a central improvement scheme at all. Had clearance of slums been the principal motivation, other areas of the city were demanding of more immediate attention, for example, along the Hawkhill. Thomson himself appears to have already been thinking on a larger canvas, and this is the first key to understanding the plans; the central improvement scheme was an element in a wider programme of improvement and urban re-design to be carried out in line with advanced contemporary thinking on town planning and urban renewal. In 1910, Thomson was already preparing a plan of all unbuilt land in the city for town-planning purposes. In November, he showed plans of this land, and areas which might be selected under the terms of the 1909 Housing and Town Planning Act, and future parks and open spaces.[41] Following a visit to the Royal Institute of British Architects (RIBA) 1910 conference on town planning, Thomson and Walsh also presented a 'plan of action', which included slum clearance, housing schemes, arterial routes, parks and open spaces, and land purchase beyond the city boundary.[42] Thomson's declared ambition was also, however, to present a vision of a civic centre which would embody not just a sense of local pride in Dundee and its achievements, but also its progressive character and leadership.

Again this needs to be seen from local and national, and even international, perspectives. Thomson's plans were at the same time bold and imaginative and decidedly conventional. Monumentalism, the architectural style he chose for his civic centre, was a key element of early discussions about town planning, especially amongst architects. It was in America rather than Britain, where the city-beautiful movement waxed most strong, that grand plans for civic centres were most common in this period, the most famous and most publicised being Daniel Burnham's 1909 plans for Chicago.[43] (Thomson and Walsh would have seen these at the exhibition which accompanied the 1910 RIBA conference on town planning.) Under Professor Stanley Adshead, the new town-planning department at Liverpool University was also sponsoring plans for civic redevelopment in Liverpool. T. H. Mawson, the landscape architect, produced an ambitious plan for a civic centre in Dunfermline in the 1900s, also exhibited at the RIBA conference in London. The civic centre was seen as the supreme expression in architectural form of civic pride; it presented an ennobling vision of the city to its citizens and to those who were visitors. It also represented a striking declaration of confidence in the city, its past, present and future. Such notions were not new, as any of the great Victorian town halls make clear, but they were articulated with great clarity in this period. There was also unexampled emphasis on the position of the civic centre and the composition of the different architectural elements which it was made up from. The civic centre should be in a position of eminence but separate from the business and commercial centres. As one historian has written:

> The civic centre was intended to be a beautiful ensemble, an architectonic triumph far more breathtaking than a single building . . . Grouping public buildings around a park, square, or intersection of radial streets allowed the visual delights of perspectives, open spaces, and the contrasts between the buildings and their umbrageous settings.[44]

Professor Adshead made a similar point at the time:

> A great city must be built on a great scale; it must have wide streets, wide sidewalks, and big buildings simply composed; it must concentrate its interest at points, and must not spread it about with reckless waste.[45]

Architects and city authorities were also urged to eschew the Gothic architecture of the previous generation in favour of a neo-classical architectural language of scale, dignity and order. Paradoxically perhaps, neo-classicism was seen as the proper language of modernity and progress.[46] Thomson had already overseen construction of a building in neo-classical style, the Coldside Library. His drawings for civic buildings show him thinking (or imagining) on an altogether grander scale.

Thomson had, as already noted, played an important role in the post-1871 improvements. His central improvement scheme was also a culmination of this process, in reality and in terms of the creation of a certain sort of image of the city. Since the 1880s, or thereabouts, the changing urban fabric had been portrayed by the civic leaders of the city and others as a text on which a myriad of improvements were inscribed. It may still have been disfigured by enormous problems of urban squalor, but the counterpoint to this was increasingly evidence of prosperity and even a degree of urban grandeur and dignity. As the *Dundee Yearbook* declared in 1890, 'it had now somewhat the aspect of a great city'.[47] It is worth recalling here that Mackison had sought to keep rigid control over the design of the facades in the upper section of Commercial Street and Whitehall Street improvements.[48] The concept – of a tall ground floor below three stories and an attic – was based on the Paris of Baron Haussmann. (It is modernisation of shop fronts in the twentieth century which has destroyed the original purpose and impact of the scheme.) In 1890, these new streets were described as containing 'many handsome buildings' and 'excellent specimens of street architecture'.[49] It was a townscape which also reflected optimism about the city's future and the capacity of the city's authorities and citizens to ameliorate urban problems and provide an improving condition of life for the bulk of the city's population. 1871 was, therefore, a key date in this unfolding narrative of improvement, increasing amenity, and architectural aggrandisement.

There had also been spasmodic discussion about the need for new civic buildings in Dundee in the years preceding 1910. Thomson himself wrote of the scarcity of public buildings of note and architectural merit in 1912.[50] The shortfall had only marginally been made good by the construction of Thomson's branch libraries at Blackness and Coldside. So far as the centre of the city was concerned, the major building in the final decades of the nineteenth century was for commercial use. In the 1880s and 1890s several insurance companies built imposing offices in Meadowside – Caledonian Insurance Company, the Prudential (the design of which may have come from the office of Alfred Waterhouse) and the Pearl Insurance. In 1907 Lord Provost Longair submitted an unsuccessful scheme for a new town house and city hall by Thomson.[51] (Thomson's drawing is stylistically similar to his later 1910–11 plans, although one major difference was that it represented an extension of the Adam townhouse.) This was partly a question of convenience; the old town hall no longer provided the space for a growing local bureaucracy. But it was also about encapsulating the 'spirit of progress and enterprise' which the civic leaders saw as infusing the city and its government. Just as the construction of Glasgow's city chambers in George Square in 1883–88 represented a declaration of confidence in Glasgow and its progressive leadership, so Dundee needed a similarly bold statement. Longair's successor as Lord Provost, Sir James Urquhart, sought to revive the proposals in 1908, although there appears to have been a widespread feeling that this was not practical politics.[52] A further important context for these proposals was a sense of strengthening civic dignity created by the conferring on Dundee of city status in 1889 and, three years later, that of a county of the city. From 1892, the leader of the municipal authorities had the title of Lord Provost and from 1894 the status of ex-officio Lord Lieutenant of the county of Dundee. From 1910, plans were also resumed for a further extension of Dundee's boundaries to include Broughty Ferry, plans which came to fruition in 1913.[53] Much of the enthusiasm for this extension on the part of Dundee's civic leaders was practical – rationalisation of services and increasing the assessable value of property within the city's boundaries. It would also facilitate town planning beyond the city's existing boundaries. But it was also motivated by the desire to bring into being a 'Greater Dundee', a city which in terms of population and prosperity could justifiably claim to be the third city in Scotland.

What did Dundonians think of Thomson's plans of 1910–11? There is no doubt that the forces of organised Labour were hostile. A citizens' meeting was held in the Gilfillan Hall and calls were made for workers' housing in preference to 'gigantic schemes for city improvement'. On 7 March 1912, a critical Labour deputation was heard by the council.[54] The central improvement was also drawn into the battle over the boundary extension, with the Broughty Ferry 'die-hards' arguing that Dundee could ill afford costly architectural schemes which would simply increase the rates and thus undermine the competitiveness of an industrial base facing an uncertain future. It was also argued, opportunistically, that they offered little to the working man, but served merely to aggrandize wealthy councillors at their expense.[55] We also start to hear a criticism which was to be levelled two years later, much more fiercely, against the central improvement scheme made possible by the jute manufacturer, Sir James Caird's gift of £100,000; namely, that more historic landmarks, and important aspects of Dundee's architectural heritage would be recklessly destroyed. This was an argument which Urquhart strongly rebuffed, in interesting terms at an anniversary meeting of the Dundee Art Society in November 1911, arguing that 'the march of progress demanded that Dundee should consider a great scheme of central improvement'. Dundonians had, he declared, 'to make the city worthy of its size and future'.[56] Some were enthusiastic, or at least impressed by the aesthetic appeal of the plans. A. H. Millar, the city's chief librarian and a prolific local historian, gave a lecture, in 1912, expounding the scope for beautification which existed. It would, he exclaimed, 'be a lasting disgrace upon this generation . . . if they did not rise to the occasion and initiate a scheme of town reform and town planning which would receive the cordial applause of coming generations'. He also talked, more unexpectedly perhaps, of opportunities 'to make the city the Venice or the Nice of Scotland'.[57] Yet the predominant reaction, at least among the ratepayers, was summed up in an editorial in the *Dundee Advertiser*: 'the whole temper of the times is against the expenditure of money or mere municipal dandiacalism'.[58] The political base for ambitious civic renewal, particularly of central areas, was simply not present in 1912.

In the event, only two parts of the scheme were proceeded with – the improvement of the areas behind the town house and the Overgate and the widening of the Overgate. Even then the Council was subject to strong criticism. The 'antique and grime laden building' earmarked for clearance, was, the editorial in the *Advertiser* declared, 'a discredit to any modern city'. Yet the issue remained of the scope of the improvement and thus the cost, and what was to be done on the cleared land. This was high value land; its creation into open space would mean foregoing significant municipal revenue through rents and rates. Urquhart strongly defended the Council's policy of incrementalism.[59] The list of opponents was, however, predictable, and included the Dundee Harbour Trustees, frequently in conflict with the Council; owners and ratepayers of Dundee; the Dundee Landlords and House Factors' Association.[60] Improvement was a political and financial minefield which councillors moved through at their peril. Well might Walsh have berated the direction of discussion at the RIBA 1910 conference on town planning for its failure to tackle the fundamental question: who was to pay and how was political support for large schemes whose benefits would only be properly felt in the long term to be created.[61]

In April 1914, Caird offered the city £100,000 to erect a new city hall. The full story of the planning and construction of the Caird Hall lies beyond the scope of this chapter. Much of the debate was about cost; even with Caird's gift, the burden on the Council finances and thus the ratepayer would be far from negligible. Property needed to be bought up, and there was the question of how far new business premises and shops would generate sufficient rental income to cover a major part of the annual charge on the Council to finance the scheme. Edwin Scrymgeour, predictably, called on the Council to reject Caird's offer. He was answered by Lord Dean of Guild Nicoll, who argued that 'The average Dundonian showed too much of a tendency to pessimism with regard to his own city, and to look forward to it being the second in Scotland'.[62] Caird, on the other hand, argued that Thomson's initial plans of 1910–11 were too ambitious and costly. His conditions were that the building should stand on the area enclosed by the High Street, Crichton Street, Shore Terrace and Tindall's Wynd; that it be 'plain but dignified' in style; that it should be completed in three years; and that the cost of the site should be balanced by rents from business properties.[63] It seems that Thomson may have fought Caird quite hard about the designs, aiming for a building of greater public worth than Caird envisaged, hence the north portico.[64] (There is a drawing from 1914 which shows the building without the portico.[65])

As the plans developed, controversy was also created, as referred to earlier, about the likely fate of the old town house, and indeed a number of buildings in the Vault, the area which lay behind the Adam town house and which was to be cleared for the new hall. Thomson appears to have been flexible about the town house; there is a drawing by him of it re-built at the junction of the Overgate and the High Street.[66] (It was eventually taken down in 1932.)

The foundation stone of the Caird Hall was laid by King George V and Queen Mary on their visit to the city in 1914, appropriately since it was an occasion of great civic pomp and display.[67] It was laid electrically by the King and Queen pushing buttons at Caird's Ashton works. The button which the King pressed was made from an emerald. It was presented to the King, but given back to the city and incorporated into the civic regalia. The symbolism is telling: the ceremony was a carefully choreographed demonstration of civic pride, together with the sense of modernity and progress on which it had been firmly based since the 1870s.

The Caird Hall was completed in 1922. The east and west sides were erected later following a design by Sir John James Burnet. The result is not an entirely happy one. As a building, the hall was hardly helped by subsequent development, particularly but not solely on the foreshore. A city centre of wide streets terminating in vistas or focused on open squares or major buildings was never properly realised. The magnificent civic centre and waterfront envisaged by Thomson in 1910–11 has remained what it was then – a teasing vision of what might have been.

Walsh resigned from his post on the Council in 1913, leaving for London and the Theistic Church in Swallow Street. Apart from the construction of the Caird Hall, Thomson's career during and immediately after the Great War was concerned increasingly with housing schemes for the working classes and his comprehensive, wide-ranging plans for the city's future development.[68] In the former element, we can detect a pattern similar to that manifested elsewhere, one shaped by an increasingly powerful political dynamic concerning the growing power of organised labour and the political salience of the housing question during and after the Great War. Already in February 1916, the Council had been forced into renewed activity with regard to housing under pressure from Scrymgeour and the Labour party,[69] while from the spring of 1917, plans were underway for housing schemes to be put into action at short notice.[70]

For Thomson and indeed Dundee it was story with a mixed outcome. Thomson was retired from his post of city architect and housing director in 1924 (the Council had re-made the post of city engineer a separate appointment in 1922), following enquiries into accounting lapses and the cost of the so-called mystery or specimen house in Glamis Road. (This was built, with initial council approval, to demonstrate how modern technology, particularly electricity, could revolutionise the home. It appears, however, that the Council had assumed that it would be built in a manner which would have made it a prototype for subsidised public housing, which it was not since it considerably exceeded the cost of such a dwelling.[71])

Whatever the truth behind the origins of the mystery house – and one senses that Thomson was perhaps impervious to the changing conditions of Council service or had become increasingly autocratic in manner – it is hard not to be impressed by the breadth of Thomson's thinking about the development of the city, although there is not scope to illustrate this in any great detail. As early as 1910, he saw town planning as a way of setting a general framework for the future, long-term development of the city. His comprehensive report of 1918 set out a plan which looked ahead fifty years. It was both ambitious and practical, reflecting a strong conviction on the part of the author about the possibilities of town planning as an instrument of social betterment and transformation. In 1912, Walsh had conjured a vision of a population dispersed beyond the outskirts of the existing city in salubrious dwellings and surrounded by open spaces and uplifting views. It was here, he wrote, '[within] the semi-circle extending from the umbrageous slopes of Balgay on the west, sweeping round by the plains of Strath Martin on the north, to the wave-washed Strips of Craigie on the east, lie all the possibilities of a real city beautiful'.[72] It was this vision which was also contained in his 1908 report on the housing question. In this context, it is interesting to recall that the claims of Dundee to achievement in interwar housing lie in terms of quality not quantity. Rents on, for example, the Logie scheme, which was provided with centrally-heated houses, were beyond what was affordable by most working-class Dundonians. Craigiebank was laid out as a neighbourhood centre, clearly influenced by garden city ideas.

How, finally, should we judge the record of town planning in Dundee in the first two decades or so of the last century? One point is fairly easily made: thanks to Walsh and Thomson, Dundee could reasonably claim to be close to the forefront of town- planning activity in Britain prior to 1914. Even before 1909, Walsh and Thomson fully appreciated the possibilities created by town planning. They also thought on a much broader canvas than that on which most councillors were prepared to do. In 1912, Thomson's plans for a garden suburb below the Law were much discussed at a Scottish conference on town planning convened in Edinburgh.[73] Both Thomson and Walsh were also appointed in 1912 to a Scottish advisory committee of the National Housing and Town Planning Society, the major national body promoting the new discipline before the war. By the end of 1911, town-planning schemes were being considered by the Scottish Local Government Board for Dundee and only five other places.[74] During the war, Thomson's expertise was recognised by national government. In December 1917, he was appointed to a committee of selection for a housing of the working classes architectural competition, held to produce specimen plans for post-war, subsidised housing. Thomson was chosen, along with Professor Adshead, first holder of the Liverpool University chair in town planning established in 1910, as 'persons having special experience in town planning'.[75]

The actual reshaping of Dundee's townscape was, like elsewhere, limited; it is the extent of Thomson's plans which highlights what was not achieved. The vision of a population happy and dispersed from inadequate housing in the central districts of the city was to be long deferred, although perhaps we should in fairness emphasise here the magnitude of the challenges facing the city's authorities in this regard. In 1908, 63% of the city's population was living in either one- or two-apartment dwellings.[76]

The image of an urban fabric worthy of the city's 'size and future' – Urquhart's vision of 1908 – was also one which retreated in interwar Britain, as the base of the local economy weakened. In this sense, it was very much a vision of its time, perhaps a final flowering of an essentially nineteenth-century frame of mind regarding the city and its prospects. It was also always a vision from above, which is not to say that it had not appeal for other sections of the local community. Like all official images, it was also subject to continual challenge, both from within the city's ruling circles and beyond them – or more accurately, it had constantly to compete with other images of the city. Dundee's visual landscape in the later nineteenth and early twentieth centuries could be read in very different ways, for example, as a manifestation of the inequalities and suffering caused by the city's major industry – jute. Yet in this Dundee was not different from other, similar cities, say, Glasgow. The imagery and moods of municipal pride and achievement were perhaps more insecurely based in Dundee, but this should not detract from their importance in any complete history of the city or from the need for historians to begin to give them rather closer attention than they have so far.[77]

Notes

Introduction

1. See *The Scotsman*, 13, 20 Jan. 1995.
2. *Scotland on Sunday*, 10 Oct. 1999; for example it is asserted that Dundee's late nineteenth-century reputation for drunkenness prompted Lord Cockburn to condemn Dundee as 'a sink of atrocity'. In fact Cockburn was writing in the early and mid-1840s. To be fair, there are signs that the tide of external opinion is beginning to turn, see Magnus Linklater in *Scotland on Sunday*, 21 Mar. 1999.
3. *People's Journal*, 2 Feb. 1867.
4. C. A. Whatley, D. B. Swinfen and A. M. Smith, *The Life and Times of Dundee* (Edinburgh, 1993), 117, 169; C. A. Whatley, 'The Making of "Juteopolis" – and How it Was', in *The Remaking of Juteopolis*, ed . C. A. Whatley (Dundee, 1992), 13.
5. *Northern Warder*, 13 Dec. 1849.
6. *Circuit Journeys of the Late Lord Cockburn* (Edinburgh, 1975 ed.), 163.
7. These ideas are outlined in M. Knight, 'She Devils: Women and Crime in Dundee 1842–1852' (unpublished M.A. dissertation, University of Dundee, 1994).
8. G. T. Stewart, *Jute and Empire* (Manchester, 1998), 122–3, 133.
9. See, for example, S. and O. Checkland, *Industry and Ethos. Scotland 1832–1914* (London, 1984), 34–47.
10. W. Ferguson, *Scotland, 1689 to the Present* (Edinburgh, 1968), 298; M. Flinn *et al.*, *Scottish Population History from the Seventeenth century to the 1930s* (Cambridge, 1977), 466.
11. L. Miskell and C. A. Whatley, ' "Juteopolis" in the Making: Linen and the Industrial Transformation of Dundee, *c.*1820–1850', *Textile History*, 30, 2 (1999), 176.
12. W. M. Walker, *Juteopolis: Dundee and its Textile Workers, 1885–1923* (Edinburgh, 1979), 85.
13. L. Leneman, 'Dundee and the women's suffrage movement', in Whatley, *The Remaking of Juteopolis*, 93.
14. E. Gordon, *Women and the Labour Movement in Scotland 1850–1914* (Oxford, 1991).
15. Edinburgh City Archives [ECA], Moses Supplementary Collection, SL 30/238.
16. P. Lindsay, *The Interest of Scotland Considered* (London, 1736), xxvii; ECA, Moses Collection, SL 30/4/6, 'Petition of the Merchants of Dundee to the Honorable Convention of Royal Burghs', 1718.

17. *The First History of Dundee, 1776,* ed. A. H. Millar (Dundee, 1923); this reputation was still intact by the mid-nineteenth century when another account proclaimed that, 'the hospitality of the merchants to strangers is almost proverbial'. See *Statistical Account of Scotland, vol. 11* (Edinburgh, 1845), 20.

18. Perth and Kinross Council Archives, MS 100, Rossie Priory MSS, Bundle 369, T. Hunter to W. Chalmers, 24 August 1783; *The Statistical Account of Scotland, XIII, Angus* (Wakefield, 1976 ed.), 148.

19. *Dundee Advertiser,* 14 Apr. 1834; C. Mackie, *Historical Description of the Town of Dundee* (Glasgow, 1836).

20. See *Dundee Trade Directory* 1782. See also R. H. Carnie, 'Provincial Periodical Publishing in Eighteenth-Century Scotland: the Dundee experience', unpublished paper. Evidence of local cultural activities is to be found in the pages of the local newspaper, the *Dundee Courier.* See for example, 27 Apr. 1804 for an advertisement for J. Stewart, dancing master.

21. I. H. Adams, *The Making of Urban Scotland* (London, 1978), 83.

22. Whatley, Swinfen and Smith, *Life and Times of Dundee,* 111.

23. C. J. A. Robertson, *The Origin of the Scottish Railway System, 1722–1844* (Edinburgh, 1983), 124–5; Dundee Public Library [DPL], LC 369 (15) 'History of Newport and the Parish of Forgan', extracts from the *Dundee Courier,* 23 Jan. 1882.

24. The *Dundee Directories* are not a fully comprehensive source of information on residential patterns. Their lists typically constituted no more than around 4.5% of the population. Also, those published before the mid-1830s tended not to specify whether the addresses listed were those of workplace, home or both. By the middle of the century, however, addresses were being recorded in a more systematic format and thus a useful analysis of the residential patterns of Dundee's commercial inhabitants is possible from this data.

25. The 1850 *Directory* included separate lists for Dundee, Broughty Ferry and Lochee. This analysis, because of its focus on those with economic and business interests in Dundee, is based solely on the Dundee list.

26. DPL, LC 369 (15) 'History of Newport'.

27. D. F. MacDonald, 'Transport', in *The Third Statistical Account of Scotland. The City of Dundee,* ed. J. M. Jackson (Arbroath, 1979), 242.

28. Eighteenth Annual Report of the Watt Institution; Twenty-fourth Annual Report of the Watt Institution. The following section draws on material from Ruth Forbes' ongoing research. The editors are grateful to her for permission to use some of it in this Introduction.

29. DPL, LC 274 (5), J. MacLauchlan, 'The Albert Institute: Its Libraries, Art Galleries, and Branches'; LC 11 (3), 'The Dundee Fine Art Exhibition, 1884–5'.

30. D. Scruton, *James Guthrie Orchar and the Orchar Collection* (St Andrews, 1988), 5.

31. DPL, Obituary Book 2, obituary of Thomas Couper, 18 Feb. 1880.

32. See for example, R. Trainor, *Black Country Elites. The exercise of authority in an industrial area, 1830–1900* (Oxford, 1993), 93–110; R. Trainor, 'Peers on an Industrial Frontier: the earls of Dartmouth and Dudley in the Black Country, *c.* 1810–1914', in *Patricians, Power and Politics in Nineteenth Century Towns,* ed. D. Fraser (Leicester, 1982), 103–6; R. J. Morris, 'The Middle Class and British

Towns and Cities of the Industrial Revolution, 1780–1870', in *The Pursuit of Urban History*, eds D. Fraser and A. Sutcliffe (London, 1983), 289.

33. L. Walsh, *Patrons, Poverty and Profit. Organised charity in nineteenth-century Dundee* (Dundee, 2000), 14–15.

34. Members of the local landed elite such as the Viscountess Duncan, an early patroness of the Orphan Institution, established in 1815, usually acted as little more than figureheads. See L. Walsh, 'The Development of Organised Charity in the Scottish Burgh. Dundee 1790–1850', unpublished Ph.D. thesis (University of Dundee, 1997), 57.

35. The names and occupations of the first police commission members are listed in the *Dundee Directory*, 1824–25.

36. Political frictions between charitable directors and other interest groups within the town, however, were common. See for example, Walsh, *Patrons, Poverty and Profit*, 30–2.

37. For details of this and other benefactions by the Baxter family, see *Dundee Past and Present*, ed. Millar, 96-8.

38. See J. E. Callison, 'Politics, Class and Water Supply in Dundee, 1831–1845', unpublished M.Phil. thesis (University of Dundee, 1985); J. A. Hassan, 'The Growth and Impact of the British Water Industry in the Nineteenth Century', *Economic History Review* 38, 4 (1986), 534.

39. DPL, LC 308 (11) cuttings on health in Dundee. Not until the passing of the Public Health (Scotland) Act, 1867 were Boards of Health a formal requirement in Scottish towns. See G. F. A. Best, 'Another Part of the Island', in *The Victorian City. Images and Realities. Vol 1*, eds H. J. Dyos and M. Wolff (London, 1973), 394.

40. DPL, LC 319 (14) Police and Improvement (Scotland) Act, 1850, section 39: 'It shall be in the power of the householders to determine by a majority of votes and to set forth on their minutes, that the magistrates and council of the burgh for the time being shall always be the commissioners for carrying this act.'

41. *Dundee Advertiser*, 4 Feb. 1851. Report of a meeting of the Chamber of Commerce on the new police bill. Comments of Thomas Neish.

42. The Dundee Working Men's Association and Trades Council was instrumental in securing the election to the Town Council of the men who presided over the 1871 improvements. See below, chapter by Louise Miskell. They also supported the movement to obtain a Free Library in the town. See for example, DPL, LC274 (4C), 'Free Libraries: the Working and Advantages. A Report Compiled from official sources and printed for gratuitous distribution by the Dundee Working Men's Association'.

43. *Dundee Year Book*, 1890, 137.

Chapter One

1. *The Topographical, Statistic and Historical Gazetteer of Scotland* (Glasgow, 1842), 372.

2. Great thanks are due to my colleagues Chris Whatley, Bob Harris and Louise Miskell; and to Pat Whatley, Jan Merchant and Jenny Tait at the University Archives. I am also very indebted to Iain Flett and his colleagues at the City Archives, David Kett at the Wellgate Library, Neil Grieve, Enid Gauldie and to

the researches of Marilyn Healy, Andrew Nicoll, Grant Buttars, and Frank Zwolinski.

3. S. A. Robertson, *A Moray Loon* (Edinburgh, 1933), 8.

4. M. Glendinning, R. MacInnes, A. MacKechnie, *A History of Scottish Architecture* (Edinburgh, 1996), 169.

5. There is extensive literature on new towns and the reasoning behind them. See particularly T. C. Smout, 'The Landowner and the Planned Village in Scotland 1730–1830', in *Scotland in the Age of Improvement*, eds N. T. Phillipson and R. Mitchison (Edinburgh, 1996); A. J. Youngson, *The Making of Classical Edinburgh* (Edinburgh, 1966); *Order in Space and Society*, ed. T. A. Markus (Edinburgh, 1984); *The Neo-Classical Town in Scotland*, ed. W. A. Brogden (Edinburgh, 1996).

6. *Proposals for carrying on certain PUBLIC WORKS In the CITY of EDINBURGH* (Edinburgh, 1751).

7. *Ibid.*

8. D. Galbraith, 'The new town in Scotland', unpublished conference paper (November, 1999).

9. See Smout, 'The Landowner and the Planned Village'.

10. Scottish Record Office [SRO], Register House Plans [RHP], 2358, 'Proposed plan for the new town of Fochabers'.

11. SRO, RHP 3/61, 'Barony of Ardrossan' by John Ainslie.

12. See P. Nuttgens, 'The planned villages of north-east Scotland', in *The Neo-Classical Town*, ed. Brogden.

13. S. Gauldie in C. McKean and D. Walker, *Dundee – an Illustrated Introduction* (Edinburgh, 1984), 3.

14. I. H. Adams *The Making of Urban Scotland* (London, 1978), 83. 'Appalling water and sewage problems and the rate and scale of industrialisation led the small middle-class population to seek new homes outside the city; the answer lay 6 km to the east in the little fishing village of Broughty Ferry. Around 1801 Charles Hunter of Burnside laid out a Georgian grid street plan.' This 'new town' remained undeveloped into the 1840s, for the demand to leave the city centre was still not manifest.

15. Dundee University Archives [DUA], MS 105 – P. 528/1, J. Leslie's 1836 holograph plan for the harbour and the proposed harbour beside the castle at Broughty Ferry to replace that at the bottom of Brook Street. It shows only 1 house outside the Fishertown.

16. DUA, MS 57 P. 6, D. Neave, untitled plan for extension of Broughty Ferry.

17. DUA, MS 17 P. 146, D. Neave, untitled, possibly Hillbank (1824); DUA, MS 57 P. 1, Neave, Maxwell ground in Hilltown (1824); DUA, MS 57 P. 2, Neave, terraces next to Hilltown (1825); SRO, RHP 1148, David Neave, Blackness (1829); DUA, MS 57 P. 13, W. Corsair, Taybank (1830); DUA, MS 105 P. 243, J. Brewster, East Hillbank (1834); DUA, MS 105 P. 575, J. Sampson, Craigie (1834); DUA, MS 11 D. 90, possibly J. Black, Dens north of Princes Street (1835) etc.

18. DUA, MS 105 P. 31.

19. DUA, K.loc, Rev. R. G. Lewis, *The Tavern Bill of Dundee* (1841). Although this paper has been taken to describe a process of social dispersal well under way when he referred to 'the newly-opened railways [which] afford new facilities to

the capitalists for uniting business through the day with retirement to the country in the evening, and threaten to convert Dundee into one great workshop' the language is quite clearly that of a forecast rather than that of a description of contemporary events. It had not yet happened, 40 years after Adams, *Urban Scotland,* 83, and Walker, 'Urban Form', 64, imply that the process had taken place.

20. *Gazetteer of Scotland* (Dundee, 1803).
21. SRO, Register of Sasines, Forfarshire, 1968, 6675. On 16 Jun. 1792, John Jobson was designated as being 'of Riga' when he began to build his house in Perth Road, before he returned to become tenant of Auchterhouse by 1811.
22. *Dundee Delineated* (Dundee, 1822), 102.
23. R. Small, *A Statistical Account of the Parish and Town of Dundee in the year MDCCXCll* (Dundee, 1793), 71. In 1555, Dundee's contribution to the king's Cess, or land tax, was second only to Edinburgh, Aberdeen being over 25% lower. It was 7 times greater than Glasgow's.
24. A. C. Lamb, *Dundee – its quaint and historical buildings* (Dundee, 1892).
25. D. A. Walker, *Dundee Architecture and Architects* (Dundee, 1976), 3.
26. Dundee City Archives [DCA], D. Shapton, 'What the seventeenth century shipping lists can tell us', unpublished paper (1998). I am grateful to Iain Flett for drawing this to my attention.
27. SRO, GD137/2334.
28. D. Defoe *A Tour through the Whole Island of Great Britain* (Folio Society reprint, London, 1976), 278.
29. W. W. Friskin, 'The Town House at Dundee', in *RIAS Quarterly,* 40 (Edinburgh, 1932). The spire had not yet begun in 1735, at which point the Council determined only to build it with the concave and panelled sides that Adam had designed if it were no more expensive than flat-sided. Unfortunately it was, so flat-sided the tower emerged.
30. B. Lenman, *From Esk to Tweed* (Glasgow, 1975), 26.
31. T. Pennant, *A Tour in Scotland* (London, 1776).
32. Brice of Exeter, *Geographical Dictionary* (1759) quoted in C. A. Whatley, D. Swinfen and A. Smith, *The Life and Times of Dundee* (Edinburgh, 1993), 76; and Lenman, *Esk to Tweed,* 26.
33. 'Report of J. Smeaton, Engineer upon the Harbour of Dundee', 15 Mar. 1770.
34. A. Carlyle, *Journal of a Tour to the North of Scotland,* ed. R. B. Sher (Aberdeen, n.d).
35. W. Crawford, *Map of the Town of Dundee* (Dundee, 1776). Many of the tanneries later became converted to flax-spinning mills *c.*1821; *Dundee Delineated* (Dundee, 1822), 19.
36. In Glasgow, the space between the arcaded front and the rear building had been a regular 11 feet, whereas in Dundee the gap between the timber frontage (which had misled visitors into believing the buildings were wholly timber) and the stone structure behind was anything between 6 and 8 feet; *Dundee Delineated* (Dundee, 1822) 142–243.
37. R. Rogers, 'Evolution of Scottish Town Planning' in *Scottish Urban History,* ed. G. Gordon and B. Dicks, (Aberdeen, 1983).
38. DCA, GD/GRW/G 1/4, Dundee Guildry Sederunt Book – what survives from a fire. Not only are some of the pages so badly damaged as to be barely legible

but it seems from chronological discontinuities that some entire sections may be missing.

39. Until the late 20th century, its postal address remained Newport, Dundee, Angus, despite its location on the shores of Fife. I am grateful to Andrew Nicoll for discovering this.

40. DCA, GD/GRW/G1/2, Guildry Sederunt Book 1696-1742. I am greatly indebted to Iain Flett for uncovering this.

41. Dundee Public Libraries [DPL], D 5080 1, miscellaneous pamphlets. Relationships with the Council, however, had remained soured after the latter's refusal to help fund St Andrew's Church. In Feb. 1776, the Trades refused to let their deacons' names be used in a bond with the Town Council 'because they are not allowed to vote in expending the town's revenue'.

42. DPL, D 5080 1, miscellaneous pamphlets. I am grateful to Marilyn Healy for finding this.

43. C. McKean, *Banff and Buchan – An Illustrated Architectural Guide* (Edinburgh, 1989).

44. A. J. Warden, *The Burgh Laws of Dundee* (London, 1872), 295.

45. DCA, Dundee Guildry Sederunt Book, 6 Oct. 1817. The petition by Deacon R. Mudie, that the Town Council disclose accounts of the last 10 years and more, which led to a formal charge against Riddoch's conduct.

46. *Ibid.*

47. *The Dundee Register* (Dundee, 1782), 41–2. There was also the Snuff and Twopenny Whist Club, founded *c.*1740 which met in the British Hotel, out of which emerged the Eastern Club in Albert Square. D. Barrie, *City of Dundee Illustrated* (Dundee, 1890), 297.

48. *The Dundee Register* (Dundee, 1782), 11–15.

49. Philetas, letter to the editor of the *Dundee Magazine* (Jul. 1799), reprinted in *Dundee Delineated,* 175.

50. D. W. Dykes, 'James Wright, junior, the Radical Numismatist of Dundee' in *Numismatic Circular* (Jul.-Aug., 1996) 195–9.

51. *The Dundee Repository* (Dundee, 1792–93).

52. W. Norrie, *Dundee Celebrities* (Dundee, 1873), 51; *Dundee Delineated* (Dundee 1822), List of Principal Inhabitants; *The Dundee Register* (Dundee, 1828), 4–5.

53. *Dundee Directory,* 1818, 190.

54. T. M. Devine *Exploring the Scottish Past* (East Linton, 1995), 114–32.

55. *Dundee Post Office Directory* (Dundee, 1845).

56. Small, *Statistical Account,* 53.

57. A. Campbell, *Journey from Edinburgh* (Edinburgh, 1802).

58. It was soon joined by other theatres in the Cowgate and Yeaman Shore.

59. DCA, Town Council Minutes [TCM], 30 Aug. 1808.

60. *Ibid.*

61. *Ibid.,* 23 Aug. 1813.

62. SRO, Register of Sasines, Forfarshire, 5219. On 3 Mar. 1806, John Glen Johnstone is designated as being 'of St Petersburg, now in Dundee'.

63. H. Colvin, *A Biographical Dictionary of British Architects 1600–1840* (London, 1978).

64. H. Cockburn, *Memorials of his Time* (Edinburgh, 1856), 287–8.

65. SRO, Register of Sasines, 1968, 6675. On 16 Jun. 1792, he is designated as 'of Riga', and returned by 1811 as tenant of Auchterhouse.
66. Dundee's statue of Neptune stood proudly on the Castle Hill overlooking the harbour, and is evident in late 18th-century views of the town taken from the sea. It vanished, presumably, with the creation of Castle Street.
67. *Dundee Delineated,* 213–40.
68. R. Chambers, *Traditions of Edinburgh* (Edinburgh, 1823).
69. J. Buchanan (J.B.), *Glasgow, Past and Present* (Glasgow, 1851), 12.
70. R. J. Morris 'Urban Space and the Industrial City' in *REFRESH 28* (Jul., 1999).
71. Small, *Statistical Account,* 48.
72. See SRO, Register of Sasines, Forfarshire, 4067, 1690, 1680 and 1691 for examples of sales of minute or larger parcels of land to carters, weavers, shoemakers and labourers in Westfield, Springfield, Chapelshade and the north side of the road from the Overgate to Scouringburn.
73. DCA, Minutes of the Dundee Police Commissioners [MDPC], 8 Aug. 1831.
74. *Ibid.,* 11 Oct. 1830.
75. *Ibid.*
76. DUA, K.loc 363.61 D. 914, Committee on the Dundee Water Works Bill: evidence of James Black, 24.
77. Small, *Statistical Account,* 11.
78. R. Forsyth, *The Beauties of Scotland* (Edinburgh, 1805).
79. *Dundee Delineated,* 16.
80. *The New Statistical Account of Scotland Vol XI* (Edinburgh, 1845). The Dundee account, 1–53, is dated Mar. 1834 but was drawn up in 1832 and revised in 1833.
81. Barrie, *City of Dundee Illustrated,* 16.
82. Small, *Statistical Account,* 33.
83. M. Watson, *Jute and flax mills in Dundee* (Newport, 1990), 192.
84. *Old Statistical Account,* (1976 reprint) 191.
85. *Dundee Delineated,* 28.
86. *Dundee Advertiser,* 12 Nov. 1819; *The New Statistical Account of Scotland Vol XI* (Edinburgh, 1845), 1–53.
87. DPL, D. 5080 1, one of the miscellaneous pamphlets, called *'Dissection of the Town Council of Dundee – demonstrating the Tricks and Transformations of MONSTER SELF ELECTION'*, published 1818, followed how Riddoch and his Councillors had maintained control year on year since 1800. I am indebted to Marilyn Healy who found this.
88. Gauldie, *Riddoch,* 19.
89. DCA, TCM, 4 Jul. 1827.
90. F. A. Walker, 'Glasgow's New Towns' in *Glasgow – the forming of a city,* ed. P. A. Reed (Edinburgh, 1993), 24 – 41.
91. *Ibid,* 37.
92. Adams, *Urban Scotland,* 83.
93. D. Graham-Campbell, *Thomas Hay Marshall and the Making of Georgian Perth* (Perth Libraries, n.d.).
94. SRO, RHP 1143, W. Crawford, Plan of the Estate of Blackness (1777).
95. SRO, RHP 1146, untitled Neave plan for feuing up Blackness Road. Mrs Watt of Crescent, for example, owned four properties in Roseangle.

96. Walker, *Dundee Architecture*, 8.

97. SRO, RHP 1147, Burn and 1148, Neave.

98. DCA, TCM, 7 Jan.1793.

99. In other words, neither set back nor gable on to the street in the old fashioned way.

100. SRO, RHP 1147. Not only was that the case along Perth Road and down into Roseangle, but virtually all of Neave's largely abortive feuing plans between 1816 and 1829 were for estates of detached houses.

101. DCA, TCM, 6 Jan. 1806.

102. Gauldie, *Riddoch*, 54.

103. DCA, TCM, 31 Oct. 1786; 31 Jan. 1787.

104. *Ibid.*, 20 Sep. 1787.

105. *Ibid.*, 5 Jul. 1808.

106. *Ibid.*, 5 Sep.1810.

107. *Ibid.*, 5 Jul. 1787. Daniel Morgan of Westfield was required to set his building back 4 feet 'as the Seagate Street is at present so very narrow'.

108. *Ibid.*, 6 Jan. 1794.

109. *Ibid.*, 30 Aug. 1808.

110. *Ibid.*, 22 May 1806.

111. *Ibid.*, 5 Jul. 1787.

112. DPL, D 5080 1, miscellaneous pamphlets.

113. DCA, TCM, 22 Jan. 1789.

114. *Ibid.*, 7 May 1801.

115. *Ibid.*, 13 Dec.1803.

116. *Ibid.*, 2 Apr. 1803.

117. *Ibid.*, 5 Sep. 1810.

118. *Ibid.*, 19 Dec. 1811.

119. *Ibid.*, 8 Nov. 1814.

120. Lenman, *From Esk to Tweed*, 76.

121. DCA, GD/GRW/G10–11, I. Flett, 'Guildry Court notices and processes', unpublished paper.

122. Warden, *Burgh Laws*, 3 Oct. 1815.

123. Gauldie, *Riddoch*, 17.

124. DCA, TCM, 1808.

125. Small, *Statistical Account*, 39.

126. Philetas, *Dundee Magazine*, July 1799, reprinted in *Dundee Delineated*, 183–91. To put that into context, J. Denholm, in his *History of Glasgow* (Glasgow, 1798) puts Glasgow's income that year at £4,000.

127. *Gazetteer of Scotland* (Dundee, 1803).

128. *Topographical, Statistical and Historical Gazetteer of Scotland*, (Glasgow, 1842), 380.

129. Youngson, *Classical Edinburgh*, 147.

130. DPL, D 5080 1, *Dissection of the Town Council of Dundee*, 1818.

131. *Dundee Advertiser*, 3 Feb.1815.

132. *Ibid.*, 28 Apr. 1815.

133. DPL, D 5080 1, miscellaneous pamphlet 1. The mediators included Robert Miller – Cowgate merchant, Alex Reid – flesher, William Baxter – Bain Square merchant, Thomas Bell, and William Small – town clerk. Those representing

the Guildry included John Baxter – agent, William Roberts – cashier, Dundee New Bank, David Miln – cashier, Dundee Union Bank, William Lindsay – corn merchant, and John Sturrock – merchant. These two groups represented a significant part of the town's elite.

134. *Ibid.*
135. DCA, Dundee Guildry Sederunt Book. The petition by Deacon Robert Mudie, 6 Oct. 1817, led to a formal charge against Riddoch's conduct.
136. *Ibid.*
137. *Ibid.*
138. DCA, TCM, 13 Oct. 1817.
139. DPL, D 5080 1, miscellaneous pamphlet 13, Dundee Harbour, 1819.
140. *Ibid.*
141. *Dundee Delineated.*
142. *Ibid.*, 81–7.
143. *Gazetteer of Scotland* (Dundee, 1803). As early as 1803, it had some 1,000 native seamen.
144. *An Act for Opening Certain Streets in the Burgh of Dundee and otherwise improving the said Burgh*, 6 George 1V: Cap.clxxxiii, passed 22 Jun. 1825.
145. DCA, TCM, 7 Jan.1824.
146. Plan of the town of Dundee, engraved in 1827, is generally thought to have been a copy of John Wood's plan. It differs substantially in what it depicts and how it is drawn (no names of building proprietors for example) and although unsigned, the 1821 original is recognisably in Neave's handwriting.
147. DCA, TCM, 17 Jan.1828.
148. *Ibid.*
149. *Dundee Delineated*, 28.
150. C. Mackie, *Historical Description of the Town of Dundee* (Dundee, 1836), 141.
151. *New Statistical Account*, and D. Walker, *Architecture.*
152. The Mathewson plan bound as a frontispiece to Mackie, *History*, in the copy in the Royal Commission on the Ancient and Historical Monuments of Scotland; and Plan of the Town of Dundee with the improvements now in progress, by Charles Edward, architect (Edinburgh, 1846). Alas, too optimistic. Not all Edward's proposals were in progress: his plans for Euclid Crescent, and the lands to the north east and north west of Dundee remained unrealised.
153. DCA,TC, MP 3, plan by J. Brewster, 1832.
154. Mackie, *Historical Description*, 154.
155. W. J. Smith, *A History of Dundee 1871* (Dundee, 1980), 53.
156. *New Statistical Account.*
157. Mackie, *Historical Description*, 154.
158. DCA, TCM, 25 Feb.1813.
159. DUA, MS 57 P 17 and P. 12/1.
160. DCA, Cowper, 'Guild Court notices and processes'.
161. *Topographical Gazetteer*, 372–3.
162. *Dundee Advertiser*, 6 May 1851.
163. *Topographical Gazetteer*, 372–3.
164. R. Chambers, *The Picture of Scotland* (Edinburgh, 1830), 372; also L. Miskell and C. A. Whatley, 'Juteopolis in the Making: Linen and the Industrial

Transformation of Dundee *c.*1820—1850' in *Textile History,* 30, 2 (1999), 176-98.

165. DUA, MS 15/114/2, Diary of T. H. Baxter – repeated references to attending public meetings in the Coffee House in the Trades Hall directed at potential subscribers.

166. DCA, DPC Registers, 3 Apr. 1834.

167. The date of the earliest drawing in the MacManus Galleries.

168. W. Beattie, *The Beauties of Scotland* (London, 1838).

169. *Topographical Gazetteer,* 372 and 375.

170. *The History of Dundee,* ed. J. MacLaren (Dundee, 1874), 335.

Chapter Two

1. G. Jackson, 'Scottish Shipping', in *Shipping, Trade and Commerce,* eds P. L. Cotrell and D. H. Aldcroft (Leicester, 1981) 121–2. Dundee was involved with the eastern Baltic yarn trade in association with her own indigenous hinterland trade in linen. This helped the volume of trade, but it was Leith which drew in the bulk of northern-European imports along the east coast before the last quarter of the eighteenth century. Dundee, however, was important in terms of coastal trade at that time, and together with Perth and Aberdeen they 'came very much into their own as major distribution and collection centres for "private" hinterlands which relied almost entirely on coastal routes for long distance trade'. As time went on however, Dundee – like Aberdeen – became a main regional centre for coastal and foreign trade); see also G. Jackson with K. Kinnear, *The Trade and Shipping of Dundee, 1780–1850* (Dundee, 1991).

2. D. F. MacDonald, 'Transport', in *The Third Statistical Account for Scotland: The City of Dundee,* ed. J. M. Jackson (Arbroath, 1979), 227.

3. *Ibid.,* 227–8.

4. For details of tonnage entering Dundee between 1790 and 1815–19, see Jackson and Kinnear, *Trade and Shipping,* 5.

5. MacDonald, 'Transport', 227.

6. *150 Years of Service to Commerce and Industry,* Dundee and Tayside Chamber of Commerce and Industry, 1835–1985 (Dundee, 1985), v.

7. E. Gauldie, *One Artful and Ambitious Individual: Alexander Riddoch (1745–1822)* (Dundee 1989), 35–6.

8. A. Campbell, *Journey From Edinburgh, Vol I* (London 1802), 380–1.

9. Dundee City Archives [DCA], Town Council Minutes, 8 Nov. 1814.

10. *Dundee Advertiser,* 6 Jan. 1815.

11. DCA, GD/DH/1/1, Original Minute Book of Harbour Committee, 2 Feb. 1814.

12. *Dundee Advertiser,* 17 Jan. 1815.

13. For details see J. H. Thompson and G. G. Ritchie, *Dundee Harbour Trust Centenary, 1830–1930* (Dundee, 1930), 7–9.

14. L. Miskell and W. Kenefick, ' "A Flourishing Seaport": Dundee Harbour and the Making of the Industrial Town, *c.*1815–1850', *Scottish Economic and Social History,* 20, 2 (2000).

15. The phrase 'the third in rank in Scotland' is noted in several articles and reports of this period, but it is most prominent in the extensive letter written to the

editor of the *Dundee Advertiser*, 6 Jan. 1815. The letter was signed under the pseudonym '*A Citizen*'.

16. C. Mackie, *Historical Description of the Town of Dundee* (Dundee, 1836), 166-7.
17. J. Thomson, *History of Dundee, from the Earliest to Present Times*, ed. J. Maclaren (Dundee, 1878), 279.
18. Mackie, *Historical Description*, 166-7.
19. G. Jackson, *The History and Archaeology of Ports* (Surrey, 1983), 137.
20. *Ibid.,* 228–9.
21. Dundee Public Library [DPL], Lamb Collection [LC] 305 (30) David Hunter, 'Observations on Mr Harrison's Report on the Harbour of Dundee' (1868).
22. Jackson, *The History and Archaeology of Ports*, 137.
23. *Ibid.,* 138.
24. W. Beattie, *The Beauties of Scotland* (1838).
25. See Miskell and Kenefick, 'A Flourishing Seaport'.
26. *Dundee Advertiser,* 1 Dec. 1825.
27. *Dundee Directory*, 1834.
28. Thomson, *History of Dundee*, 279–80.
29. *Ibid.*
30. Inquiry into the Wages and Conditions of Employment of Dock and Waterside Labour, xxiv (PP, 1920), vol. II. See appendices, documents, and indexes. By 1918 the trade gap between Dundee and Leith had shortened significantly, principally due to Leith losing a substantial amount of its previous trade. Dundee's profitable position was almost entirely due to the trade in flax, hemp and jute which, before the 'Great War', accounted for almost 40% of the total volume of traffic through the port, rising, perhaps predictably, to almost 60% by the end of hostilities in 1918.
31. J. M. Jackson, 'Leading Industries', in *Third Statistical Account,* 104.
32. *Ibid.,* 106.
33. Calculated from Jackson, *The History and Archaeology of Ports,* 167.
34. Jackson, 'Scottish Shipping', 122, 134.
35. *Ibid.,* 235–7; see also Appendix C, Table 10.5 for Traffic Statistics.
36. W. M. French, *The Scottish Ports* (Glasgow, 1938), 65–9.
37. MacDonald, 'Transport', 230.
38. French, *The Scottish Ports,* 69–70.
39. S. J. Jones, 'The Site and its Development' in *Third Statistical Account,* 25–6.
40. S. G. E. Lythe, 'The Historical Background: The Early Nineteenth Century' in *Third Statistical Account,* 80.
41. *Ibid.,* 74.
42. Miskell and Kenefick, 'A Flourishing Seaport'.

Chapter Three

1. *Dundee Advertiser,* 24 Nov. 1868.
2. See for example, I. H. Adams, *The Making of Urban Scotland* (London, 1978), 82; T. M. Devine, 'Urbanisation', in *People and Society in Scotland, volume 1, 1760–1830,* eds T. M. Devine and R. Mitchison (Edinburgh, 1988), 41; *Scottish Population History from the Seventeenth Century to the 1930s,* ed. M. Flinn (Cambridge, 1977), 466.

3. See for example, R. Trainor, *Black Country Elites. The Exercise of Authority in an Industrialised Area, 1830–1900* (Oxford, 1993); R. J. Morris, *Class, Sect and Party. The Making of the British Middle-class, Leeds, 1820–1850* (Manchester, 1990); T. Koditschek, *Class Formation and Urban Industrial Society. Bradford, 1750–1850* (Cambridge, 1990).

4. B. Lenman and K. Donaldson, 'Partners' Incomes, Investment and Diversification in the Scottish Linen Area, 1850–1921', *Business History*, 13, 1 (1971), 17–18.

5. See B. Lenman, C. Lythe, and E. Gauldie, *Dundee and its Textile Industry* (Dundee, 1969), 80.

6. J. T. Ward, 'Trade Unionism in Dundee', in *Third Statistical Account of Scotland. The City of Dundee*, ed. J. M. Jackson (Arbroath, 1979); E. Gordon, *Women and the Labour Movement in Scotland, 1850–1914* (Oxford, 1991).

7. M. J. Wiener, *English Culture and the Decline of the Industrial Spirit, 1850–1980* (Cambridge, 1981).

8. S. Nenadic, 'Businessmen, the urban middle classes, and the "dominance" of manufacturers in nineteenth-century Britain', *Economic History Review*, 44, 1 (1991), 66-85.

9. A. Durie, *The Scottish Linen Industry in the Eighteenth Century* (Edinburgh, 1979), 66.

10. *First History of Dundee*, ed. T. Y. Miller (Dundee, 1923), 158.

11. B. Lenman and E. Gauldie, 'The Industrial History of the Dundee Region from the Eighteenth to the Early Twentieth Century', in *Dundee and District*, ed. S. J. Jones (Dundee, 1968), 165.

12. A. J. Warden, *The Linen Trade, Ancient and Modern* (London, 1864), 592.

13. J. H. Thompson and G. G. Ritchie, *Dundee Harbour Trust Centenary* (Dundee, 1930), 9 and 11.

14. S. G. E. Lythe and J. Butt, *An Economic History of Scotland, 1100–1939* (Glasgow, 1975), 245.

15. *Ibid.*

16. Lenman, Lythe and Gauldie, *Dundee and its Textile Industry*, 11.

17. D. Bremner, *The Industries of Scotland* (Trowbridge, 1969), 231–2.

18. Lenman, Lythe and Gauldie, *Dundee and its Textile Industry*, 30.

19. J. M. Jackson, 'Population' in *The Third Statistical Account of Scotland. The City of Dundee*, ed. J. M. Jackson (Arbroath, 1979), 90.

20. E. Gauldie, *One Artful and Ambitious Individual. Alexander Riddoch (1745–1822)* (Dundee, 1989), 20.

21. A. J. Warden, *Burgh Laws of Dundee* (London, 1872), 106.

22. See for example, W. Norrie, *Dundee Celebrities of the Nineteenth Century* (Dundee, 1873), 32–5.

23. For details see Dundee Public Library [DPL], Lamb Collection [LC] 241(15) cuttings on the Town Council.

24. *New Statistical Account*, 10–11.

25. For biographical information on William Hackney, see *Roll of Eminent Burgesses of Dundee*, ed. A. H. Millar (Dundee, 1887), 259.

26. Norrie, *Dundee Celebrities*.

27. Includes council members who could be positively identified in *Dundee Directories*, 1818, 1834 and 1850.

28. See DPL, LC 248(1) Harbour and Docks, for details of the make up of the Harbour Board.
29. Table excludes Board members who were employees of the Harbour Trust.
30. DPL, LC 319(25b) Abstract of an Act for the Better Paving, Lighting and Watching and Cleansing of the Burgh of Dundee (Dundee, 1824).
31. See D. Fraser, *Urban Politics in Victorian England* (Leicester, 1976), 91–5; Koditschek, *Class Formation*, 158–9.
32. See R. J. Morris, 'The Middle Class and British Towns and Cities of the Industrial Revolution, 1780–1870' in *The Pursuit of Urban History*, eds D. Fraser and A. Sutcliffe (London, 1983), 291–2.
33. J. Garrard, *Leadership and Power in Victorian Industrial Towns, 1830–1880* (Manchester, 1983), 14–19.
34. Problems with the use of data from trade directories are discussed in P. J. Corfield and S. Kelly, 'Giving directions to the town: the early town directories', *Urban History Yearbook* (1984), 22–35; G. Shaw, 'Directories as sources in urban history: a review of British and Canadian material', *Urban History Yearbook* (1984), 36-44.
35. Bank of Scotland Archive, 1/70/3, Treasurer's Private Reports and Statements, 90.
36. L. Miskell and C. A. Whatley, ' "Juteopolis" in the Making. Linen and the Industrial Transformation of Dundee, 1820–1850', *Textile History*, 30, 2 (1999), 188.
37. The *1834 Leeds Directory* used by Morris was wide in scope, incorporating approximately 7.4% of the population of the town as opposed to the 4.7% encompassed by the 1850 *Dundee Directory*.
38. T. Koditschek, 'The dynamics of class formation in nineteenth century Bradford', in *The First Modern Society. Essays in English History in Honour of Lawrence Stone*, eds A. L. Beier, D. Cannadine and J. M. Rosenheim (Cambridge, 1989), 514. Bradford's population grew from 26,000 in 1821 to over 100,000 by 1851. Over the same period Dundee's population grew from 30,000 to 79,000. See J. M. Jackson, 'Population', in *Third Statistical Account of Scotland. The City of Dundee*, ed. J. M. Jackson (Arbroath, 1979), 90.
39. Koditschek, *Class Formation*, 116-17.
40. See M. Hewitt, *The Emergence of Stability in the Industrial City: Manchester, 1832–67* (Aldershot, 1996), 36.
41. Morris, *Class, Sect and Party*, 25.
42. Koditschek, *Class Formation*, 116.
43. Figures from *Dundee Directory*, 1850.
44. Morris, *Class, Sect and Party*, 26.
45. Koditschek, *Class Formation*, 116-17.
46. *Dundee Directories*, 1818 and 1850.
47. Teachers were not included in this category unless it was clear from their occupational description that they held a post such as a subject teacher in the public seminaries or rector of an academy, for which formal educational qualifications would have been necessary. Here I am following the practice set out in Morris, *Class, Sect and Party*, 23.
48. Morris, *Class, Sect and Party*, 26.

49. See for example, S. Nenadic, 'Businessmen, the urban middle classes, and the "dominance" of manufacturers, 66-85; Koditschek, *Class Formation*, 116-17.

50. Exceptions to this are K. Donaldson, 'The Cox Family, the Linen Trade and the Growth of Lochee to 1921', unpublished M.Phil. thesis (University of Dundee, 1972); *Baxter's of Dundee*, ed. A. Cooke (Dundee: University of Dundee, 1980); and D. Chapman, 'William Brown of Dundee, 1791–1864: Management in a Scottish Flax Mill', *Explorations in Entrepreneurial History*, 4, 3 (Feb. 1952), 119–34.

51. See for example, W. G. Rimmer, *Marshalls of Leeds. Flaxspinners, 1788–1886* (Cambridge, 1960); and P. L. Payne, 'Industrial Entrepreneurship and Management in Great Britain', in *Cambridge Economic History of Europe*, 7, 2, eds P. Mathias and M. M. Postan (Cambridge, 1978).

52. Koditschek, *Class Formation*, 165–6.

53. See Miller, *Dundee Past and Present*, 94–5.

54. Dundee University Archives [DUA], MS 6, Diary of James Cock, 65.

55. E. Gauldie, *The Dundee Textile Industry, 1790–1885, from the papers of Peter Carmichael of Arthurstone*, (Edinburgh, 1969) 16.

56. Norrie, *Dundee Celebrities*, 242.

57. *Religious Census of Great Britain, 1851.* Religious Worship and Education, Scotland (London, 1854), 25.

58. C. G. Brown, 'Religion, Class and Church Growth', in *People and Society in Scotland volume 2, 1830–1914*, eds W. H. Fraser and R. J. Morris (Edinburgh, 1995), 320; and A. A. MacLaren, *Religion and Social Class in the Disruption Years in Aberdeen* (London, 1974), 213.

59. DUA, MS11/5/14, C. Mackie, 'Reminiscences of Flaxspinning from 1806-1866', 56.

60. DUA, MS15/45/1, J. R. L. Halley, 'Business in Dundee in the Nineteenth Century'.

61. C. A. Whatley, *Onwards from Osnaburgs: the rise and progress of a Scottish textile company, Don and Low of Forfar, 1792–1992* (Edinburgh, 1992), 112.

62. DUA, MS11/5/14, Mackie, 'Reminiscences', 56.

63. DPL, LC 391(46) Biographical note on George Thoms.

64. DPL, Dundee Obituary Book 1, 113–15, obituary of Patrick Hunter Thoms, June 1882.

65. *Dundee Year Book* 1882, 87, obituary of William Thoms, May 1882.

66. G. Anderson, *Victorian Clerks* (Manchester, 1976), 11.

67. See R. Guerriero Wilson, 'Office workers, business elites and the disappearance of the "ladder of success" in Edwardian Glasgow', *Scottish Economic and Social History*, 19, 1 (1999), 55–6.

68. DPL, LC398, 96-105, obituary of George Duncan, 6 January 1878.

69. For biographical information on Patrick Anderson see Millar, *Eminent Burgesses*, 242. For Symers, see Norrie, *Dundee Celebrities*, 269–70.

70. For a discussion of the marriage patterns of Black Country elites see Trainor, *Black Country Elites*, 121.

71. See Norrie, *Dundee Celebrities*, 49–50.

72. See Millar, *Eminent Burgesses*, 259.

73. Scottish Record Office [SRO], SC45/31/6, Inventory and Will of Thomas Bell of Belmont. Died 9 Jan. 1844.

74. SRO, SC45/31/38, Inventory and Will of Thomas Bell, junior, of Belmont, died 2 Feb. 1887.

75. For biographical information on Charles Boase, see Millar, *Eminent Burgesses*, 268; and for William Lindsay see DPL, LC 398, 208–12.

76. For biographical information on Thomas Nicholson, see DPL, Dundee Obituary Book 1, 10 Aug. 1882, 87–8.

77. V. A. C. Gatrell, 'Incorporation and the pursuit of Liberal hegemony in Manchester, 1790–1839', in *Municipal Reform and the Industrial City*, ed. D. Fraser (Leicester, 1982), 24.

78. For example, James Carmichael, engineer, was said to be 'so thoroughly devoted to his own profession' that he had little time for anything else. *Dundee Courier and Argus*, 19 Jun. 1876.

79. See J. Garrard, *Leadership and Power*, 65–71.

80. Miller, *Dundee Past and Present*, 97.

81. Lenman, Lythe and Gauldie, *Dundee and its Textile Industry*, 80.

82. See Miller, *Dundee Past and Present*, 104; *Dundee Year Book* 1894, obituary of Joseph Grimond, 57–60.

83. DPL, Obituary Book 2, obituary of Alexander J. Buist, 15 Apr. 1901.

84. A. Elliot, *Lochee: as it was and as it is* (Dundee, 1911), 14–20.

85. See J. Thomson, *The History of Dundee* (Dundee, 1874), 339.

86. DUA, MS6, Diary of James Cock, 62.

87. Gauldie, *The Dundee Textile Industry*, 126-9.

88. DUA, MS6, Diary of James Cock, post-1834 section, 3.

89. DUA, MS15/45/1, Halley, 'Business in Dundee'.

90. W. D. Rubinstein, *Elites and the Wealthy in Modern Britain. Essays in Social and Economic History* (Brighton, 1987).

91. See SRO, SC45 Confirmations and Inventories, various volumes.

92. C. A. Whatley, D. Swinfen and A. Smith, *The Life and Times of Dundee* (Edinburgh, 1993), 110.

93. I. Maver, 'Glasgow's Civic Government', in *Glasgow, volume 2, 1830–1912*, eds D. Fraser and I. Maver (Manchester, 1997), 443.

94. See A. A. MacLaren, 'Class formation and class fractions. The Aberdeen bourgeoisie, 1830–1850', in *Scottish Urban History*, eds G. Gordon and B. Dicks (Aberdeen, 1983), 113.

95. For a discussion of this issue see *Dundee Advertiser*, 24 Nov. 1868.

96. Lenman and Gauldie, 'Industrial History of the Dundee Region', 169.

97. G. T. Stewart, *Jute and Empire. The Calcutta Jute Wallahs and the Landscapes of Empire* (Manchester, 1998), 2–3.

98. Bremner, *Industries of Scotland*, 252.

99. Jackson, 'Population', 90.

100. Fraser, *Urban Politics*, 91–2.

101. DPL, LC 319(14), Police and Improvement (Scotland) Act, 1850, section 39.

102. J. E. Callison, 'Politics, Class and Water Supply in Dundee, 1831–1845', unpublished M.Phil. thesis (University of Dundee, 1985), 158.

103. *Dundee Year Book*, 1914, obituary of William Brownlee.

104. *Dundee Advertiser*, 3 Nov. 1868.

105. *Ibid.*, 27 Nov. 1868.

106. *Ibid.*, 24 Nov. 1868.

107. *Dundee Year Book*, 1889, obituary of Frank Henderson, 53–6.

108. Reprinted in *Dundee Advertiser*, 4 Dec. 1868.

109. J. Kemp, 'Red Tayside? Political Change in Early Twentieth Century Dundee'.

110. *Dundee Advertiser*, 27 Nov. 1868.

111. C. A. Whatley, 'Altering Images of the Industrial City: the case of James Myles, the "factory boy" and mid-Victorian Dundee'.

112. *Dundee Advertiser*, 1 Dec. 1868.

113. Nenadic, 'Business, the Urban Middle Classes and the "dominance" of manufacturers', 67.

114. DPL, LC 217(63) newspaper cuttings on Alexander H. Moncur, 10 Jan. 1883.

115. For details, see D. M. Walker, 'The Architecture of Dundee' in *Dundee and District*, ed. S. J. Jones, (Dundee, 1968), 291–2.

Chapter Four

1. Nevertheless, Scottish working-class autobiographies from the nineteenth century are not hard to find, see D. Vincent, *Bread, Knowledge and Freedom: A Study of Nineteenth-Century Working Class Autobiography* (London, 1981), 8; the book has also been placed within the genre of propaganda tracts written by and in support of factory reformers such as Michael Sadler and Richard Oastler, J. T. Ward, 'The Factory Movement', in *Popular Movements*, ed. J. T. Ward (London, 1970), 70.

2. E. P. Thompson, *Customs in Common* (London, 1993 ed.), 389–90.

3. See B. Lenman, C. Lythe and E. Gauldie, *Dundee and its Textile Industry 1850–1914* (Dundee, 1969), 18; W. M. Walker, *Juteopolis: Dundee and its textile workers 1885–1923* (Edinburgh, 1979), 103, 118; E. Gordon, *Women and the Labour Movement in Scotland 1850–1914* (Oxford, 1991), 155; T. C. Smout and S. Wood, *Scottish Voices 1745–1960* (London, 1991 ed.), 69–72; the present author has used the source too, describing it as 'a vivid account of a system which was bad enough in the towns but even worse in the countryside', C. A. Whatley, 'The Experience of Work', in *People and Society in Scotland, I, 1760–1830*, ed. T. M. Devine and R. Mitchison (Edinburgh, 1988), 245. See too C. Beveridge and R. Turnbull, *Scotland After Enlightenment* (Edinburgh, 1997), 132–3.

4. A. Noble, 'Urbane Silence: Scottish Writing and the Nineteenth-Century City', in *Perspectives of the Scottish City*, ed. G. Gordon (Aberdeen, 1985), 73.

5. Such depictions of Dundee are to be found in Walker, *Juteopolis*, 121; S. and O. Checkland, *Industry and Ethos: Scotland 1832–1914* (London, 1984), 45–7; R. J. Morris, 'Urbanisation and Scotland', in *People and Society in Scotland Volume II, 1830–1914*, ed. W. H. Fraser and R. J. Morris (Edinburgh, 1990), 80.

6. See W. H. Fraser, 'The Working Class', in *Glasgow, Volume II: 1830 to 1912*, ed. W. H. Fraser and I. Maver (Manchester, 1996), 318–9; for a recent survey of economic and social conditions in the period see W. W. Knox, *Industrial Nation: Work, Culture and Society in Scotland 1800–Present* (Edinburgh, 1999), 81–126.

7. W. W. Knox, 'Whatever Happened to Radical Scotland? the Economic and Social Origins of the Mid-Victorian Political Consensus in Scotland', in *People and Power in Scotland: Essays in Honour of T. C. Smout*, ed. R. Mason and N. Macdougall (Edinburgh, 1992), chapter 10.

8. E. F. Biagini and A. J. Reid, 'Currents of radicalism' in *Currents of Radicalism. Popular radicalism, organised labour and party politics in Britain, 1850–1914,* ed. E. F. Biagini and A. J. Reid (Cambridge, 1991), 5.

9. J. Horst, *Victorian Labour History. Experience, identity and the politics of representation* (London, 1998), 63–70.

10. For a brief, comprehensible discussion of what is a complex debate, see M. Hewitt, *The Emergence of Stability in the Industrial City: Manchester, 1832–67* (Aldershot, 1996), 1–22; working-class poets in Dundee were exhorted by their main newspaper publishers to stick to practical topics, about which they knew something, and in this sense they can be considered as first-hand evidence.

11. *Northern Warder*, 3 Jan., 28 Mar.1850.

12. W. Norrie, *Dundee Celebrities of the Nineteenth Century* (Dundee, 1873), 132–3.

13. *People's Journal*, 23, 30 May 1903.

14. Vincent, *Bread, Knowledge and Freedom*, 23.

15. J. Myles, *Chapters in the Life of a Dundee Factory Boy* (Dundee, 1980 ed), 74.

16. Norrie, *Dundee Celebrities*, 132–3; S. Strap, *Feasts of Literary Crumbs* (Dundee, 1848).

17. *New Moral World*, 18 Sep. 1841, 14 Jan., 11, 18 Feb., 1 Apr. 1843; W. H. Fraser, 'Owenite Socialism in Scotland', *Scottish Economic & Social History*, 16 (1996), 70–9; I am grateful to Professor Fraser for drawing my attention to the material in the *New Moral World*.

18. J. Myles, *Rambles in Forfarshire or Sketches of Town and Country* (Dundee, 1850), 70; Norrie, *Dundee Celebrities*, 383–9; L. C. Wright, *Scottish Chartism* (Edinburgh, 1853), 152–3, 210.

19. Fraser, 'Owenite Socialism', 78–80.

20. *The Reasoner*, 4, 92 (Mar. 1848), 184–6.

21. M. Vicinus, *The Industrial Muse: A Study of Nineteenth Century British Working-Class Literature* (London, 1974), 95; R. Gray, *The factory question and industrial England, 1830–1860* (Cambridge, 1996), 142–3.

22. W. Donaldson, *Popular Literature in Victorian Scotland: language, fiction and the press* (Aberdeen, 1986), 77–83.

23. *Ibid.*, 88–92.

24. Myles, *Chapters*, 20.

25. *Northern Warder*, 14 Feb. 1850.

26. G. Morton, 'The Most Efficacious Patriot: The Heritage of William Wallace in Nineteenth-Century Scotland', *Scottish Historical Review*, 77 (Oct. 1998), 225–6.

27. E. F. Biagini, *Liberty, Retrenchment and Reform. Popular Liberalism in the Age of Gladstone, 1860–1880* (Cambridge, 1992), 37; *People's Journal*, 14 Jan. 1865.

28. Myles, *Chapters*, 69.

29. *Ibid.*, 55.

30. A. Elliot, *Lochee: As it Was and Is* (Dundee, 1911), 35.

31. C. W. Munn, *The Scottish Provincial Banking Companies 1717–1864* (Edinburgh, 1981), 75–7; *The Dundee Textile Industry 1790–1885*, ed. E. Gauldie (Edinburgh, 1969), 76-7.

32. Myles, *Chapters*, 60–1.

33. T. C. Smout, *A Century of the Scottish People* (London, 1986), 234; W. H.

Fraser, 'The Scottish Context of Chartism', in *Covenant, Charter and Party. Traditions of Revolt and Protest in Modern Scottish History*, ed. T. Brotherstone (Aberdeen, 1989), 70.

34. For Myles on the urban working classes see his *Picture of a Political Demagogue: A Sketch From Life &c., &c.* (Dundee, 1850).

35. Myles, *Rambles*, 17–18.

36. Vicinus, *The Industrial Muse*, 32.

37. Donaldson, *Popular Literature*, 92–9.

38. Knox, *Industrial Nation*, 81.

39. M. St John, *The Demands of the People. Dundee Radicalism 1850–1870* (Dundee, 1997), 13–31.

40. *People's Journal*, 21 Mar. 1863.

41. *Ibid.*, 11 Jun. 1859, 1 Jul. 1865.

42. *Ibid.*, 4 Mar. 1865.

43. *Ibid.*, 25 Feb., 10, 31 Mar. 1860, 7 Jan. 1865.

44. *Ibid.*, 21 Nov. 1868.

45. C. McGurk, 'Burns and Nostalgia', in *Burns Now*, ed. K. G. Simpson (Edinburgh, 1994), 33, 60–1; see too R. J. Finlay, 'The Burns cult and Scottish identity in the nineteenth and twentieth centuries', in *Love & Liberty*, ed. K. G. Simpson (East Linton, 1997), 72–3.

46. E. Johnston, *Autobiography: Poems and Songs of Ellen Johnston, The 'Factory Girl'* (Glasgow, 1867), 102–3.

47. *Dundee Advertiser*, 10 Sep. 1863; *Fife Herald*, 10 Sep. 1863

48. *Northern Warder*, 11 Apr. 1850; *Perth and Cupar Advertiser*, 27 May, 7 Jun. 1853; C. A. Whatley, '"The privilege which the rabble have to be riotous": carnivalesque and the monarch's birthday in Scotland *c.*1700–1860', in *Labour and Leisure in Historical Perspective, Thirteenth to Twentieth Centuries*, ed. I. Blanchard (Stuttgart, 1994), 89–100.

49. Dundee University Archives [DUA], MS 101/1/2, Peter Carmichael, Life and Letters, Vol. 2, 326-30; Ward, 'Trade Unionism in Dundee', 250.

50. J. T. Ward, 'Trade Unionism in Dundee', in *The Third Statistical Account of Scotland. The City of Dundee*, ed. J. M. Jackson (Arbroath, 1979), 247–83; Gordon, *Women and the Labour Movement*, 102–36.

51. M. Knight, 'She-Devils: Women and Crime in Dundee 1842–1852', unpublished M.A. dissertation (University of Dundee, 1994), 10, 19–38.

52. R. J. Morris, 'The middle class and British towns and cities in the industrial revolution', 1780–1870', in *The Pursuit of Urban History*, ed. D. Fraser and A. Sutcliffe (London, 1983), 290–3.

53. Anon., *Memorandum of the Chartist Agitation in Dundee* (Dundee, 1889), 29–50; Dundee City Archives [DCA], General Committee Minutes, vol. 3, 1839–1843.

54. Perth and Kinross Council Archives, PE16/360, Major General Lord Greenock to John Graham, 22 Sep. 1837.

55. *Northern Warder*, 15 Aug. 1850; G. Gilfillan, *Letters and Journals, with Memoir*, ed. R. A. and E. S. Watson (London, 1892), 187. Aileen Black kindly supplied me with this reference.

56. Gauldie, *Dundee Textile Industry*, 84, 110–12.

57. Ward, 'Trade Unionism in Dundee', 249–50.

58. S. G. Paul, 'Dundee Radical Politics 1834–1850', unpublished M.Phil. thesis (University of Dundee, 1998), 23.
59. Gauldie, *Dundee Textile Industry*, 84.
60. J. Ireland, *The Life of a Dundee Draper* (Dundee, 1878), 22–33.
61. C. A. Whatley, 'The making of "Juteopolis": and how it was' in *The Remaking of Juteopolis, Dundee c.1891–1991*, ed. C. A. Whatley (Dundee, 1992), 11; T. M. Devine, 'Urbanisation and the Civic Response: Glasgow, 1800–30', in *Industry, Business and Society in Scotland Since 1700*, ed. A. J. G. Cummings and T. M. Devine (Edinburgh, 1994), 191–4.
62. Paul, 'Dundee radical Politics', 185.
63. L. C. Wright, *Scottish Chartism* (London, 1953), 153; Norrie, *Dundee Celebrities*, 101–2; W. Thom, *Rhymes and Recollections of A Hand-Loom Weaver* (London, 1845 ed.), 3, 72–6.
64. Knox, *Industrial Nation*, 83; P. Joyce, 'Work', in *The Cambridge Social History of Britain 1750–1950, Volume 2, People and their environment*, ed. F. M. L. Thompson (Cambridge, 1990), 168–9; the classic account is Joyce's *Work, Society & Politics: The culture of the factory in later Victorian England* (London, 1982 ed.).
65. DUA, MS 105/XI/1, Minute Book of Baxter Park, vol 1, 1863–1901, 4.
66. Dundee Public Library [DPL], Lamb Collection [LC], 228 (24), notes and cuttings on Balgay Hill; on localism, see C. M. M. Macdonald, 'Weak roots and branches: class, gender and the geography of industrial protest', *Scottish Labour History*, 33 (1998), 7–9, and 'The vanduaria of Ptolemy: place and the past', in *Image and Identity: The Making and Re-making of Scotland Through the Ages*, ed. D. Broun, R. J. Finlay and M. Lynch (Edinburgh, 1998), 177–8.
67. DCA, General Committee Minutes, vol. 4, 1842–54, 17 Feb. 1851, vol. 5, 1854–64, 13 Dec. 1854, 31 Mar. 1855, 12 Jul. 1856.
68. L. Walsh, 'The Development of Organised Charity in the Scottish Burgh: Dundee 1790–1850, unpublished Ph.D. thesis (University of Dundee, 1997), 51–2, 227.
69. Myles, *Rambles in Forfarshire*, xiii; *People's Journal*, 31 Jan. 1863; P. Joyce, *Visions of the People. Industrial England and the question of class 1848–1914* (Cambridge, 1991), 59; T. Koditschek, 'The dynamics of class formation in nineteenth-century Bradford', in *The First Modern Society*, ed. A. L. Beier, D. Cannadine and J. M. Rosenheim (Cambridge, 1989), 538.
70. J. V. Smith, *The Watt Institution, Dundee 1824–49* (Dundee, 1978), 44.
71. C. A. Whatley, D. B. Swinfen and A. M. Smith, *The Life and Times of Dundee* (Edinburgh, 1993), 121; see G. Gilfillan's introduction in J. Easson, *Select Miscellany of Poetical Pieces* (Perth, 1856); and *City Songs* (Dundee, n.d.).
72. DUA, MS 15/114/2, Diary of Thomas Handyside Baxter, 29 Apr. 1830.
73. See W. W. Knox, *Hanging By a Thread: The Scottish Cotton Industry c.1850–1914* (Preston, 1995).
74. *Myles' Forfarshire Telegraph*, 4 Jan. 1851; *People's Journal*, 4 Jan. 1862, 24 May 1862, 28 Jan. 1865.
75. H. J. C. Gibson, *Dundee Royal Infirmary, 1798–1948* (Dundee, 1948), 72.
76. DPL, LC, 196 (14), newspaper clippings on the opening of Manhattan Works, 16 Jul. 1874.
77. DPL, LC 196 (14) MS note on Gilroy's works, n.d; M. Watson, *Jute and Flax Mills in Dundee* (Tayport, 1990), 56.

78. Material drawn from M. Watson's comprehensive *Jute and Flax Mills In Dundee*; see too G. Jackson and K. Kinnear, *The Trade and Shipping of Dundee 1780–1850* (Dundee, 1991) and Whatley, Swinfen and Smith, *Life and Times of Dundee*, 65–71.

79. *People's Journal*, 2 Nov. 1867.

80. This is summarised in Knox, *Hanging By a Thread*, 121–2.

81. *People's Journal*, 30 Aug. 1862, 27 Apr. 1861.

82. M. Savage and A. Miles, *The Remaking of the British Working Class 1840–1940* (London, 1994), 43.

83. Walsh, 'The Development of Organised Charity', 123.

84. For a case study of class reciprocity in the civilising of the city see A. J. Croll, 'Civilising the Urban: Popular Culture, Public Space and Urban Meaning, Merthyr *c.*1870–1914', unpublished Ph.D. thesis (University of Wales, 1997).

85. DPL, LC, 103(9), Rev. J. MacPherson, 'A Word to the People of God in Dundee on the Opening of Baxter Park on Sabbath-Day' (1863); *People's Journal*, 21, 28 Feb. 1863.

86. DPL, LC, 228 (24), cuttings on Balgay Park; *Hand Book to the Places of Public Recreation in Dundee* (Dundee, n.d.).

87. *Dundee Advertiser*, 27 Jan. 1863.

88. Biagini, *Liberty, Retrenchment and Reform*, 20–8.

89. Donaldson, *Popular Literature in Victorian Scotland*, 23–34.

90. *People's Journal*, 28 May 1859.

91. DPL, LC, 196 (A), 39, letter to editor of *People's Journal* (n.d.).

92. Anon., *Dundee and Dundonians Seventy Years Ago* (Dundee, 1892), 53; Norrie, *Dundee Celebrities*, 385; Donaldson, *Popular Literature*, 28.

93. Biagini, *Liberty, Retrenchment and Reform*, 31–41.

94. C. G. Brown, *Religion and Society in Scotland Since 1707* (Edinburgh, 1997), 111–12.

95. E. W. McFarland, *Protestants First: Orangeism in 19th Century Scotland* (Edinburgh, 1990), 99.

96. J. Wolffe, *The Protestant Crusade in Great Britain 1829–1860* (Oxford, 1991), 150–1, 160; C. A. Whatley, *The Diary of John Sturrock, Millwright, Dundee, 1864–65* (East Linton, 1996), 49.

97. DUA, MS 15/114/2, Diary of Thomas Handyside Baxter, 19, 25 Feb. 1829; Whatley, *Diary of John Sturrock*, 45.

98. McFarlane, *Protestants First*, 9.

99. Whatley, *Diary of John Sturrock*, 14–15, 98–9; *People's Journal*, 30 Jun. 1860; Biagini, *Liberty, Retrenchment and Reform*, 372–5.

100. G. Morton, *Unionist Nationalism: Governing Scotland, 1830–1860* (East Linton, 1999), 155–88.

101. *Ibid.*, 135–54; see too DCA, General Committee Minutes, vol. 5, 1854–1864; *People's Journal*, 25 May 1867.

102. *People's Journal*, 28 Sep. 1860.

103. Fraser, 'The Scottish Context of Chartism', 71–2.

104. This differs from the explanation given for the anti-aristocratic element of popular liberalism provided by Biagini, *Liberty, Retrenchment and Reform*, 50–60; see too T. Koditschek, *Class Formation and Urban Industrial Society: Bradford 1750–1850* (Cambridge, 1990), 23–31.

105. *Dundee and Dundonians Seventy Years Ago*, 8–9.

106. *People's Journal*, 20 Aug. 1859

107. *Ibid.*, 29 Sep., 20 Oct. 1860.

108. *Scottish population history from the 17th century to the 1930s*, ed. M. Flinn (Cambridge, 1977), 466-9.

109. *People's Journal*, 25 May 1867.

110. Flinn, *Scottish population history*, 467.

111. C. W. J. Withers, *Urban Highlanders. Highland-Lowland Migration and Urban Gaelic Culture, 1700–1900* (East Linton, 1999), 96-105.

112. Joyce, 'Work', 140–3.

113. *Dundee and Dundonians Seventy Years Ago*, 54.

114. Whatley, 'Experience of Work', 242.

115. Whatley, 'The Making of "Juteopolis"', 7.

116. DUA, MS 15/26/1, W. Brown, 'Essays on Flax Spinning and Remarks on the Management of East Mill, Dundee' (1819–23), 9–10; MS 102/1/2, P. Carmichael, 'Life and Letters', vol. 2, 44, 260.

117. *Ibid.*, 86-99, 344; see too, for example, National Archives of Scotland, GD1/879/1, Diary of William Stephen, 1 Sep. 1870.

118. C. A. Whatley, *Onwards From Osnaburgs: The Rise & Progress of a Scottish Textile Company* (Edinburgh, 1992), 78–86, 122–5.

119. Lenman, Lythe and Gauldie, *Textile Industry*, 67; Whatley, *Diary of John Sturrock*, 5–7; Gordon, *Women and the Labour Movement*, 170.

120. Knight, 'She-Devils', 35.

121. Whatley, *The Diary of John Sturrock*, 8; *Dundee and Dundonians*, 60.

122. DCA, GD/X99/10, Memoir of Alexander Moncur, 1869.

123. M. Gray, *Scots on the Move. Scots Migrants 1750–1914* (Glasgow, 1990), 14–23.

124. B. Collins, 'The Origins of Irish Immigration to Scotland', in *Irish Immigrants and Scottish Society in the Nineteenth and Twentieth Centuries*, ed. T. M. Devine (Edinburgh, 1991), 5–6.

125. N. Murray, *The Scottish Handloom Weavers 1790–1850: A Social History* (Edinburgh, 1978), 203.

126. R. J. Morris, 'Urbanisation', in *Modern Scottish History, 1707 to the Present, Volume 2: The Modernisation of Scotland, 1850 to the Present*, ed. A. Cooke, I. Donnachie, A. MacSween and C. A. Whatley (East Linton, 1998), 132–4; R. J. Morris, 'Clubs, societies and associations', in *The Cambridge Social History of Britain 1750–1950*, ed. F. M. L. Thompson (Cambridge 1993), 416-8; *Dundee and Dundonians*, 57–61.

127. N. Murray, 'The Regional Structure of Textile Employment in Scotland in the Nineteenth Century: East of Scotland Hand Loom Weavers in the 1830s', in *Industry, Business and Society*, ed. Cummings and Devine, 229; Gauldie, *Dundee Textile Industry*, 84; Myles, *Rambles in Forfarshire*, 80–92.

128. B. E. Collins, 'Aspects of Irish Immigration into Scottish Towns (Dundee and Paisley) During the Mid-Nineteenth Century', unpublished M.Phil. thesis (University of Edinburgh, 1979), 120, 171–4; *People's Journal*, 18 Apr. 1868.

129. Collins, 'Aspects of Immigration', 194.

130. Myles, *Rambles in Forfarshire*, 20; Walker, *Juteopolis*, 118; Walsh, 'The Development of Organised Charity', 115–16.

131. DUA, MS 102/1/2, P. Carmichael, 'Life and Letters', vol. 2, 45.

132. Walker, *Juteopolis*, 121, 122–34; Collins, 'Aspects of Irish Immigration', 180–93, 236; E. W. McFarland, 'The Fenian Panic in Mid-Victorian Scotland', *Scottish Historical Review*, 77 (October 1998), 202–3.

133. Whatley, ' "Juteopolis" ', 11–13; Whatley, Swinfen and Smith, *The Life and Times of Dundee*, 105–9; more forceful are Lenman, Lythe and Gauldie, *Textile Industry*, 77–102.

134. *Dundee Advertiser*, 7 Jun. 1853.

135. G. Lewis, *The Tavern Bill of Dundee, and What Might be Made of It* (Dundee, 1841), *The Filth and Fever Bills of Dundee, and What Might be Made of Them* (Dundee, 1841).

136. Whatley, *Diary of John Sturrock*, 53; *People's Journal*, 28 Dec. 1867.

137. Calculated from R. Rodger, 'Employment, wages and poverty in the Scottish cities 1841–1914', in *Perspectives of the Scottish City*, ed. G. Gordon (Aberdeen, 1985), 29.

138. See Gordon, *Women and the Labour Movement*, 141–2.

139. Knox, *Hanging By a Thread*, 115–43.

140. J. M. Beatts, *The Municipal History of Dundee* (Dundee, 1878), xvii-xxvii.

141. *People's Journal*, 11 Jul. 1903.

142. For a wider discussion see P. Joyce, 'A people and a class: industrial workers and the social order in nineteenth-century England', in *Social Orders and Social Class in Europe Since 1500: Studies in social stratification*, ed. M. L. Bush (London, 1992), 212–7.

143. See W. H. K. Turner, 'The development of flax spinning mills in Scotland, 1787–1840', *Scottish Geographical Magazine*, 98 (1982), 11; DUA, MS 102/1/3, P. Carmichael, 'Life and Letters', vol. 3, 75, 135, 147; G. T. Stewart, *Jute and Empire* (Manchester, 1998), 66-7.

144. Gordon, *Women and the Labour Movement*, 170–211.

Chapter Five

1. In its annual report, the Infirmary congratulated itself on its success in dispensing healthcare 'from the Grampians to the Firth of Forth'. See Dundee Public Library [DPL], Lamb Collection [LC] 404(2), Dundee Royal Infirmary [DRI] *Annual Report* (1825).

2. St Andrews University Archives [StAUA], M 415, DRI minute book vol.1, 28 Jun. 1794.

3. *Ibid.*, general meeting, 10 Jun. 1799.

4. DPL, LC 36(1), *List of Subscribers to the Dundee Dispensary* (1795–6).

5. StAUA, M 415, DRI minute book vol.1, 11 Aug. 1800.

6. *Ibid.*, 9 Feb., 2 Mar., 8 Jun. 1801.

7. *Ibid.*.1, 6 Feb. 1797; 18 Jun. 1798.

8. *Ibid.*, 26 Jan. 1795.

9. *Ibid.*, 11 Jan. 1802; 6 Dec. 1802.

10. DUA, THB 1/2/2, DRI *Annual Report* (1839).

11. Dundee City Archives, GD/X207/1, *Handbook to the Charitable Institutions of Dundee* (n.d.).

12. S. G. E. Lythe and J. Butt, *An Economic History of Scotland, 1100–1939* (Glasgow, 1975), 96.

13. B. Lenman, C. Lythe and E. Gauldie, *Dundee and its Textile Industry, 1850–1914* (Dundee, 1969), 11.
14. British Association *Handbook and Guide to Dundee and District* (Dundee, 1912), 45.
15. See C. McKean and D. Walker, *Dundee. An Illustrated Architectural Guide* (Edinburgh, 1993), 116.
16. DPL, LC 404 (1), DRI *Annual Report* (1828).
17. See description in DUA MS11/5/14, C. Mackie, 'Reminiscences of Flax Spinning', c.1866.
18. DUA, THB 1/2/2, DRI *Annual Report* (1848).
19. DUA, MS 15/26/1, Essays on Flax-Spinning and Remarks on the Management of East Mill, Dundee (1819).
20. DUA, THB 1/2/5, DRI *Annual Report* (1875).
21. Figures from DRI Annual Reports, 1865–1900.
22. See Glasgow Royal Infirmary Annual Reports, 1865–1900.
23. For a discussion of the activities of these and other societies in Scotland see O. Checkland, *Philanthropy in Victorian Scotland. Social Welfare and the Voluntary Principle* (Edinburgh, 1980), 298–309.
24. See M. Baillie, 'The Greylady of Dundee'.
25. L. Walsh, 'Subscribers to the Sick: the role of the nineteenth-century medical charity', unpublished paper.
26. DUA, MS 15/28, D. Lennox, *Working Class Life in Dundee for Twenty Five Years 1878–1903*, 251.
27. DUA, THB 1/2/6, DRI *Annual Report* (1892).
28. B. Abel-Smith, *The Hospitals 1800–1948. A Study in Social Administration in England and Wales* (London, 1964), 135.
29. Aberdeen University Archives [AUA], Lper Aa LI. 3 AI r, Aberdeen Royal Infirmary [ARI] *Annual Report* (1899).
30. DPL, LC 404 (1), DRI *Annual Report* (1831).
31. DUA, THB 1/5/2, DRI Admissions and Discharge Register (1848–58).
32. DUA, THB 1/3/1, DRI minute book 1902–1912, 155.
33. *Ibid.*, Jan. 1911.
34. Greater Glasgow Healthboard Archives [GGHBA], HB 14/2/9, Glasgow Royal Infirmary [GRI] *Annual Report* (1891).
35. GGHBA, HB 14/2/10, GRI *Annual Report* (1899).
36. *Ibid.* (1901).
37. K. Waddington, ' "Grasping Gratitude": Charity and Hospital Finance in Late-Victorian London' in *Charity, Self-Interest and Welfare in the English Past*, ed. M. Daunton (London, 1996), 187.
38. *British Medical Journal*, 26 May 1889, 1187, in Abel-Smith, *The Hospitals*, 136.

Chapter Six

1. With thanks to Professor Christopher A. Whatley for his suggestions and help with this chapter.
2. *People's Journal*, 20 Apr. 1872.
3. Dundee Public Library [DPL], Lamb Collection [LC], 278 (1–4), cuttings on Dundee maidservants.

4. *People's Journal,* 27 Jan., 3 Feb. 1872.
5. DPL, LC, 278 (1), cuttings on Dundee maidservants.
6. *People's Journal,* 10 Feb. 1872.
7. DPL, LC, 278 (1–4), cuttings on Dundee maidservants.
8. *Ibid.,* LC, 278 (2); Dundee Resident Sample, 1871 from J. Merchant, 'The Maidservant and the Female Labour Market in late Victorian and Edwardian Dundee', unpublished Ph.D. thesis (University of Dundee, 1998), 33–40.
9. DPL, LC, 278 (1–4), cuttings on Dundee maidservants.
10. *Ibid.*
11. J. Lewis, *Women in England 1870–1950* (London, 1984), 81; E. Gordon, *Women and the Labour Movement in Scotland* (Oxford, 1991), 2; C. Hall, *White, Male and Middle-Class: Explorations in Feminism and History* (Cambridge, 1992), 75–93.
12. Gordon, *Women and the Labour Movement.*
13. Classic texts are W. Walker, *Juteopolis: Dundee and its Textile Workers 1885–1923* (Edinburgh, 1979); B. Lenman, C. Lythe and E. Gauldie, *Dundee and its Textile Industry 1850–1914* (Dundee, 1969). More wide-ranging analyses include C. A. Whatley, D. B. Swinfen and A. M. Smith, *The Life and Times of Dundee* (Edinburgh, 1993) and *The Remaking of Juteopolis,* ed. C. A. Whatley (Dundee, 1992).
14. *Chambers's Journal,* various years.
15. *People's Journal,* 1892.
16. P. Horn, *The Rise and Fall of the Victorian Servant* (Stroud, 1996), 188.
17. *Ibid.,* 171.
18. L. Jamieson, 'Rural and Urban Women in Domestic Service', in *The World is Ill Divided. Women's Work in Scotland in the Nineteenth and Early Twentieth Centuries,* eds E. Gordon and E. Breitenbach (Edinburgh, 1990), 137; Gordon, *Women and the Labour Movement,* Table 1.4, 25. In 1891, the proportion of domestic servants was 29.6%. But this is an unreliable figure as the census included female family members who were enumerated as servants. Their terms of employment were different and require separate investigation.
19. Merchant, 'The Maidservant and the Female Labour Market', 158–77.
20. T. C. Smout, *A Century of the Scottish People 1830–1950* (London, 1987), 89–92.
21. Hall, *White, Male and Middle-Class,* 75–93; Carol Dyehouse, 'Mothers and daughters in the Middle-Class Home *c.* 1870–1914', in *Labour and Love: Women's Experience of Home and Family, 1850–1940,* ed. J. Lewis (Oxford, 1986), 28; E. Breitenbach and E. Gordon, 'Introduction' in *Out of Bounds: Women in Scottish Society 1800–1945,* eds E. Breitenbach and E. Gordon (Edinburgh, 1992), 5–8; S. Nenadic, 'The Rise of the Urban Middle-classes', in *People and Society in Scotland, Vol. 1, 1760–1830,* eds T. M. Devine and R. Mitchison (Edinburgh, 1988), 121. Many of these sources also note the failure of the domestic ideal and outline the difficulties encountered by the mistress in the middle-class home.
22. J. Harris, *Private Lives, Public Spirit: A Social History of Britain 1870–1914* (Oxford, 1993), 70–71; Dyehouse, 'Mothers and daughters', 34; M. M. Boase, *I Stir the Poppy Dust* (Cupar and St Andrews, 1936), 16, 23.
23. Smout, *A Century of the Scottish People,* 89–92; R. Gray, 'Thrift and Working

Class Mobility in Victorian Edinburgh', in *Social Class in Scotland: Past and Present*, ed. A. A. McLaren (Edinburgh, 1976); R. Gray, 'Religion, Culture and Social Class in Late Nineteenth and Early Twentieth Century Edinburgh', in *The Lower Middle-class in Britain 1870–1914*, ed. G. Crossick (London, 1977), Table 5.2, 155.

24. Gordon, *Women and the Labour Movement*, 80–1.
25. E. Roberts, *A Woman's Place: an oral history of working class women, 1890–1940* (Oxford, 1990); Gordon, *Women and the Labour Movement*, 80; Dundee Social Union [DSU], *Report on Housing and Industrial Conditions and Medical Inspection of School Children* (Dundee, 1905).
26. DSU, *Report on Housing*, 72.
27. J. Rendall, *Women in an Industrialising Society: England 1750–1880* (Oxford, 1990), 57, 60–2; Gordon, *Women and the Labour Movement*, 75, 136-7; V. A. Phillips, 'Classing the Women and Gendering the Class', in *Defining Women: Social Institutions and Gender Divisions*, eds L. McDowell and R. Pringle (Cambridge, 1992), 96-8.
28. Gordon, *Women and the Labour Movement*, 20, 142; DPL, LC, 196 (D).
29. DPL, LC, 196 (A).
30. Dundee University Archives [DUA], MS 15/28(1), D. Lennox, 'Working Class Life in Dundee for 25 Years 1878–1903', 169.
31. *1911 Census of Scotland Vol. II*, Table XXVIII.
32. *People's Journal*, 21, 28 Feb., 6 Jun. 1903; PP (1893), *The Employment of Women on the Conditions of Work in Various Industries in England, Wales, Scotland and Ireland*, C.6894–XXIII, 318; The Mitchell Library, C.239454, M. Irwin, *Women Shop Assistants* (1901).
33. Merchant, 'The Maidservant and the Female Labour Market', 84–124.
34. L. Davidoff, *Worlds Between, Historical Perspectives on Gender & Class* (Blackwell, 1995), 22.
35. Rendall, *Women in an Industrialising Society*, 100–1; Roberts, *A Woman's Place*, 54–6.
36. *People's Journal*, Jun.-Jul. 1903.
37. *Useful Toil: Autobiographies of Working People from the 1820's to the 1920's*, ed. J. Burnett (London, 1976), 165.
38. Walker, *Juteopolis*, 148.
39. Gordon, *Women and the Labour Movement*, 162.
40. Whatley, Swinfen and Smith, *Life and Times of Dundee*, 123.
41. PP (1893), Employment of Women in Scotland, 313, 318.
42. *People's Journal*, 6 Jun. 1903.
43. Gordon, *Women and the Labour Movement*, 156-61.
44. DPL, Dundee Oral History Project [DOHP], 040/A/2.
45. Burnett, *Useful Toil*, 171; DPL, LC, 278 (1–4), cuttings of Dundee maidservants.
46. DSU, *Report on Housing*, 49; Merchant, 'The Maidservant and the Female Labour Market', 84–124.
47. Interviews conducted by the author with Mrs P., Mrs D. and Mrs B., Dundee; DPL, DOHP, 011/B/1.
48. Interview with Mrs B.; Merchant, 'The Maidservant and the Female Labour Market', 116-20.

49. Interviews with Mrs B. and Mrs D.; DPL, DOHP, Tape no. 9.
50. Merchant, 'The Maidservant and the Female Labour Market', 111–12.
51. Walker, *Juteopolis*, 46; DPL, LC, 196 (A), (D).
52. C. H. Bull, 'Who are the Subalternists? A Study of Dundee's Millworkers from 1850–1885', unpublished M.Phil. thesis (University of St. Andrews, 1989), 27–9; Gordon, *Women and the Labour Movement*, 169–211.
53. *Dundee Advertiser*, 26 Mar. 1912.
54. Gordon, *Women and the Labour Movement*, 162.
55. DSU, *Report on Housing*, 41.
56. *Dundee Year Book*, 1909, 76.
57. *People's Journal*, 11 Jul. 1903; DSU, *Report on Housing*, 41.
58. Gordon, *Women and the Labour Movement*, 160; *People's Journal*, Jun.–Jul. 1903; PP (1893–94), Employment of Women in Scotland, *Minutes of Evidence, Group C*, XXXIV C.6894–IX, 96.
59. Gordon, *Women and the Labour Movement*, 152–3; PP (1893), *Employment of Women in Scotland*, 307, 309–10; *People's Journal*, 11 Jul. 1903; *Dundee Year Book*, 1884, 63.
60. For a discussion of the different models of maidservant employment related to requirements and social class see Merchant, 'The Maidservant and the Female Labour Market', 183–96, 200–13.
61. *People's Journal*, 4 May, 1872; *People's Journal*, 2 Jul. 1892.
62. Interviews with Mrs B. and Mrs D.; DPL, LC, 278 (1–4), cuttings on Dundee maidservants.
63. Interviews with Mrs B. and Mrs D.; Dyehouse, 'Mothers and daughters', 32; DPL, LC, 278 (1); Horn, *Rise and Fall*, 66, 129; M. C. Scott Moncrieff, *Yes Ma'am! Glimpses of Domestic Service 1901–51* (Edinburgh, 1984), 13, 16, 29, 56-58, 61.
64. *Dundee Advertiser*, 21 May, 1872.
65. *People's Journal*, 9 Mar. 1872.
66. DPL, LC, 278 (2), cuttings on Dundee maidservants.
67. *People's Journal*, 9 Jul. 1892.
68. DPL, LC, 278 (2), cuttings on Dundee maidservants.
69. *People's Journal*, 27 Jun. 1903.
70. DPL, LC, 278 (1), cuttings on Dundee maidservants.
71. *Chambers's Journal*, Apr. 1906.
72. PP (1893–94), Employment of Women in Scotland, *Minutes of Evidence*, 445.
73. *Dundee Year Book*, 1901, 207; *People's Journal*, 23 Mar. 1872.
74. DPL, LC, 278 (1), cuttings on Dundee maidservants.
75. PP (1919), *Report of the Women's Advisory Committee on the Domestic Service Problem*, XXIX, 28–9.
76. DPL, LC, 278 (2), cuttings on Dundee maidservants.
77. *Ibid.*, 278 (1).
78. *Ibid.*
79. Merchant, 'The Maidservant and the Female Labour Market', 263–26, 278–80.
80. *People's Journal*, 3 Feb. 1872.
81. *1871 Census of Scotland, Vol. 1*, 314.
82. Merchant, 'The Maidservant and the Female Labour Market', 39.

83. Census of Dundee (Enumerator Books), 1871.

84. *People's Journal*, 10 Sep. 1892

85. Lewis, *Women in England*, 113.

86. *People's Journal*, 23 Jul. 1892.

87. Mrs Beaton, quoted in Horn, *Rise and Fall*, 18.

88. Census of Dundee, P397 2821, Bk. 7, 1871.

89. Merchant, 'The Maidservant and the Female Labour Market',106, 111–12.

90. *Ibid.*, 158–62.

91. *Ibid.*

92. For a discussion on the mobility of maids, see *Ibid.*, 237–44.

93. *Ibid.*, 160.

94. DPL, LC, 278 (1–4), cuttings on Dundee maidservants.

95. *Ibid., Dundee Advertiser*, 21 May, 1872.

96. E. Higgs, 'Domestic Servants and Households in Rochdale, 1851–1871', unpublished D.Phil. thesis (University of Oxford, 1979), 40–5.

97. DPL, LC, 421 (54), *The Scottish Records Association Conference Report* (1985), 8, 10.

98. DUA, K.loc. 941.31 W319, *The Wasp: the Dundee Flagellator* (1897–98), 55.

99. *People's Journal*, 6 Mar. 1858.

100. DPL, LC, 231 (3), *Dundee Advertiser, Centenary Number 1801–1901*, 1.

101. *Ibid.*

102. *Ibid.*, 8.

103. DUA, K.loc, 052 L 218, A. C. Lamb, *Bibliography of Dundee Periodical Literature* (*c.*1891), 29–30.

104. *People's Journal*, various years.

105. *Dundee Year Book*, 1899, 68–71.

106. *People's Journal*, 23 Mar. 1872.

107. *Ibid.*, 4 May 1872.

108. *Ibid.*, 11 May 1872.

109. *Dundee Advertiser*, 30 Apr., 21 May 1872.

110. DPL, LC, 278 (1), cuttings on Dundee maidservants.

111. *Ibid.*, LC, 278 (4).

112. *People's Journal*, 3 Feb. 1872.

113. *Ibid.*, 6 Apr. 1872.

114. *Ibid.*, 13 Apr. 1872.

115. E. H. Hunt, *British Labour History 1815–1914* (London, 1981), 264–8.

116. *Dundee Advertiser*, 12 Jan. 1872.

117. *People's Journal*, 27 Jan. 1872.

118. *Dundee Advertiser*, 2 Jan., 13, 19 Mar. 1872; *People's Journal*, 10 Feb. 1872.

119. DPL, LC, 278 (1), cuttings on Dundee maidservants.

120. *Ibid.*, LC, 278 (1–4).

121. *Dundee Advertiser*, 30 Apr., 19, 21 Jun. 1872; *People's Journal*, 11 May 1872.

122. *People's Journal* (Perth and Stirling edition), 9 Mar. 1872.

123. *People's Journal* (Perth and Stirling edition), 23 May 1872.

124. PP (1893–94), Employment of Women in Scotland, *Minutes of Evidence*, 444; Horn, *Rise and Fall*, 179.

125. Bull, 'Who are the Subalternists?', 19.

126. Davidoff, *Worlds Between*, 22.

127. Merchant, 'The Maidservant and the Female Labour Market', 245; *1871 Census of Scotland,* 796.
128. Higgs, 'Domestic Servants and Households', 213, 214, 216, 237.
129. Horn, *Rise and Fall,* 180.
130. Gordon, *Women and the Labour Market,* 211.
131. Gordon, *Women and the Labour Market,* 169–211; DPL, LC, 196 (D).
132. DUA, MS 15/28 (1), Lennox, 'Working Class Life'.
133. Gordon, *Women and the Labour Market,* 142; Merchant, 'The Maidservant and the Female Labour Market', 299.
134. Gordon, *Women and the Labour Market,* 20.
135. Merchant, 'The Maidservant and the Female Labour Market', 113–24.
136. *People's Journal,* 16 Mar. 1872.
137. Merchant, 'The Maidservant and the Female Labour Market', 77–78, 246-48.
138. *Ibid.,* 299.
139. DPL, LC, 278 (1–4), cuttings on Dundee maidservants.
140. *Dundee Advertiser,* 10 May 1872.
141. DPL, LC, 278, (4), cuttings on Dundee maidservants.
142. Merchant, 'The Maidservant and the Female Labour Market', 160.
143. *People's Journal,* 18 May, 29 Jun. 1872.
144. DPL, LC, 278 (1–4), cuttings on Dundee maidservants.
145. *Ibid.,* LC, 278 (1).
146. Scottish Record Office [SRO], FS.1/16/89, Glasgow Gentlemen Servants Society; SRO, FS4/1077, West of Scotland Domestic Servants Friendly Society; PP (1893–94), Employment of Women in Scotland, *Minutes of Evidence,* 44–5.
147. Gordon, *Women and the Labour Movement,* 105, 183–4.

Chapter Seven

1. E. Gauldie, *Cruel Habitations: a History of Working Class Housing, 1780–1918* (London, 1974); B. P. Lenman, E. Gauldie, C. Lythe, *Dundee and its Textile Industry, 1850–1914* (Dundee, 1969).
2. J. Harris, *Private Lives, Public Spirit: Britain, 1870–1914* (London, 1993), 51.
3. A. McIvor, 'Gender Apartheid?': Women in Scottish Society', in *Scotland in the Twentieth Century,* ed. T. M. Devine and R. J. Finlay (Edinburgh, 1996), 188–209.
4. J. A. Hobson, 'The Social Philosophy of Charity Organization', *Contemporary Review* (1896), 710–27; G. Stedman-Jones, *Outcast London* (London, 1971), Part III, 239–336.
5. C. Booth, *Life and Labour of the People in London,* 17 vols, 1892–1904, reprint (New York, 1970); S. Rowntree, *Poverty: a Study of Town Life* (1901).
6. P. Clarke, *Liberals and Social Democrats* (Cambridge, 1978).
7. Dundee Social Union [DSU], *Annual Report* (1896), 19.
8. PP (1910), xlvi, Royal Commission on the Poor Laws, Minutes of Evidence (Scotland), Cd. 4978. Evidence of Walker, Q63373–63688; evidence of Kerr, Q62335–62559; evidence of Hadwen, 61831–61903; evidence of Bannatyne, Q59727–59986; evidence of Haldane, Q60748–61007.
9. *Ibid.,* evidence of Carlaw-Martin, Q63386-9, Q63487–9; evidence of Kerr, Q62336(5)-(8), Q62401–4.

10. M. L. Walker, 'Women and Children in Dundee', *Charity Organization Review* (1910), 31–42.
11. R. D. Anderson, *Education and Opportunity in Victorian Scotland* (Oxford, 1983), 255–7.
12. Dundee University Archives [DUA], UCD Calendars, 1884–85, 1885–86, 1886–87, 1887–88, 1888–89; DUA, RECS A/122,UCD Principal's Scrapbooks.
13. Gauldie, *Cruel Habitations,* 220; M. Shafe, *University Education in Dundee* (Dundee, 1982), 19.
14. *Dundee Advertiser,* 11 Dec. 1896.
15. DSU, *Annual Report* (1896), 19.
16. *Ibid.* (1899), 2.
17. *Ibid.* (1891), 13; calculated from DSU, *Annual Report* (1896), 11.
18. DSU, *Annual Reports.*
19. *Dundee Advertiser,* 7 Mar. 1905, 30 Mar.1906, 1 Apr. 1913.
20. St Andrews University Archive [StAUA], D'Arcy Wentworth Thompson papers [DWT], MS 44648.
21. *Ibid.,* MSS 44658, 44673.
22. DSU, *Annual Report* (1899), 2–3.
23. *Ibid.* (1901), 2.
24. *Dundee Advertiser,* 28 Oct. 1902.
25. DUA, T-GED 9/2327, photocopy of Geddes papers.
26. DSU, *Annual Report* (1902), 15–6, 1–2.
27. Dundee City Archives [DCA], GD/OC/GL 4/6/5, 'The work already undertaken by the DSU'.
28. *Dundee Advertiser,* 26 Mar. 1909.
29. W. Picht, *Toynbee Hall and the English Settlement House Movement* (London, 1914), 240–4.
30. C. M. Kendall, 'Higher Education and the Emergence of the Professional Woman in Glasgow, c.1890–1914', *History of Universities* 10 (1991), 199–223.
31. DCA, GD/OC/GL 4/6/5.
32. Royal Commission on Housing in Scotland, Evidence, 4 vols (Edinburgh, 1921), evidence of Rutherford, Q22,107–22, 377; evidence of Walker, 35,103 (1)-(63).
33. Kendall, 'Higher Education', 214.
34. DSU, *Report on Housing and Industrial Conditions,* vi-vii; for Wilson's work prior to Dundee, see M. Wilson, 'Employers' Liability and Workmen's Compensation', *Westminster Review* 149 (1898), 194–203; *Our Industrial Laws: Working Women in Factories, Workshops, Shops and Laundries, and How to Help Them* (London, 1899).
35. *Mary Lily Walker of Dundee: Some Memories,* ed. M. M. Paterson (Dundee, 1935), 17.
36. *Dundee Advertiser,* 30 Mar. 1906.
37. Inscription on the flyleaf of the copy held in the library of Northwestern University, Illinois, USA.
38. *Dundee Advertiser,* 11 Oct. 1905; DCA, Dundee Town Council Minutes, (1905–6), 111.

39. *The Times*, 2 Mar. 1907.
40. City of Edinburgh Charity Organization Society, *Report on the Physical Condition of Fourteen Hundred School Children in the City* (London, 1906).
41. DSU, *Report on Housing and Industrial Conditions*, 66-75.
42. *The Times*, 26 Dec. 1905; Paterson, *Mary Lily Walker*, 21.
43. DCA, GD/OC/GL 1/1/1, DSU Minute Book, 1906-20, 8 Mar. 1906.
44. Walker herself claimed that Dundee's restaurants were the first in Britain: M. L. Walker, 'Work among Women', *Handbook and Guide to Dundee and District* (Dundee, 1912), 72.
45. DCA, Dundee Town Council Minute Book, 16 Apr. 1908, 9 Jun. 1908, 31 Aug. 1908, 13 Oct. 1908, 4 Oct. 1910.
46. *Dundee Advertiser*, 24 Mar. 1908, 26 Mar. 1909, 17 Mar. 1911.
47. W. L. MacKenzie, *Scottish Mothers and Children: The U.K. Carnegie Trust Report on Physical Welfare (Scotland)* (Dunfermline, 1917), 303, 145–50, 155–7, 318, 575–8.
48. Paterson, *Mary Lily Walker*, 15.
49. H. Marland, 'A Pioneer in Infant Welfare: the Huddersfield Scheme, 1903–1920', *Social History of Medicine*, 6 (1993), 37.
50. DCA, GD/OC/GL 4/6/5, DSU Minute Book.
51. DSU, *Annual Report* (1902), 15–6; *Dundee Advertiser*, 28 Oct. 1902, 26 Feb. 1904.
52. *Dundee Advertiser*, 26 Feb. 1904; DCA, Dundee School Board Minutes, 20 Feb. 1905, 27 Mar. 1905, 24 Apr. 1905, 4 May 1905, 26 Apr. 1906, 10 May 1906, 14 Sep. 1906, 20 Sep. 1906, 11 Oct. 1906, 22 Oct. 1906; *Dundee Year Book* (1912), 50.
53. DSU, *Report on Housing and Industrial Conditions*, 110, Tables I-XVI.
54. *Dundee Advertiser*, 26 Mar. 1909.
55. *Ibid.*, 19 Mar. 1912; DCA, Dundee School Board Minutes, 11 Mar. 1912.
56. StAUA, DWT, MSS 14737, 14747, 14750.
57. DCA, Dundee School Board Minutes, 13 Apr. 1908.
58. DCA, GD/OC/GL 1/1/1, DSU Minute Book, 19 Apr. 1910, 19 May 1910, Feb. 1912, May 1912.
59. L. Leneman, 'Dundee and the Women's Suffrage Movement: 1907–1914', in *The Remaking of Juteopolis: Dundee c. 1891–1991*, ed. C. A. Whatley (Dundee, 1992), 80–95.
60. DCA, Dundee Distress Committee Minutes, 4 Dec. 1905, 9 Feb. 1906, 18 Dec. 1906, 20 Feb. 1906.
61. DCA, TC/SF/254, Children's Welfare Committee papers.
62. Royal Commission on Housing in Scotland, evidence of Walker, Q35103(1); Paterson, *Mary Lily Walker*, 9.
63. For example, *Dundee Advertiser*, 20 Dec. 1894, 27 Dec. 1895, 11 Dec. 1896.
64. M. Vicinus, *Independent Women: Work and Community for Single Women, 1850–1920* (London, 1985), 244.
65. M. Moore, 'Social Work and Social Welfare, the Organization of Philanthropic Resources in Britain, 1900–1914', *The Journal of British Studies*, 16 (1977), 92.
66. StAUA, DWT, MS 44654.
67. *Ibid.*, MSS 14724–5; Scottish Record Office [SRO], Register of Wills, SC 45/34/26, 242.

68. Dundee Public Library [DPL], Dundee Charity Organisation, annual report (1886): 3, 7; PP (1910), xlvi, Royal Commission on the Poor Laws, evidence of Walker, Q63,422.
69. Edinburgh Public Library, YHV 250E, Edinburgh Social Union, annual reports.
70. DCA, GD/OC/GL 3/1/1, Grey Lodge Settlement Committee.
71. DCA, GD/OC/GL 2/2 – 2/5, Dundee School of Social Study and Training, annual reports.
72. I would like to thank Dr. Richard Rempel for his help and encouragement, and the H. L. Hooker Fellowship for financing the archival research for this chapter.

Chapter Eight

1. E. Gauldie, *The Dundee Textile Industry, 1790–1885: from the papers of Peter Carmichael of Arthurstone* (Edinburgh, 1969), 228–9. Thanks must go to Lesley Lindsay for drawing my attention to the significance of this society.
2. See F. Young, *The Coming of Age of the Dundee Naturalists' Society* (Dundee, 1895); Dundee Public Libraries [DPL], Lamb Collection [LC] 378 (8).
3. DPL, LC 142(26), 8–12, Membership list appended to *Dundee Naturalists' Society, Tenth Annual Report, 1882–83*.
4. *Dundee* Advertiser, 31 Jul. 1835.
5. Emile Garcke, Managing Director of the British Electric Traction Company.
6. 'Electricity Supply', *Encylopaedia Britannica*, 11th edition, vol. 9, 198–9.
7. Gauldie, *Dundee Textile Industry*, 228–9.
8. DPL, LC, 142(25), 4, *Dundee Naturalists' Society, Ninth Annual Report, 1881–82*.
9. P. Boardman, *The Worlds of Patrick Geddes: Biologist, Town Planner, Re-educator, Peace-Warrior* (London, 1978), 55.
10. P. Abrams, *The Origins of British Sociology* (Chicago, 1968). Abrams notes also the influence of Geddes's close collaborator Victor Branford, whose contribution to the early formations of sociology was substantial, but has been little researched. Branford's papers are held at Keele University.
11. Boardman, *Geddes*, 78; and P. Kitchen, *A Most Unsettling Person: An Introduction to the Ideas and Life of Patrick Geddes* (London, 1975), 84.
12. Proposed by Professors Rutherford, Stirling, Turner and Sir Wyville Thomson. All fellowship information reported here is courtesy of Dr Lesley Campbell, Fellowship Officer, Royal Society of Edinburgh, who located it in the archive of the Society.
13. Young's other proposer was Professor Alleyne Nicholson.
14. DPL, LC 142(25), 4, *Dundee Naturalists' Society, Ninth Annual Report, 1881–82*.
15. Professor A. D. Peacock, quoted in Boardman, 54.
16. The membership list published with the DNS annual report for 1882–83 shows Geddes to be one of only 7 honorary members, another of whom was James Geikie.
17. Kitchen, *Unsettling Person*, 84 ff.
18. *Ibid.*, 85.
19. D. Southgate, *University Education in Dundee* (Edinburgh, 1982), 31.

20. Kitchen, *Unsettling Person*, 85.
21. G. F. Barbour, *The Life of Alexander Whyte* (London, 1923), 203. Whyte is himself quoting from the biography of Robertson Smith by G. S. Chrystal and J. S. Black. One can note that G. S. Chrystal is the already mentioned Professor Chrystal.
22. Barbour, *Life of Whyte*, 203–4.
23. *Ibid.* 201.
24. Robertson Smith continued to be a figure of international reputation. Some indication of his overall influence can be found in the work of his younger contemporary Sigmund Freud, who devoted a substantial section of *Totem and Taboo* to a discussion of Smith's work (and that of Smith's pupil James Frazer).
25. It was Hill's desire to make a painting to commemorate the founding of the Free Church that led Brewster to suggest to him that he made use of the newly-invented technique of photography to ease the task. In the next few years this led to the development of programmatic documentary photography by Hill and the chemist Robert Adamson.
26. Kitchen, *Unsettling Person*, 85.
27. *Ibid.*, 86.
28. D. Nash, *Secularism, Art and Freedom* (Leicester, 1992), 22–3.
29. M. Lutyens, *Krishnamurti: The Years of Awakening* (Boston, 1997), 13–14.
30. N. Mears *Intimations and Avowals* (Edinburgh, 1944).
31. Boardman, *Geddes*, 437.
32. 11 Mar.; DPL, LC, 142(27), *Dundee Naturalists' Society Twelfth Annual Report, 1884–5.*
33. *Ibid.*
34. T. M. Devine, *The Scottish Nation, 1700–2000* (Edinburgh, 1999), 296.
35. Kitchen, *Unsettling Person*, 87–8.
36. National Library of Scotland [NLS], MS 10524, fos.71,72.
37. For example, NLS, MS 10530, fo.209, from White to Geddes dated 20 Sep. 1898, details the arrangement for a loan which seems to relate to the completion of Ramsay Garden, and NLS, MS 10533, fos.222–24, a letter from White dated 12 Nov. 1902 seems to relate to repayments of the same loan.
38. M. Baillie, 'The Grey Lady: Mary Lily Walker of Dundee'.
39. Significant but as yet unpublished research has been carried out on this topic by Ann Prescott, and my thanks to her for drawing my attention to it. Prescott has pointed out that the scheme failed to gain council approval by the narrowest of margins in 1909.
40. NLS, MS 10537, fo.56; Balruddery, 22 Sep. 1904.
41. A. S. Mather, 'Geddes, Geography and ecology: The Golden Age of Vegetation Mapping in Scotland', *Scottish Geographical Journal*, 115, 1, (1999), 35–52.
42. R. Smith, 'Botanical survey of Scotland. I. Edinburgh District', *Scottish Geographical Magazine*, 16, (1900a) 385–415; R. Smith, 'Botanical survey of Scotland. II. North Perthshire District', *Scottish Geographical Magazine*, 16, (1900b), 441–67.
43. P. Geddes, 'Robert Smith BSc, University College Dundee', *Scottish Geographical Magazine*, 16 (1900), 597–9.
44. W. G. Smith, 'A botanical survey of Scotland', *Scottish Geographical Magazine*,

18 (1902), 132–9; W.G. Smith, 'Botanical survey of Scotland III and IV: Forfar and Fife', *Scottish Geographical Magazine*, 20 (1904), 617–28; and 21, 4–23, 57–83 and 117–26.

45. P. Geddes 'A Great Geographer: Elysée Reclus', *Scottish Geographical Magazine*, 21 (1905), 490–6, 548–55.

46. Another Geddes student in Edinburgh, W. G. Burn Murdoch, had accompanied Bruce. He recalls how during a lunch in the hall in Mound Place, Bruce suddenly invited him to go to the Antarctic. A week later they left from Dundee. Burn Murdoch writes: 'This was away back in 1892. Fifty years previously to this Dundee expedition of 1892–93, Sir James Ross had reported seeing great numbers of right whales in the Antarctic regions and the Dundonians having whaling vessels almost idle owing to the scarcity of right whales in the Arctic, fitted out this expedition to get these whales in the South; and our scientific bodies selected promising scientists to go as doctors on board three of the vessels and supplied them with scientific equipment'. Burn Murdoch writes of the return of that first expedition to Camperdown Dock in Dundee, noting that they were met by Geddes and his wife. W. G. Burn Murdoch in R. N. Rudmose Brown, *A Naturalist at the Poles* (London, 1923), 31

47. *Ibid.*, 31.

48. P. Speak, introductory chapters to W. S. Bruce, *The Log of the Scotia* (Edinburgh, 1992).

49. P. Geddes, *A Study in City Development: Parks, Gardens and Culture-Institutes* (Dunfermline, 1904). The title page as a whole is of interest. It continues: 'A report to the Carnegie Dunfermline Trust by Patrick Geddes, Professor of Botany, University College Dundee (St Andrews University), President of the Edinburgh School of Sociology'.

50. NLS, MS 10538, fos.67–70.

51. See, for example, F. Novak, ed., *Lewis Mumford and Patrick Geddes: The Correspondence* (London, 1995).

52. See, for example, P. Abercrombie, *Town and Country Planning* (London, 1933).

53. NLS, MS 10534, fos.29, 35. Letter dated 16 Feb. 1903.

54. *University of London: The Historical Record 1836-1912*, (London, 1912), 184–7.

55. Geddes, *City Development*, 145.

56. J. Kemplay, *John Duncan a Scottish Symbolist* (San Francisco, 1994), 12.

57. *Ibid.*, 15

58. NLS, MS 9987, fo.11. Letter of 3 Aug. 1885, written from *Dundee Advertiser* Office. 'Any reply to addresses to John T. Duncan, Artistic Department, *Advertiser* Office'.

59. E. A. Sharp, *William Sharp (Fiona Macleod): A Memoir* (London, 1910), 249–55.

60. NLS, MS 9987, fo.32, letter of 25 Apr. 1893.

61. NLS, MS 10588, fo.96, (1895–6). This fragment of letter from Duncan suggests that the Claverhouse mural was painted.

62. Strathclyde University Archives [SUA], T GED9/137. Letter of 10 Jul. 1895, written from 13 Union Street, Kirkcudbright.

63. NLS, MS 10588, fo.24, 30 Jul. 1895.

64. *The Meal Poke*, eds H. B. Baildon & R.C. Buist (Dundee, 1903).
65. For example a copy of *The Evergreen: Book of Spring*, in the author's possession, awarded to Charles Somerville, as a special prize in the Practical Botany Class in Jun. 1895.
66. Kemplay, *Duncan*, 18–19.
67. Also notable here is Edinburgh-based Helen Hay, an artist about whom even less is known, but whose work merits further research.
68. NLS, MS 10530, fo.122 (1898), 5 May 1898, 31 Albert Square Dundee.
69. SUA, TGED9/2175. This letter from 'Margaret M. Mackintosh' to 'Mrs Geddes' is written from 6 Florentine Terrace, Hillhead, Glasgow. It has no date but is datable to 1912–14 inclusive. The Duncans moved into their new house in St Bernard's Terrace, Edinburgh, in 1912. The Mackintoshes left Glasgow in 1914.
70. See, for an excellent guide to Dundee in 1912, *Handbook and Guide to Dundee and District: Prepared for the Members of the British Association for the Advancement of Science, on the occasion of their visit to Dundee, under the direction of the Local Publications Committee*, eds A. W. Paton & A. H. Millar (Dundee, 1912). For proceedings, abstracts of papers, programmes, membership, etc. see *British Association for the Advancement of Science, Dundee Meeting 1912* (London, 1913). For popular interest in the British Association meeting, see, for example, *The Piper o' Dundee*, various issues for Aug. and Sep., 1912; DUA, MS 88/11/6.
71. *Geographical Journal*, 40, 537–50, Jul.-Dec. 1912; papers by E. A. Reeves, C. Markham, W. S. Bruce.
72. See, for example, F. Spufford, *I May be Some Time: Ice and the English Imagination* (London, 1996), 273 ff.
73. Speak, introduction, *Log of the Scotia*. See also Don Aldridge, *The Rescue of Captain Scott* (East Linton, 1999).
74. *Geographical Journal*, 40 (1912), 548.
75. *Geographical Journal*, 40 (1912), 549.
76. SUA, TGED 1107.
77. *Illustrated Catalogue of a Loan Collection of Paintings Watercolours and Engravings in the Victoria Galleries Dundee on the Occasion of the British Association Meeting with an introduction by A. H. Millar* (Dundee, 1912).
78. At first in its own right, and, from 1890 under the broader wing of St Andrews University.

Chapter Nine

1. M. Dyer, *Capable Citizens and Improvident Democrats: The Scottish Electoral System 1884–1929* (Aberdeen, 1996), 65.
2. *Ibid.*, 68.
3. *Ibid.*, 137.
4. D. Lowe, *Souvenirs of Scottish Labour* (Glasgow, 1919), 83.
5. I. Sweeney, 'Local Party Politics and the Temperance Crusade: Glasgow, 1890–1902', *Scottish Labour History Society Journal* (1992), 51.
6. K. D. Buckley, *Trade Unionism in Aberdeen* (Edinburgh, 1955), 154.
7. W. Walker, *Juteopolis: Dundee and its Textile Workers, 1885–1923* (Edinburgh, 1979), 237.

8. I. G. C. Hutchison, *A Political History of Scotland, 1832–1924, Parties, Elections and Issues* (Edinburgh, 1986), 277.

9. C. Harvie, 'Before the Breakthrough, 1886-1922', in *Forward! Labour Politics in Scotland 1888–1898*, eds I. Donnachie, C. Harvie and I. S. Wood, (Edinburgh 1989), 14; J. J. Smyth, 'From Industrial Unrest to Industrial Debacle', in *Roots of Red Clydeside 1910–1914?*, eds W. Kenefick and A. McIvor (Edinburgh, 1996), 253–4; M. Fry, *Patronage and Principle: A Political History of Modern Scotland* (Aberdeen, 1987), 161; Dyer, *Capable Citizens*, 68; T. M. Devine, *The Scottish Nation 1700–2000* (London, 1999), 306.

10. Hutchison, *Political History of Scotland*, 245.

11. T. C. Smout, *A Century of the Scottish People* (London, 1986), 259; J. Smith 'Taking Leadership of the Labour Movement', in A. McKinlay and R. J. Morris, *The ILP on Clydeside, 1893–1932: from foundation to disintegration* (Manchester, 1991), 61; Kenefick and McIvor, *Roots of Red Clydeside*, 14.

12. W. W. Knox, *Industrial Nation. Work, society and culture in Scotland, 1800 to the present* (Edinburgh, 1999), 179.

13. P. Joyce, *Visions of the People* (Cambridge, 1991).

14. J. J. Smyth, 'The ILP in Glasgow, 1888–1906', in McKinlay and Morris, *The ILP on Clydeside*, 47.

15. Smyth, 'The ILP in Glasgow', 33; W. Miller, 'Politics in the Scottish City', in *Perspectives of the Scottish City*, ed. G. Gordon (Aberdeen, 1985), 188.

16. Walker, *Juteopolis*, 282.

17. D. G. Southgate, 'Politics and Representation in Dundee', in *Third Statistical Account of Scotland: The City of Dundee*, ed. J. M. Jackson (Arbroath, 1979), 305.

18. N. Morgan and R. Trainor, 'The Dominant Classes', in *People and Society in Scotland, vol II*, eds W. H. Fraser and R. J. Morris (Edinburgh, 1990), 106.

19. *Dundee Advertiser*, 25 Oct. 1887.

20. *Ibid.*, 25 Oct. 1904.

21. *Ibid.*, 2 Nov. 1897.

22. Southgate, 'Politics and Representation', 309.

23. *The Dawn of Peace*, 1 Nov. 1871.

24. *The Dilettante*, 8 Nov. 1884.

25. *Dundee Advertiser*, 20 Oct. 1890.

26. *Ibid.*, 15 Aug. 1876.

27. *Ibid.*, 10 Nov. 1876.

28. *Ibid.*, 30 Oct. 1877.

29. *Ibid.*, 13 Oct. 1886.

30. *Piper O' Dundee*, 9 Oct. 1895

31. Dundee Public Library [DPL], Lamb Collection (LC), Dundee Citizens Assoc. Papers, letter from J. Hart to Dr R. C. Buist, Oct. 1895.

32. *Ibid.*.

33. DPL, Edwin Scrymgeour's scrapbook, cutting, Oct. 1896.

34. Buckley, *Trades Unionism in Aberdeen*, 122.

35. W. H. Fraser, 'Trades Councils in the Labour Movement in Nineteenth Century Scotland', in *Essays in Scottish Labour History*, ed. I. MacDougall (Edinburgh, 1978), 18.

36. Walker, *Juteopolis*, 91.

37. *Dundee Advertiser*, 24 Oct. 1890.
38. *Ibid.*, 2 Oct.1890.
39. Lowe, *Souvenirs of Scottish Labour*, 69.
40. *Dundee Advertiser*, 11 Aug. 1889.
41. *Piper O' Dundee*, 2 Mar. 1892.
42. *Ibid.*, 10 Aug. 1892.
43. *Dundee Advertiser*, 2 Nov. 1886.
44. Dundee City Archives [DCA], GD/DLT, Minutes of Dundee Wine, Spirit and Beer Trade Protection Association, 21 Nov. 1902.
45. *Ibid.*, 19 Dec. 1905.
46. *Dundee Advertiser*, 2 Nov. 1904.
47. *Ibid.*, 14 Oct. 1904.
48. DPL, Election Address for Edwin Scrymgeour, 1904 in volume of cuttings on Scrymgeour 1904–5.
49. *Dundee Advertiser*, 29 Oct. 1904.
50. National Library of Scotland [NLS], Acc. 4682, STUC Minutes, minutes of Scottish Workers' Parliamentary Election Committee, 22 Sep. 1900.
51. *Ibid.*, 16 Aug. 1902; *Dundee Advertiser*, 8 Aug. 1902.
52. Archives of the ILP, Francis Johnson Correspondence (Harvester Press Microform, Brighton, 1979) 1902/27(i), James Reid to J. Keir Hardie, 26 Sep. 1902.
53. Archives of the ILP, Francis Johnson Correspondence, 1904/16(i), W. F. Black to F. Johnston, 9 May 1904.
54. *Ibid.*, 1904/10, J. Henderson to W. F. Black (n.d.).
55. *Ibid.*, 1905/23, J. Carnegie to J. Keir Hardie, 12 Dec. 1905.
56. *The Wasp*, Nov. 1904.
57. *Dundee Advertiser*, 31 Oct. 1904.
58. *Ibid.*, 1 Nov. 1904.
59. *The City Echo*, Oct. 1907.
60. DPL, Scrymgeour Papers, Election Address, 1905.
61. *Dundee Advertiser*, 30 Oct. 1906.
62. *Ibid.*, 9 Aug. 1902.
63. *Piper O'Dundee*, 19 Jan. 1906.
64. Southgate, 'Politics and Representation in Dundee', 304.
65. *Dundee Advertiser*, 16 Jan. 1906
66. *Piper O'Dundee*, 2 Mar. 1892.
67. Walker, *Juteopolis*, 284.
68. NLS, Acc. 5490, Joseph Duncan Papers, J. Duncan to M. Saunders, 9 Nov. 1906.
69. *Forward*, 25 Jan. 1908.
70. Archives of the ILP, Francis Johnson Correspondence, 1905/23, J. Carnegie to J. Keir Hardie, 12 Dec. 1905.
71. *Forward*, 18 Apr. 1908.
72. Archives of the ILP, Francis Johnson Correspondence, 1902/27(i), J. Reid to J. Keir Hardie, 26 Sep. 1902.
73. *Dundee Advertiser*, 9 Oct. 1906.
74. Dundee University Archives, MS6, Diary of James Cock. See chapter by L. Miskell, 'Civic Leadership and the Manufacturing Elite: Dundee, 1820–1870'.
75. *Forward*, 27 Oct. 1906.

76. *Dundee Advertiser*, 22 Oct. 1906.
77. NLS, Acc. 5490, Joseph Duncan Papers, J. Duncan to M. Saunders, 1 Nov. 1906.
78. Walker, *Juteopolis*, 204.
79. *Scottish Prohibitionist*, May 1909.
80. NLS, Acc. 5490, Joseph Duncan Papers, J. Duncan to M. Saunders, 9 Nov. 1906.
81. *Ibid.*, 14 Jan. 1908.
82. *Scottish Prohibitionist*, May 1908.
83. *Dundee Advertiser*, 19 Oct. 1907.
84. *Dundee Courier*, 6 Jan. 1906.
85. *Forward*, 25 Jan. 1908.
86. Walker, *Juteopolis*, 231.
87. See the collection of undated photographs in DPL, Scrymgeour Papers, box 9.
88. *The Wasp*, Nov. 1904.
89. *Dundee Advertiser*, 27 Oct. 1906.
90. *Dundee Courier*, 31 Oct. 1906.
91. *Dundee Advertiser*, 6 Oct. 1876.
92. *Forward*, 29 Feb. 1908.
93. Joyce, *Visions of the People*, 56.
94. *Forward*, 30 May 1908.
95. NLS, Acc. 4682, STUC Minutes, Minutes of Scottish Workers' Representation Committee, 6 Jun. 1908.
96. *Dundee Advertiser*, 21 Oct. 1920.
97. W. Walker, 'Dundee's Disenchantment with Churchill: A comment on the downfall of the Liberal Party', *Scottish Historical Review*, 49 (1970), 91.
98. *Forward*, 23 May 1908.
99. DCA, GD/DLA/4/6 Election Address, Winston Churchill, 28 Dec. 1909.

Chapter Ten

1. An excellent introduction is P. Hall, *Cities of Tomorrow* (revised edn., London, 1996). Scottish developments are briefly described in M. Glendinning, R. Macinnes and A. Mackechnie, *A History of Scottish Architecture: from the Renaissance to the Present Day* (Edinburgh, 1996), chs. 7 & 8.
2. For Thomson's career, see C. McKean and D. Walker, *Dundee: An Illustrated Introduction* (Edinburgh, 1984); see also J. K. Young, 'from "Laissez-faire" to "Homes fit for Heroes": Housing in Dundee 1868–1919', unpublished Ph.D. thesis (University of St Andrews, 1991).
3. For the political and fiscal background, see esp. R. Rodger, 'Crisis and Confrontation in Scottish Housing 1880–1914', in *Scottish Housing in the Twentieth Century*, ed. R. Rodger (Leicester, 1989), 25–53.
4. For contemporary reflection on the extent of the improvements by 1886, see 'Dundee Improvement Schemes – Recent and Prospective', *Dundee Year Book 1886* (Dundee, 1887), 149–53. See also the comments in D. Barrie *The City of Dundee Illustrated* (Dundee, 1890).
5. The need to remove obstructions resulted in the demolition in 1878 of two of the town's most important Georgian buildings – the Union Hall and Samuel

Bell's Trades' Hall – the former from one end of the High Street and the latter from the end of the Murraygate leading into the High Street.

6. A. W Paton and A. H. Millar, *British Association Handbook* (Dundee, 1912), 180–2.

7. The 1871 Improvement Act incorporated several clauses from the 1862 Police of Towns (Scotland) Act (Lindsay Act). For the 1882 act, see *Dundee Municipal Statutes: being the Acts of Parliament Administered by the Corporation of Dundee 1872–1898* (Dundee, n.d.), 54–291.

8. Local responses to the erection of these new buildings can be followed in the local newspapers and in the *Dundee Year Book.*

9. Paton and Millar, *British Association Handbook*, 153.

10. For improvements to the Law and to Baxter Park, see Dundee University Archives [DUA], MS 5/3/14, Dundee Town Council Minutes, 1907–8 [DTCM], esp. 133–4, 1,338; MS 5/3/9, DTCM, 1902–3, 1329–31 (Report on Baxter Park by the Superintendent of Parks, &c.). The work on the Law and Baxter Park was proposed as part of job creation schemes for the unemployed.

11. DUA, MS 5/13/13, DTCM, 1906-7, 397–8.

12. Comparisons need to be made not just in respect of the chronology and scope of municipal activity, but also in terms of the quality and price of municipal services, for example, electricity and the trams.

13. Rodger, 'Crisis and Confrontation', 38. Between 1890 and 1914, combined general, school, poor and police rates rose by respectively 64%, 51%, 30% and 27% in Edinburgh, Glasgow, Aberdeen and Dundee.

14. Lord Provost Urquhart, 'The Future of Dundee', *Dundee Year Book 1911* (Dundee, 1912), 53–4.

15. DUA, MS 5/2/11, Minutes of Meetings of the Police Commissioners of Dundee, 1890–1901 (Dundee, 1891), 241; MS 15/3/7, DTCM, 1900–1, 542–5 (Proposed scheme of sanitary reform by Alexander Elliot, convenor of the sanitary committee); MS 15/3/8, DTCM, 1901–2, 121–3, Report of the Town Clerk of Dundee on Part III of the Housing of the Working Classes Act, 1890. In February 1901, delegates from Dundee and the surrounding region attended a housing-reform conference which urged local authorities to use powers available to them under the 1890 Act to acquire land and build houses for the working classes, as well as to clear slum areas, DTCM, 1900–1, 437–8.

16. See DUA, MS 5/3/11, DTCM, 1904–5, 511, 646, 1,170. For Thomson's eventual plans, which envisaged a 4–storey tenement, with six 1–room flats to each floor, see MS 5/13/13, DTCM, 1906-7, 455–6. That the plans were a source of considerable division and debate is suggested by comment in the *Dundee Year Book, 1908* (Dundee, 1909), 7, that 'A committee is cudgelling its brains over the provision of a model tenement'.

17. W. Walsh, *A Tale of the Trick and the Gist of the Matter* (Dundee, 1908), 14. Note, where Walsh writes, 'A scheme of Housing, to be satisfactory, must be comprehensive, embracing a variety of site, types of dwelling, and management, and providing for the development of the city in different directions'.

18. DUA, MS 5/13/13, DTCM, 1906-7, 244.

19. See W. Walker, *Juteopolis* (Edinburgh, 1979), 368–72. In February 1908, Thomson found himself entangled in these developments, when Scrymgeour led an attack on a proposal to increase Thomson's salary, broadening his target

to include the 'cronie' system which he alleged prevailed on the Council. In the municipal elections of that year, 7 councillors stood down, while 9 new members were elected.

20. For the planning and construction of Logie, see esp. J. Frew, 'Cottages, Tenements and "Practical" Idealism: James Thomson at Logie, 1917–1923', in *The Architecture of Scottish Cities*, ed. D. Mays (Edinburgh, 1997), 171–80.
21. *Ibid.*
22. For Nettlefold, see G. E. Cherry, *Birmingham: A Study in Geography, History and Planning* (Birmingham, 1994).
23. W. Walsh, 'The Dwellings of Dundee', in Paton and Millar, *British Association Handbook*, 94. The onslaught against insanitary dwellings was to be resumed, on an even more systematic basis, in 1916, DUA, MS 5/3/20, DTCM, 1915–16, 365; MS 5/3/21, DTCM, 1916-17, 363–5.
24. *The Rise of Modern Urban Planning, 1800–1914*, ed. A. Sutcliffe (London, 1980).
25. For Geddes, see H. Meller, *Patrick Geddes, Social Evolutionist and City Planner* (London, 1990).
26. A. Prescot, 'A Botanic Garden for Dundee' (unpublished paper).
27. DUA, MS 5/3/18, DTCM, 1911–12, 1338–9, Report of Sub-Committee of the Improvement Committee on Proposal for City Survey. The sub-committee was convened and chaired by Walsh. The proposed survey followed a format very much in the Geddes' mould, encompassing situation and topography; archaeology and antiquities; historic development; means of communication; manufactures and commerce; town conditions and requirements.
28. *Illustrated Catalogue of a Loan Collection of Paintings, Water Colours & Engravings in the Victoria Art Galleries, Dundee on the Occasion of the British Association Meeting, with an Introduction by A .H. Millar, LL.D.* (Dundee, 1912).
29. DUA, DTCM, 1900–1, 888.
30. For Walsh's political career, see esp. Walker, *Juteopolis*, 269–85.
31. DUA, MS 5/3/13, DTCM, 1906-7, 467.
32. *Ibid.*, 1202.
33. DUA, MS 5/3/15, DTCM, 1908–9, 1,294.
34. *Dundee Telegraph*, 8 Mar. 1911; *Dundee Advertiser*, 9 Mar. 1911.
35. Dundee City Archives [DCA], TC/SF 200, Report of the Special Housing Committee, 1908.
36. For Walsh's account of the affair, see Walsh, *The Tale of a Trick*.
37. Walsh, *A Tale of a Trick*, 5.
38. DUA, MS 5/3/14, DTCM, 1907–8, 67, 139, 337, 457.
39. Copies of all these reports are contained in the relevant volumes of the council minutes.
40. For reasons of speed, final approval for the Logie scheme was given by telephone from the Scottish Local Government Board. The race was won in July 1919 when Sir George McRae, vice president of the Board, came to Dundee to cut the first sod for Logie.
41. DUA, MS 5/3/17, DTCM, 1910–11, 86.
42. *Ibid.*, 88–9.

43. See Hall, *Cities of Tomorrow*, ch. 6. See also W. H. Wilson, *The City Beautiful Movement* (Baltimore and London, 1984).

44. Wilson, *The City Beautiful Movement*, 92.

45. *The Builder* (1910), 476.

46. See for example, *Town Planning Review*, 1 (1910), 188–204.

47. *Dundee Year Book 1890* (Dundee, 1891), 5.

48. B. Walker and W. Sinclair Gauldie, *Architects and Architecture on Tayside* (Dundee, 1984), 147; Dundee Public Library, Lamb Collection, DAA3, Mackison's 1871 elevation for buildings on Murraygate and Commercial Street.

49. Barrie, *City of Dundee Illustrated*, 92.

50. Paton and Millar, *British Association Handbook*, 389.

51. *Dundee Year Book 1907* (Dundee, 1908), 5, 26, 102. Opponents included members of the local Independent Labour Party, who called instead for the erection of municipal dwelling houses for the working classes, DUA, MS 5/3/ 17, DTCM, 1906-7, 565.

52. See *Dundee Year Book, 1908* (Dundee, 1909), 7.

53. C. J. Davey, *The End of Broughty Ferry: The Dundee Boundaries Act of 1913*, Centre for Tayside and Fife Studies, Occasional Pamphlet No. 4 (Dundee, 1992).

54. DUA, MS 5/3/18, DTCM, 1911–12, 505.

55. See for example, *Dundee Advertiser*, 29 Oct. 1912.

56. *Dundee Courier*, 10 Nov. 1911.

57. Ibid., 15 Nov. 1912.

58. *Dundee Advertiser*, 27 Sept. 1912.

59. *Dundee Courier*, 15 Nov. 1912.

60. *Ibid.*, 3 Jan. 1913.

61. *The Builder* (1910), 615.

62. *Dundee Courier*, 10 Apr. 1914.

63. *Ibid.*

64. Personal communication between Professor C. McKean and James Thomson's granddaughters, Gertie and Trixie Thomson, 3 Mar. 1999. As a jute man, Caird apparently instructed Thomson to 'design me a hall that looked like a jute factory, for that is how I made my money'.

65. See also the illustration in the *Dundee Year Book, 1914* (Dundee, 1915), 90.

66. A copy is on display in the McManus Galleries, Dundee.

67. See *Dundee Courier*, 6 Jun. 1914.

68. See Frew, 'Cottages, Tenements and "Practical" Idealism'. See also N. Subedi, 'James Thomson: His Early Twentieth Century Proposals for the Development and Re-development of Dundee', in *Art, Design and the Quality of Life in Turn of the Century Scotland 1890–1910*, ed. C. J. Carter, Proceedings of Symposium held at Duncan of Jordanston College of Art, Dundee, 1982.

69. This involved identifying systematic action areas for inspection and maintaining a register of inspections (DUA, MS 5/3/22, DTCM, 1916-17, 363–5).

70. DUA, MS 5/3/22, DTCM, 1916-17, 513–34.

71. DCA, TC/SF 17 & 20.

72. Walsh, 'The Dwellings of Dundee', 97.

73. DUA, MS 5/3/18, DTCM, 1911–12, 1,045–6.

74. The other places were Rosyth; Inverkeithing; Edinburgh (Fountainbridge); Gourock; and Greenock.

75. National Archives of Scotland, Edinburgh, dd6/661. I owe this reference to Dr K. Young.

76. R. J. Morris, 'Urbanization and Scotland', in *People and Society in Scotland. Vol II, 1830–1914*, eds W. H. Fraser and R. J. Morris (Edinburgh, 1990), 84.

77. I would like to acknowledge the very generous help provided in the preparation of this chapter by Dr Kay Young. I would also like to thank Dr Nutan Sebedi for providing slides of some of the illustrations which accompany this chapter.

Index